PAINTING THE MENTAL CONTINUUM

Perception and Meaning in the Making

Acknowledgements

I want to thank good friends Susan Felter, Bill Mastin, Molly McFadden and Arn Henderson for their many helpful editorial comments. Sara Liu, my neighbor and a recent Literature Ph.D. from the University of California, Berkeley, improved expression, helpfully challenged, and housebroke some of my idea pets. Congratulations to authors who get to work with publisher and editor John Strohmeier. He brims with energy, learning and publishing savvy.

I also thank Lisa Schulz for her fine cover designs.

Thanks to Jim Gresham, who first introduced me to Vermeer while we shared an apartment at college; Mary Greene for her master's thesis on movement and compressions of language in the narrative of Huckleberry Finn; Nanine Hilliard Greene for the title; and Ken Rice for fifteen years of taking photographs of my ever-changing images.

List of Figures

All collages by the author are done on canvas or hardboard with acrylic ground, casein, pastel, tempera and acrylic, fixed with acrylic matte medium and varnish.

21. Author Collage: *Hitler,* with photo of Hitler from *Life's Picture History of World War Two* and Cartier-Bresson's photos of Soviet athletes

22. Author collage: *Texas Mother,* with a Farm Security Administration photo by Russell Lee and a print of Vermeer's *The Love Letter*

23. Rembrandt: *The Jewish Bride,* Rijksmuseum, Amsterdam

24. Author: Cunningham House, exterior from golf course

25. Author: Cunningham House, interior photo by Julius Shulman

26. Author: Prairie House, photo by Robert Alan Bowlby

27. Author collage: *Crying Frenchman,* with photos of a weeping man at the surrender of French flags to the Nazis, and German troops riding on a tank, from *Life's Picture History of World War Two,* and a photo of a crocodile by Emil Shulthess

28. Author collage: *Ships and the Feminine Gender,* with photos of the Churchills from *The Churchill Years, 1874-1965* by Viking Press and *The London Times,* and a print of Turner's *First Rate Taking on Stores*

29. Author collage: *Beginning to End,* with Nilsson's photo of a fertilized human egg attached to the uterine wall and Michaelangelo's Sybil from the Sistine ceiling

30. Author collage: *Konorak,* with photos of Hindu goddesses at Konorak, Giselbertius' *Eve from Atun* and Vermeer's *The Procuress*

31. Author collage: *Collaborateur,* with photo by Cartier-Bresson

32. Author: Post Office design, 1952

33. Author: Prairie House Norman, Oklahoma, 1960-1962. Photo by Julius Shulman

34. Author: *Energy, Mass and Air*

35. Picasso: *Baboon and Young,* Museum of Modern Art, New York, Mrs. Solomon Guggenheim Fund

36. Author collage: *The Evolution of Eve* detail, with Michaelangelo's *Eve* from the Sistine ceiling

37. Author collage: *The Evolution of Eve,* with Michaelangelo's *Eve* from the Sistine ceiling

38. Author collage: *The Becoming of Consciousness* detail, with print of Vermeer's *Milkmaid*

39. Author collage: *Texas Man* detail, with Farm Security Administration photo by Dorothea Lange of a Depression-era Texas farmer and an Emil Shulthess photo of a skua

40. Author collage: *Collage With Vermeer's* Girl in a Red Hat detail

41. *Mayan Maize God* (Dumbarton Oaks, Pre-Columbian Collection, Washington, DC)

42. Author collage: *Collage with Vermeer's* Girl in a Red Hat

43. Vermeer: *Head of a Young Girl* detail

44. Author collage: *Vietnam,* with photo of a migrant family by Dorothea Lange for the Farm Security Administration, and Marines in Vietnam photographed by Larry Burroughs

45. Author collage: *Collage with Vermeer's* Woman Reading a Letter detail

46. Author collage: *Decoy Fish,* with a photo of a "Decoy Fish" from *National Geographic* detail. Collection of Robert and Toby Bowlby

Part One

Issues and Examples

CHAPTER ONE

Motives and Methods

The main objective in writing this book is to reach people who feel the power of images but have not taken the time to ask what is in the image, and in themselves, to make them feel this power. I hope to point out cues that influence thought and feeling, and to show how imagination, in processing contrasts and identities stimulated by these cues, shapes them into meaning. Imagination is no longer simplistically opposed to perception and reason. Perception and reason are more and more coming to be recognized as always informed by imagination.

In my analysis of imagination, I will investigate how we see and ultimately interpret a perceived object in terms of other things not ostensibly present in the object. This process has been found by Whitehead and many current cognitive scientists and neurobiologists to be the common ground effecting both meaning and emotion. For example, there is an abstract outdoor sculpture near the Oakland Museum that I find lighthearted and even humorous in feeling, and rather obscure in meaning. It resembles an old-fash-

ioned gate that is used to bar baby from the stairway. The sculpture, about twenty feet high and twenty long, is made of welded steel pipe about five or six inches in diameter and formed into crossed diagonals. A sphere about a foot in diameter is located at each of its four exterior corner junctions. Crescent shapes, perhaps a foot and a half in length, are placed in a somewhat jaunty fashion at its two highest extensions. I joked to my wife that the sculpture might be entitled "Dentistry at Dawn." She smiled and continued to refer to the phrase for several weeks. I suppose the symmetry of the sculpture's pipe frame, punctuated by balls and crescents, suggested a certain purpose and gaiety, and that the balls and crescents reminded me of suns, moons and dentists' tools. The word "dentistry" sounds a bit like "destiny," and perhaps adds notes of humorous expectancy and pomposity to my title, while the word "dawn," in context with destiny, might add something of the portentous. My evolving yet enduring personality, energized by my subjective aims or overview, including a propensity to find humor in images, was responsible for my attempt to map my responses to the sculpture and its details into a humorous entity of meaning.

This incident can point to important questions about how we metaphorically generate feeling and meaning out of any data that is perceived as real or imagined. Metaphor is not to be limited to humor and literary purpose, but is found to be endemic to all imaginative thought.

Giving expression in words and in pictures to qualities and thoughts about the objects of perception, including amusing sculptures, has occupied philosophers and artists throughout history. In this century thoughts and feelings have been found to issue from a body-mind in which any perceived response must be understood within physical, psychological and cultural contexts. We are also discovering genetic and developmental influences on our responses that may be applicable to the entire race, as well as to cultures and individuals. Our explanations of these concerns are informed by our expanding knowledge of what physical and thought objects are, of their life in space-time, and in our mental process. These concerns, possibly forever beyond the reach of complete and satisfying explanations, form the province of this book.

Instead of using sculptures to initiate the discussion, I use images selected from art and photography that persistently move me or otherwise hold my interest. I combine these images — a photograph by Henri Cartier-Bresson of an aged man entering a cab, an electron photograph of a human neuron by Lennart Nilsson, a print of Vermeer's *Woman Holding a Balance* — with my own painted interpretive forms to produce collage paintings. It often takes me years to complete a painting, and I favor photographed images with which I can commune, or that I feel have some compelling and timeless interest.

I have been influenced by Alfred North Whitehead, whose theory of events enables us to break down our interactions with an image into details, parts, and wholes that span the feelings, ideas, and the incredible variety of contexts and circumlocutions of our response. For example, after transferring an image to canvas I surround and overpaint it with a visual commentary, an organized rumination stemming from details, parts, and wholes that respond to what seems to me some of its important forms and messages. In figure 1, I ask what accounts for the perfect poise and delicacy of the hands, or the particular sense of an enveloping wholeness that I experience when I view this painting. How can I communicate particulars about the significance of the woman that seems to be embodied in her pregnancy? In context with the beatific quality of light washing over her serene face and figure, I mentally collage these particulars into a symbol of "everlasting life." How can such thoughts and impressions, subject to digressions and unconscious guidance, be conceptualized and projected in my painted response? I try to do so in figure 2, where large scale fingers reach out as if to touch the tactile garment, Vermeer's woman, and in the same gesture suggest my reaching out in an attempt to understand the events in Vermeer's painting. Further, can or should I evoke something of my disbelief in the benign universe that Vermeer projects, or of the sympathy I have for the feeling of rationality that pervades the painting?

To refer to these questions about how the mind works, I have chosen the term "mental continuum." This term suggests that there is both continuity and open-endedness to thought as we confront the active and evolving world and make sense out of its vast diversity. I hope that the reader will find the term useful as a locus for talking about relationships in the unconscious-liminal-conscious gradient by which we access our past experience to connect the object, perceived through our body-mind, to the rest of the world. The term can also direct us to ideas of enjoyment and wonder, since the analysis of images within the mental continuum may be considered as a kind of game with flexible strategies that allow individual viewers, when presented with a painting or an explanation, to bring their own feelings and thought processes into focus. By adapting images such as Vermeer's woman that have generated interest in a wide audience, I hope to encourage readers to become involved in my commentaries and to go on to make their own.

We know that individuals cannot have congruent perceptions to the same events. *The Deptford Trilogy* (1986) by the late Canadian novelist Robertson Davies is based on the idea that reality resides in a public plurality of interacting scenarios, rather than an authorial and individual omnipotence. The novel's success attests to an acceptance of this notion in a culture where Einstein proved that

space and time are different for every single observer, and Gertrude Stein conceived a daily life made up of thousands of occasions that are different from those of everyone else. All artists can hope for, she concluded, is that an audience will recognize the force and consistency of their efforts.

Even as we absorb the latest knowledge of indeterminacy and relativity in physical and mental activity, the recognition of similarities among differences experienced by ourselves and others is possible because we share so much in common as we touch wool, taste sugar, interpret body language and other sources of embodied metaphors such as darkness and light. Consequently, we respond to countless works of art that communicate feeling and thought among individuals across cultures without need for further explanation.

Nevertheless, as we share some of our thoughts and feelings in looking at a Vermeer we may be only dimly aware of how our responses are produced. Shapes, colors, objects and subjects depend on many associations for their meaning. These associations depend on a living, evolving culture. Further, analyzing our response to an art image that contains multiple and ambiguous themes can be puzzling. We may miss or misinterpret important clues that the artist has left us in his work.

It wasn't until I saw Vermeer's original painting (figure 1) in the National Gallery that I noticed an oversized shadow-hand worked into the woman's headdress. Although the hand has only three discernible fingers, the heightened clarity of the thumb helps me to

Figure 1. Vermeer, *Woman Holding a Balance* (Detail)

Figure 2. Herb Greene, *The Shadow Hand in the Vermeer #3* (Detail)

make the visual closure. The boundaries and shading of the hand meld into the shadow of the headdress. Because of Vermeer's subtle handling and our expectation that we should see a shadow, we may fail to recognize the hand, and yet there it is. Once we recognize the hand, for a moment, it may be difficult to see anything else. In my mind, after weighing alternative possibilities, it suggests the act of comforting, and a godlike protecting presence. The shadow-hand was in my mind as I decided to use outreaching fingers as a metaphor for addressing Vermeer's image in figure 2.

When a congenial and soft-spoken child psychologist friend recognized this dark and murky shadow-hand, he thought it heavy and oppressive, while his wife emphatically offered reasons why the hand should be read as supportive and comforting. The context that we create for a symbol or a sign is critical to these contrasting interpretations. It would be interesting to test a number of male and female subjects to see if there might be a correlation by gender of interpretations of the shadow-hand. My wife tells me that her first impression of the hand suggested a mother supporting a child's head. A male student in a college seminar thought it might be a sign of the husband. Science tells us that during evolution we have adapted to see what seems to be in our practical interest, what conforms to our preconceived ideas of things rather than what is merely raw data in the visual field. Perhaps my wife's response to the hand was initiated by her unusually deep interest in children and mothering. Usually we are unaware of how the mind networks

associations among raw data and our notions of things.

Today we might consider Vermeer's shadow hand to be a benign forerunner of effective yet subversive subliminal images used in magazine advertising. Artists have designed human skulls and black color fields into liquor ads to stimulate latent fears of death and, consequently, liquor consumption in heavy drinkers.[1] Nike has been accused[2] of employing not-quite-hidden swastikas and Nazi colors in a sales campaign directed at young, inner city males. As I look at a pattern of four circles filled with black, placed symmetrically on the diameter of a larger black circle, an image of Mickey Mouse ears intrudes into my consciousness. This is an association that I imagine many Americans and, perhaps more recently, other nationalities would recognize, and suggests how most any visual cue repeated in a sustained public context can become associated with cultural connotations.

Subliminal cues fit very well into Whitehead's event theory. Perception gives us far more information than we can consciously process. We normally narrow down our selection of data to conform to predigested interpretations that allow us to expedite thought and action. Yet we may respond to conflicting or supporting data on unconscious levels, which can effect behavior and feeling.

Whitehead brought feelings to the forefront of philosophy. He found all cognitive acts to be interactions of feelings and ideation. According to Whitehead, our initial awareness of a sculpture's resemblance to dentists, tools, the sacramental light in Vermeer's painting (figure 1), and the Mickey Mouse ears, combine feelings and cognition into what he called "prehensions," or acts of apperception. Consider my prehension of an odor of gas when I awake in a darkened room in a cheap motel. In the case of the gas, by qualifying my initial prehension with prehensions of other features of the situation — that there is no flame, and what should I expect after checking into a motel with so many burned out letters on its neon sign? — I subdue my feeling of fear and breathe more easily while admonishing myself for being so stingy. This suggests that prehensions do not keep pre-harmonized contexts at bay but are dependent on them. A baby perusing its mother's face for smiles rather than frowns exemplifies prehensive processing directed by genetic programming. The complex neural process of mapping and evaluating unifications of prehensions including subliminal images has begun to be described by Gerald M. Edelman[3] and other neuroscientists. The issue as it relates to both our conscious, liminal and unconscious responses to the qualities and features of images is taken up in my presentation of Whitehead's theory of prehension in Chapters Seventeen and Nineteen, *Events* and *The Act of Perception*.

Returning to the hand of Vermeer's woman that lightly but firmly touches the table in figure 2: My evaluations of this gesture acknowledge a solid, physical world. Vermeer's harmonious proportions, sense of balance, and composition of diverse visible objects — table, wall, picture on wall, hand, balance, hooded garment, and pregnant woman — create the feeling of an ensemble that, together

with his precision, naturalism, and projection of verisimilitude, I can process into concepts of an order imposed by the supreme being described by Vermeer's near contemporaries, Newton and Spinoza. The woman's pregnancy, her bodily gestures and her sublime face may together be taken as signs of the continuity of life and of life's preciousness, a preciousness qualified by the delicacy of the hand that holds the scale, the gentle tilt of the woman's head, and the beatific quality in her expression. Even before I noticed the shadow-hand with its connotations of support and protection, I felt, with perhaps millions of others who have missed the hand, a sense of the benign, of life and its preciousness, and a spiritualized materiality in the painting. When recognized in these contexts, the hand becomes a chord in Vermeer's already potent orchestration and a further indication of his probable world-view.

Kenneth Clark sheds light on Vermeer's shadow hand.

> In the seventeenth century the triumph of the Sacrament (a projection of a state of grace) . . . was still thought to be reconcilable with a faith in natural order, and this gave an extraordinary wholeness to all phenomena. The human mind had begun to conceive a universe governed by beneficent cause and effect but had not subjected it to analysis.[4]

It is this sense of unchallenged benign cause and effect that

Vermeer projects and that the shadow hand, with its implications of a protecting, personal Western God, enforces.

Upon having the shadow hand and its link to "beneficent cause and effect" pointed out, a Marxist might, nonetheless, interpret the hand as he might the painting of *The Last Judgment* on the wall directly behind the woman in the Vermeer, a sign of religious beliefs that have been used to block social progress. Gregory Bateson,[5] the late distinguished researcher of entomology, biology and cybernetics, tells us that communication among and within brains may be characterized as the production of a sequence of contexts in which each is continually being corrected with respect to each previous context. While some relationships between particular signals may be confused, understanding may emerge at another level guided by the mind's continuation or exclusion of contexts. For example, the actual lilting figures in the painting of *The Last Judgement* on the wall in back of Vermeer's woman may provide conceptual feelings of positive life, dancing motion and human scope that uplift and enhance Vermeer's creation, rather than merely remind of judgement day and the conservatism of the traditional church.

Regarding the shadow-hand, many acculturated viewers are likely to find corrected contexts that override the Marxist's view. For example, they may know that upon his marriage, Vermeer converted to Catholicism, fathered over a dozen children, received financial aid from his mother-in-law, and began his career by painting convincing religious pictures. These facts can suggest that in his painting

Vermeer was projecting cultural and religious beliefs in his world view, or even that he might be buttering up his Catholic mother-in-law. But, in addition to our knowledge and guesses about Vermeer's world, we can deduce from the actual contextual cues in the painting before us, such as the woman's hand firmly touching the (material) table and the light that caresses her face and garment, that Vermeer has constructed his image out of details that speak of "a guiding spirit present in the material world." The shadow-hand image builds upon this possibility, while introducing references such as "godlike" and "support" into potential meaning.

The shadow-hand analysis indicates that prehensions cross-fertilize one another. They cut through the dualisms of mind and body, objective and subjective thought and feeling, and past, present and future time. Prehensions give access to the concrete. The analysis of prehensions allows us to directly discover contrasts and identities among various modes of thought and sensation, and to hold in the mix of meaning important excluded alternatives as we move thought along to conclusions and satisfactions.

Vermeer's shadow-hand is not an optical illusion or an allegorical symbol, the use of which was prevalent in Renaissance and Baroque painting. The hand initiates emotional and intellectual content directly associated with comfort, support, and a benign superintending presence, ideas that are close to the heart of what we feel about the painting. Vermeer melds his projection of this inheritance with the naturalism, scientific objectivity and study of optics that flourished in the seventeenth century. He projects feelings about these subjects to give his picture, as Clark suggests, a kind of wholeness and uniqueness that could only have been produced at that time and place in European history, when the budding modern rational mind still subsumed something of the Medieval belief in an omnipotent God.

My response that began with public data in the image, which I find embodied with metaphoric meanings such as sacramental light, lovely face projected in a state of grace, touching hands, stable table, comforting garment, body language that expresses calm, contemplation, rising up, and Vermeer's keen sense of geometric balance, is infused with my private qualifications. For example, living amidst twentieth-century science, I am unable to believe that the universe is subject to a beneficent superintending presence. I do have feelings of wonder and love in my response to the expressive alchemy of the painting's details in form and idea. As far as I can express it, my private synthesis of the image includes its ability to connect me with ideas of an authentic, humane religious spirit developing in *Homo sapiens* that is more durable than any theology. By this I mean the generic human urge for security, protection, and to be unified with an immortal stream of life. This reading can become a public fact just as well as the Marxist's view. Obviously there is a vast spectrum of interpretation that is conditioned by our individual overviews through which we interpret perceptual data according to our subjective aims. The interplay of the public and private aspects of

our response to our prehensions of images conditioned by our subjective aims is taken up in Chapter Twenty-Three, *Public and Private*.

During the 'eighties and 'nineties my reading in cognitive and neuroscience confirmed my belief in the continuing appropriateness of Whitehead's insights in his book, *Process and Reality* (1929). By applying tenets from his theory of perception, with its emphasis on the role of prehensions, feeling, imagination, and our dependence on the experience of the body as it is incorporated in the mind as a basis for interpretive thought, I hope to gain fresh content and precision in my explanations. I have already appropriated one of Whitehead's terms, "the enduring personality," in the opening paragraphs of this chapter, which suggests the changing yet ongoing uniqueness of an individual within the passage of time. While my enduring personality narrows the channel of the verbal and painted expressions that follow, I hope they call attention to the ideas that I find to be so exciting.

Since 1955, as an architect, painter and professor, I have been drawn to Whitehead's critique of scientific materialism and his rendition of organic process. Whitehead offered a correction to explanations of perception given by Aristotle's fixed categories, Plato's ideal forms, Descartes' thought or mind separated from nature and, I would add, the leveling of value of much post-modernist thought. Descartes held that the real structure of nature was impervious to change and to the ambiguities of sense perception —

a world with timeless laws, a permanent material stuff, and a mind independent of nature and the body. In Whitehead we see mind evolving in creatures within an evolving nature that produces us. The fixed archetypes, fixed categories, absolute essences, ideal forms, primary subjects with secondary predicates and mathematical certitudes that were thought to define the structure of nature and of mind have been deconstructed and revised.

Instead of treating a visual perception as if it were an isolated instant, as, for example, in a glance at a wood wall with termite damage, Whitehead finds us participating in an event through a duration which is an actual, perceived occasion happening through time — an analog to Heidegger's famous "Being in Time." In Whitehead's process we select particulars from aspects of the wood wall, as in our cognizance of flaking studs, musty presence, roughly rectangular shapes, knowledge of "woodiness," and termites, which we derive from the selected particulars and our embodied experience of them. The meaning of these derivations is based on the outlooks and perceptual and mental equipment of particular organisms, whether humans or termites. For myself it is postmodern sophistry to insist that the values of termites and humans should be aesthetically, intellectually, ethically and morally flattened to a common plane, even as we realize that termite mounds are important to the ecosystem.

Human gestalts within durations of a stone, a termite-infested wall, or the shadow-hand are processed into wholes that are more important to us than their parts. Whitehead accounts for the human abilities, limitations, aspirations and culture that influence our feelings and concepts during the act of perception. His approach to feelings can help us as we determine whether finding the shadow-hand is the satisfaction of finding Waldo in a comics page puzzle, or a sign of deeply harmonized cultural significance and of abiding mystery.

For myself the shadow hand illustrates Edward O. Wilson's[6] discussion of genetics, where regularities of sensory perception and mental development animate and channel the acquisition of culture. Wilson uses statistical examples to confirm how biogenetic dispositions interact with cultural dispositions. He cites mythologies arising from the human fear of snakes and the narratives different cultures have developed to rationalize this fear. He also discusses incest avoidance, the interpretations of color, and the establishment of perceptual order through pottery designs in tribal cultures. Most likely Vermeer had been nurturing the idea of forming the shadow-hand for some time, because there is a faint suggestion of a similar hand in the headdress of the woman in an earlier painting, *Woman with a Water Jug*. The "supporting" hand can be seen as a polysemic symbol that is capable of several meanings in Western culture. We select among their possibilities to map pre-harmonized connotations of "the hand of God" and conceptual feelings such as support, comfort and security. Such symbols can link discourses of meaning that build strength of experience.

Advancing cultural continuity through symbolic form is, of course, vividly illustrated by examples from the arts. Whitehead suggests that, among our early ancestors, sound could have been the strongest internally felt sense modality because of the resonance of sound throughout the body.[7] I was once both viscerally and intellectually affected by a film in which the camera slowly panned along a narrow Appalachian valley, among scattered shacks and rundown houses, to the haunting and wailing sounds of old-world bagpipes slowly transforming into sounds of new-world, country music violins. The timbre of the bagpipes maintained in the tones of the violins indicates how deep cultural links to multitudes of pre-harmonized experiences are maintained in evolving forms of expression. In the Vermeer, God as "father," "superintendent" and "authority" represent Western archetypes that allow feelings of cultural identity, order and well-being to be realized. While symbols of these archetypes may be banal in some contexts, in figure 1, Vermeer invokes them in contexts with nuances and cross references that can move us.

Hoping the reader can bear one or two more discursive connections in this section, I would note that in this century the term "archetype" has taken a psychological turn. Jung has probably been the most influential figure in discussing archetypes. I want to make a distinction between what I take to be his interpretation and a Whiteheadian interpretation. For all his fame, Jung's notions are undermined by presuppositions of idealized origins of meaning, and by a specifically romantic imagery, such as his multi-storied house atop its cellar and nearly hidden cave below. Jung's cave image became a cushioned Procrustean bed into which, with what today must be considered a megalomaniacal ego, he could fit the collective unconscious, and himself as a paragon of sexual force to female patients and colleagues, a reincarnated Goethe, a reincarnated Nordic warrior-god, and as a player in the Germanic state conceptualized as a will to power expressing superiority of spirit and blood.[8] I find necessary contrasts in Whitehead's archetypes, such as the "enduring personality," which are more subject to the findings of organic development in anthropology and biology, and to a civilizing morality. Most importantly, Whitehead's archetypes are mutable.

Yet Whitehead's "evolutionary" and mutable approach actually preserves value in contrast to the relativism of some post-modernists. While both approaches constantly revise our mental scenarios in quest of meaning, using the former approach means that we need not radically deconstruct the depth of our feeling for Vermeer's religious and cosmic archetypes because of our changing perceptions of religion and the validity of knowledge. Consider Shakespeare's characters in *The Merchant of Venice*. Via our prehensions of historical change, we readjust rather than negate our feelings for Shylock and Portia, who are given the play's most poignant and human lines. We qualify our negative feelings of Elizabethan male views about women and Jews without losing the strength and scope of Shakespeare's characterizations of human nature.

The current emphasis of civilizing feminist values on philosophy, sociology, art and politics would have been welcomed by Whitehead because, as Professor Albert Levi[9] explains, in Whitehead's universe of energy transformations, within space-time nothing is lost. Our characterizations of electrons and Shakespeare are only reconfigured. Our current filters of behavioral psychology, scientific relativity and gender issues are lenses for reconfiguration.

Attempts to form connections among the world-views of science, philosophy and art are often forced or oversimplified to prove a point. Yet connections between art and scientific relativity can have real efficacy. Such connections are inevitable as common influences, ideas and technologies find expression in the varieties of human endeavor. Art historian John Gage[10] has shown how Turner's contacts with Faraday could have led him to embrace the notion that all things were made up of heat, light and electricity. Turner's mature work is characterized by the powerful expression he gives to the homogeneity of all things, an expression that seemed to parallel Faraday's theory. See, for example, the fusion of textures and the sense of one stuff that permeates the light, movement of air, fluids, earth and steam engine in his painting *Rain, Wind, and Speed* in figure 4. My approach in the book is to attempt such connections, as in treating the painted ground in my collage as a symbol of the embodied experience that fills in appearance as described by Whitehead and current cognitive science. For example, science gives us the image of an actual human neuron. In figure 3, I want to

express my bodily (physical) and mental (conceptual) feelings in reaction to the arresting scale, texture, form and spatial perspective of the neuron. I want to use my hand-drawn background with human profiles and metaphors of tensioned balance to give rise to physical and conceptual feelings — a voice to my intuition that we instinctively seek signs of the human in all that we perceive, no matter what the scale or subject of perception.

In Part One, after this introduction and two prefatory chapters on looking at photographs and the idea of figure and background, I present my painted responses to a variety of photographs and prints that I have introduced into collages. I hope to provide brief yet informative interpretations of the images. In explanations of devices and symbols in a collage, I call attention to features of the introduced image that I have reiterated in the surrounding painted ground, as I have in the white shape of the smoke stack (figure 4), or, in spite of my doubts about a too literal analogy, as I place a photograph of a human heart in the center of the white engine to see if I can make it work metaphorically with the fire at the center of Turner's black engine. Again metaphor is not limited to literary embellishment, but is considered fundamental to the process of understanding any concept or feeling through imagining and correcting contexts and interrelating meanings — seeing one thing in terms of others as we process prehensions. To me, the spatial framework of whitish tubes in the collage (figure 4) is intended to suggest the implosion of the connecting and interrupted thoughts

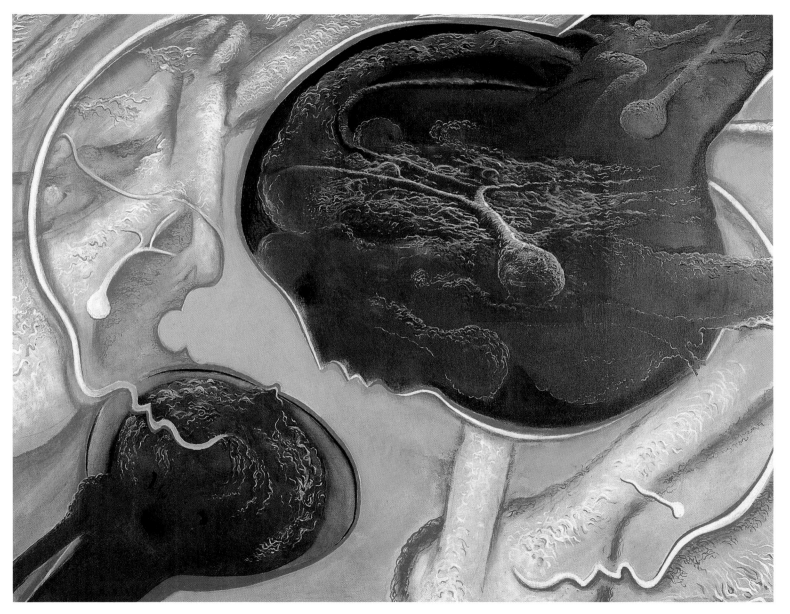

Figure 3. Herb Greene, *The Human Neuron*

that I experience while responding to Turner's engine. I describe these responses and my expressions of them — that the tubes also suggest bones, hands, and creatures — to represent the unifying body-mind that underlies all feeling and thought.

My imagination and my painting style are both influenced by the vibrating, physiologically-inspired, figure ground images of Pavel Tchelitchew's painting, *Hide and Seek* (figure 8), which was executed in 1941-2. This exceptionally intricate and arresting painting, incorporating multiple perspectives that seem to suggest scientific relativity, conveys the illusion of one living organism transforming into another, which dramatizes organic continuity. This work is perhaps not as well known today as it was when Tchelitchew's art was featured on a cover in *Life* and in art histories of the period. Nevertheless, the museum postcard of *Hide and Seek* (figure 8) continues as a top seller, and I continue to meet artists and lay people who strongly admire this particular work, which confirms my belief in its lasting attraction and importance.

My personal endeavor to suggest the complexity of cognition owes something to a search for a way to express the unceasing activity of the physiological and neurological processes that effect even our calmest states of being and the most serene appearance of perceptual objects. Further, I am attempting to express meanings as overlapped, contiguous and extended. For whatever reason, I find nervousness in some of my paintings that disturbs. Could daily Depression-era shouting matches about money during my early

childhood dinners have caused nervousness transmitted to canvass? While others have mentioned an expression of line, mass and metaphor in my work, I never hear acknowledgement of serenity or simplicity. Nonetheless, I remain enthusiastic about my idea, which is to devise a painted ground as an art symbol of the imaginative process by which we grasp thoughts and feelings arising out of perception.

For example, in figure 5, a famous snapshot of Anne Frank is integrated with hand-drawn indications of feelings and ideas initiated by details in the photograph. These include my responses to her sensitive, uplifted face, and to her arresting and expectant gaze with its glimmer of aspiration. A prehension of morbidity in Anne's face that can be associated with ideas about her death finds expression in the birdlike figures rising above Anne's head that are down-turning, as if in mourning, or in the curve of her hair, which echoes the curves of birds in an adjoining photograph. I see the preening birds as a sign of caring programmed into creatures, and the evolution of that behavior into human love, which is an embodied "offstage" feature informing our interpretation of Anne. My intent is to emphasize a selection of references, and to suggest overlappings and extensions among them. In confronting my additions, readers will, I hope, freshen the image of Anne Frank for themselves, and feel both confirmation and surprise.

In Part Two of the book I present the major tenets of Whitehead's theory of the perceiving mind. My method is to utilize

Figure 4. Herb Greene, *Collage with Turner's* Wind, Rain and Speed

Figure 5. Herb Greene, *Homage to Anne Frank* (Detail)

quotations and paraphrases from *Process and Reality* and Whitehead's other writings. I want the reader to come away with experience of Whitehead's original expression. There is a book[11] containing a selection of Whitehead's memorable quotations on science, history, philosophy, education and other topics. At times Whitehead is capable of breathtaking prose and I hope to have included several examples.

I comment on each Whitehead selection, applying the concept, sometimes supported by recent findings in the cognitive and neurosciences, to the analysis of the images in the collage paintings. Thus there are selections pertaining to his theory followed by applications to the concrete. This allows a fresh and more precise vocabulary with which to discuss how we feel and think about images, as well as forming a presentation of Whitehead's thought and terminology.

To assist the reader with Whitehead's terms, I have placed a section on terminology at the beginning of Part Two. A better sense of Whitehead is gained as one acquires an overview of his system, and this presentation and placement, I believe, is preferable to a more conventional glossary at the end of the book.

In the 1950s, when I began reading Whitehead, one could easily find Bantam Books paperback editions of his *Science and the Modern World*, *Adventures of Ideas*, *Modes of Thought* and *The Aims of Education*. Now in most bookstores we are likely to see few of his titles compared to many by his student, collaborator and friend,

Bertrand Russell. Russell's output was enormous, widely-admired for both simplicity and clarity, and he received a Nobel Prize for literature. One reason for a decline in Whitehead's academic and bookstore popularity is that the process of perception and a metaphysics suitable for treating the mental process of ideation are not simple, and neither could Whitehead's explanations be simple. Another reason is that Russell's passion for analytic-logical reductions and positivist programs as the most effective descriptions of reality still dominates philosophy and science. With positivism, meaning is limited to expressions of technical, scientific language, and verifiability couched in conventional subject-predicate form, supposedly free of subjective value assertions. As Whitehead has stated, Humpty Dumpty did not precede the wall that he sat on, nor can his act of falling be expressed without recourse to an embodied background of sensation, spatial modeling, bodily containment, and metaphors of the consequences of falling currently inadmissable to analytic philosophy.

Finally, many academics are put off by Whitehead's connection of concepts of immanence, aesthetic and moral consistency, beauty and adventure to the realizations of human creatures in their attempts to understand their world. For Whitehead, choice in aesthetic and moral decisions is required as we evolve our understanding and imaginative enjoyment. Finding no materialist explanation to account for choice, Whitehead gives the name "the consequent nature of God" to this agency, not as a traditional theological requirement, but out of deference to historical connotations of God as the maker and organizer of harmony in our higher mental satisfactions. Whitehead's God becomes a metaphysical necessity. The influence of this doctrine on image interpretation is taken up in Chapter Twenty-Five, *Creativity and Novelty*.

Currently, metaphysics are not in fashion and Whitehead's are seen as outside the boundaries of post-modern philosophy. My intuition, buttressed by the opinions of many others, is that Whitehead, the intensely private sage who destroyed all his correspondence and unpublished writing, was on the right track. Given time, when mental process and concepts of metaphor and embodied experience are more fully understood, his views will be found to be closer to human truth and understanding than those of the brilliant, but sometimes flighty Russell, who was so often in the public eye, and of the post-modernists and multiculturalists who argue for the leveling of values and meanings.

Nevertheless, Russell's positivist approach to our understanding of a stone shows that long established habits of language and common sense pervade our simplifications of everyday perception. A stone does in important ways possess seemingly discrete, enduring and verifiable qualities. I can, with familiar language, compare its weight, color and shape to other objects right now without concern about its decay during the next million years. With Whitehead I can reflect on the stone's coming dissolution, that its present shape reminds me of a Cycladic head, and that some creative agency is required to explain why certain thoughts or feelings about the stone may be cherished over others.

The sensibility for appreciation of Whitehead's universe, where any event, object or quality can have some structural and emotional bearing on any other via prehensions of the body-mind cutting through the continuum of space-time, is dramatized by our exposure to the surprising comparisons and unifications made evident in film, collage and information processing. I have just turned from a television commercial for automobile tires where, in the space of about five seconds, the image moves in computer-generated transformations from the calm surface of a lake to an emerging bubble, after which the tire emerges as a well-defined watery image of a tire, and then to the tire emerging in full realism on a car. The ad popularizes the idea of linking diverse and unexpected combinations of events within the flux of an ever-changing world, and of our constantly shifting foci and associations. More instructive than the advertising fantasy with its suspect juxtaposition of a realistic lake and a brand name auto tire, are Lennart Nilsson's images, often shown on public television, that allow us to perceive the developing human fetus during its continuum of incredible changes in scale and form. Nilsson's films and photographs shows how the fetus interacts with minute particles introduced into its environment from far and near.

Organisms tend to adjust their interactions within their environment to further their self-interest. Whitehead gives the name "subjective aim" to the agency that directs the organism's adjustments. I apply his explanations of subjective aim in my analysis of the budding feeling of aspiration that we recognize in the photograph of Anne Frank. Because Whitehead's system provides a comprehensive approach utilizing modern biological and physical interpretation, and a technique for probing the anatomy of a feeling through the analysis of its prehensions, it can enlarge our understanding of aesthetics, the assembling of meaning, and of organic process in various disciplines.

Contrary to the current academic mainstream's limited teaching of Whitehead, scientists, ecologists and many of the rest of us are seeing the world in terms of process and holistic relationships. In this context, there is continuing interest in Whitehead's work. Well over 700 articles and books on Whitehead, published from 1970 to 1996, are listed at the University of California. As I have applied Whitehead's ideas of subjective aim to the analysis of images, Jeremy Rifkin in his 1983 book, *Algeny,* incidentally, not included in the list above, applies Whitehead's concepts of time and subjective aim to genetic engineering.[12] I refer to a few of these and other sources where they further my discussion, and to suggest that Whitehead's work will gain appreciation as obsolete conceptions about sense perception and the derivation of meaning give way to recent studies in neurobiology, cognitive process and the functions of metaphor.

Finally, one might ask why a painter would seek to produce a book explaining his art. I have never considered painting as a vocation, nor am I sure that what I am doing is art in a conventional sense. I see myself as an individual with a certain imagination coming out of architecture attempting to investigate a few philosophic and aesthetic ideas. I see the deep, continuous space found in the work of Rembrandt and Frank Lloyd Wright as a sign of immanence and the necessity to create a symbol of the unseen mental background that informs appearance. This is one such idea: how different aspects of separate visual and thought objects can commingle in thought and art represents another. To apply Whitehead's concepts to the explanation of images is my primary objective. While my painting technique is related to current media where photographs, film, hand-drawn fantasy and real actors are merged in one expression, I have not been enough satisfied with most of my results to seek a gallery and have not exhibited since 1976. I have continued to keep and revise many of my works. A book offers the best opportunity to present the thoughts that have motivated me and the current state of my efforts.

While skipping through art history, philosophy, cognitive research, neuroscience, and Whiteheadian explanations of my efforts will lack competency to some, I can only say that selective skipping is what my intellectual and artistic life has been like since high school, when I first cut out items on Picasso and Frank Lloyd Wright from *The New York Times,* and read my first articles in *Scientific American* on bird navigation by star patterns, and on Harlow's baby monkeys going to a wire mother with cloth attached more than a wire mother with nursing bottle attached (a point which underlies my intuition to emphasize the importance of texture and symbols of touching in my architecture and painting). Connecting these subjects with my reading of Whitehead and art history to images is what I have to offer.

As the selection of photographs makes plain, my collages often deal with tragedy, and with socio-emotional and moral concerns. To make a masterly painted expression of the synthetic nature of mind in the face of such concerns is beyond my talent. Nor can my hand painted additions compete with the complexities of interest and miracles of some of the great photographs and art works that I include in my collage paintings. But when so much art in the twentieth century has proffered alienation and surface, there may be at least sympathy for an approach that is concerned with feeling, perceptual process, and with delving into our responses to photographed events as a way of understanding ourselves and our world.

CHAPTER TWO

Lenses for Seeing:
Sensationalist Objectivity and Organic Process

I remember an early documentary film showing lions after feeding, with bloodied faces, pausing with vacuous stares. Some were sleeping on their backs with paws outstretched at unexpected and humorously incongruous angles. My youthful conceptions of leonine dignity, formed by stories, statues, circuses, and encyclopedias, were dispelled by an unattended telescopic camera.

The camera has educated us by showing both the familiar and unfamiliar natural world in a new light. It has greatly enlarged the realm of what is visible through the use of new kinds of technological aids, such as satellite computer-assisted photography and the electron microscope. But most important for this discussion, the photograph can provide a reality that has the presence of an archaeological artifact — a happening that was really there and yet is also here — somehow a double focus within space-time. By providing us with a stabilized image that allows us leisure and opportunity to find information that we might overlook with the often hurried and habituated eye, the photograph enables us to study events taken from nature with a concentration that enriches our understanding. Through the documentary on lions, my discoveries enlarged my knowledge of the way lions look and of what they are.

Even family snapshots can supply a sense of unsupervised truth, in contrast to preconceived and stereotyped dispositions. In my wife's candid sequence (figure 6), her two-year-old granddaughter is shown picking up a stone, losing or throwing it over her shoulder, and apparently coming to a state of mirth over her actions. In frame 3, I see her upturned face and react to positively felt prehensions of the body metaphor "up is good," her look of expectancy, and her face and arms remind me of a beautifully drawn cherub in a Tiepolo. In frame 2, I see her twisted mouth and pigeon-toed feet. Is she about to drool? These are among my mildly negative prehensions that are gently overpowered by my positive prehensions. For example, her coloring and modeling in light, wispy blond hair, feminine dress, and possible "what to do next" expression are positive prehensions. I also carry over positive prehensions from

1   2   3

4   Figure 6. Nanine Hilliard Greene, *The Joy of Being Two*   5   6

other photos in the sequence as I continue my perusal in search of satisfaction and understanding. In frame 4, I am mildly shocked by the large size of her head and the absence of neck. My surprise is mingled with my conceptual feelings that confirm the "truth" of the child's age and how she still retains her baby shape. Has she tossed the stone over her shoulder or unwittingly lost it? In frames 5 and 6, is her apparent mirth related to her losing the stone in the midst of a pleasurable act, joy over the mysterious disappearance of the stone, awareness of her act, or something else?

Photographs seem to offer a sense of a stable reality. We are prone to feel that a photograph lets us know and control its contents, that we can manipulate photographs as if they were slices of the world we can actually possess. Respecting this qualification in doing collage, I use the photograph primarily for the feeling of fact that it communicates. Of course, photographers impose their values on the selection and treatment of facts, but one of the principal virtues of photography is that it can record what happens without prejudice. We can then, guided by subjective aim, select treasures such as the crying Frenchman (figure 27), edited from a filmstrip showing the surrender of French flags to the Nazis in Marseille at the fall of France, or the haunting image of Anne Frank, (figure 4) selected from a series of snapshots made in an automatic photo booth and enlarged for the cover of *Life*.

The intellectual side of our response to photographs is grounded in the belief that we are looking at the presence of sheer fact. As we respond to the events of hair, gaze, shadows and dress ornament in the photograph of Anne, we can pause to examine both our objective and our subjective feelings. We seize upon details — this uplifted head is more aspiring than the other heads included in the photo booth series. Those dark shadows around the eyes add gravity and appear ominous. I have a prehension of something morbid about the face in the photo. Our knowledge of Anne Frank's history influences our interpretation of those shadows and feelings of morbidity and fills them with significance. Editing the photos of the Frenchman and Anne Frank enables us to idealize. We bring the resources of our bodily and mental life — our knowledge of gazing out, the uplifted head, hair styles, fashion, femininity, and Jewish and Nazi history — which we network and bring to the photograph as we are continually compelled to notice the surprise, complexity, sources of emotional feeling and beauty in the events around us.

Susan Sontag[1] says that photographs make us chronic voyeurs, which can result in a leveling of meaning for all events. This leveling represents an attitude that is enhanced by artists like Robert Rauschenberg who use photographs to suggest the contemporaneous and random. The immortality Rauschenberg gives to a collage of photographs that might include Jackie Kennedy, an astronaut floating in space and street debris, implies an intellectual attitude that holds one phenomenon to be as "good" or "valuable" as the next. This attitude is derived largely from science's preference for "objective evaluation" and the twentieth-century determination to avoid the romantic and sentimental. There is also a movement to escape from anthropomorphic humanism exemplified by a side of Heidegger's philosophy[2] where he stresses primary essences of thought, ontologies of thought, and the neutrality of thought, as if these are the sought after fundamental characteristics of knowing and being. Heidegger usually holds these fundamentals as separate from nature, or at least free of an obligation to conform to instances of nature.

These attitudes are often taken to imply that an artist should project a sense of the neutrality of things as a goal, and should avoid overtly directing the historical, emotional or other associative connections of things. Let the viewer freely form associations with the floating astronaut image without the artist's personal experience and vision getting in the way. This sounds democratic and reasonable, but the position of "objectivist-neutrality" is itself a product of subjective aim, and seems to ignore the premise that "calculated" exclusion of the artist's subjective world and overview would delete often rich and informative content in the artist's work, such as Picasso's need to "destroy" the subject of his painting or Redon's need to express his urge to move from darkness into light.

To return to tracing the roots of objective neutrality, the effect of what Whitehead calls "sensationalist" ideology descending through Descartes' separation of mind and body is probably the most important factor still contributing to the reification of neutrality in twentieth-century science, philosophy and high art. This ideology inherited the belief in ideal forms from Greek philosophy and of absolutes from Medieval scholars. It separated mind from matter and the biological organism of which the mind is an outgrowth. By a strict process of mental abstraction that purged the life out of thought, Plato and many philosophers following him found universals to be predominantly causative. The universal "essence" was considered to be more real than any piece of actual nature.

This view has been extremely influential on the treatment of rectangular "ideal" forms in much modern art and architecture. The rectangles of color that hang in our most prominent museums are subject to similar influence. The photographically-realistic but very "neutral" and "flat" paintings of urban streets by Richard Estes, and the even flatter watery stripe abstracts of Morris Louis, where the pigment has been thinned to the utmost, exemplify the ideals of "flatness" and neutrality that were propelled by critics and artists in the 'sixties. Described in Tom Wolfe's *The Painted Word,*[3] and *From the Bauhaus to Our House,*[4] these "flat" forms are considered as expressions of "primary essences," "primary forms" and "primary ideas" that we clothe with various temporary qualifications from our mental wardrobe. While my version of Whitehead's criticism of sensationalist dualism will be familiar to many, I want to recast it briefly, since, in contrast to Descartes' separation of logic and feeling, I emphasize Whitehead's interpretation of perception and mental process. With Whitehead there is a prismatic fluctuation of the objective with the subjective and a symbiosis of the linguistic intellectual construct with feelings, intuitions and emotions that characterize our normal response to images, roses and everything else. In this approach there are no primary or secondary forms, no permanent essences, only forms in an emerging, submerging and shifting play in which no form, feeling or idea can permanently preempt another.

In *Science and The Modern World,* Whitehead shows the development of thought that led to seventeenth-century science, in which nature was conceived as irreducible brute matter — an impermeable material with its stuff or particles disconnected from the causes and ends of their situations. Such material was thought to be spread throughout space in configurations such as stones and roses. The material of these entities was thought to be senseless, valueless and purposeless. Descartes was influenced by Galileo's theory of primary substances and secondary attributes, and was writing during a time that sought certainty and civil order after decades of religious slaughter. With his appetite for the "rational" and for permanence, he held that stones and roses possessed sup-posedly permanent, objective characteristics, such as mass, location, number and, perhaps, outlines. These primary characteristics were qualified by impermanent subjective secondary factors such as colors, smells and sounds. We access the secondary factors as if from a super-rolodex in the mind, to recast Whitehead in popular terms. The color and scent of a rose were not integral to the irreducible matter of the rose, but were considered to be products of the mind's

ability to recover these qualities in the rolodex. Wordsworth should have written an ode to himself rather than the nightingale. The nightingale's matter was believed to be physically outside the mind and had to obey Newton's laws, which required that matter be discretely located and measurable while the song remained within the mind. "Nature is a dull affair, soundless, scentless, colorless; merely the hurrying of material, endlessly, meaninglessly."[5]

Whitehead calls this theory of dualism the sensationalist view of perception because temporary sensations produced by the mind clothed the theoretically neutral, durable, primary configurations of matter. This view gave matter a reality of permanence, a permanence that was also attached to formulations of abstract thought such as Newton's laws, or to later art theories such as the doctrine of flatness as an essence, which held that the essential fact of a painting is its flat surface and not the illusion of three-dimensional space familiar to previous centuries of Western painting. Lakoff and Johnson[6] suggest that the world as we "know" it contains no primary qualities but only embodied qualities. They state that the mind works by metaphor, and demonstrate how the mind is embodied in the deep sense that our conceptual systems and our capacity for thought are shaped in terms of physical acts like moving, seeing, manipulating objects and eating, as well as adding, speaking, writing and making objects. We cannot comprehend or reason without such metaphors. The meta-phoric mind is part of the very structure and fabric of our interac-tions with our world, in which we build meaning by seeing things in terms of other things. It is these embodied qualities — that "up" is usually processed as good and that down is "bad" — that we can approach through Whiteheadian prehensions.

Overstating the concreteness and permanence in ideal forms, natural laws and conceptual doctrines such as "flatness" is the principal legacy of sensationalist ideology, reflecting a more than two-thousand-year tradition of belief in eternal ideal forms and Aristotelian fixed categories of thought. The increasingly accepted, Whiteheadian view integrates the concept of the universe and its creatures as if both are undergoing evolutionary adventures within the physical field. Our own descriptions of events within the field are limited by the neurobiological and conceptual-linguistic filter that determines human experience. Such experience is built up by an evolving nervous system, brain, mind, and culture that continuously reconstitutes meaning in a changing environment. Gertrude Stein's early twentieth-century projection of consciousness in a continuous present where there is no exact repetition exemplifies her sensitivity to the continuous reconstitution of meaning that characterizes actual perception. Whitehead, her admired acquaintance, in conversation with Lucien Price,[7] remarked that there are no natural laws, only temporary habits of nature. He cautioned about constants in science such as Newton's laws of motion or the speed of light. While these constants may prevail for most of our observations on earth, we cannot be sure that they are the only interpretation, or that they hold for all regions or for all times in the universe. The discovery of

black holes would seem to confirm Whitehead. We must also account for our body in the mind-experience of gravity, bending, forces, containers, extenders, speed, light, geometry, metaphors of consistency, and more, to give the background meaning necessary to interpret Newton's forces and the speed of light.

Of course, in order to function we must narrow down experience. When I look at the aged man in figure 7, I pay attention to selected ideas about the man just as I would when I step out into the garden and immerse myself in the pleasurable green leaves. My mind is structured so that it can come to closures of pleasurable greenness by bypassing multitudes of potentially relevant information — that the leaves do not appear threatening or that they make chlorophyll. But in searching for an accurate rendering of our responses to the leaves or the aged man, and in many situations that require practical or aesthetic judgments, connections among the multitude of their possible meanings and metaphors cannot be dismissed.

The influence of sensationalist doctrine, with its idealization of the separate, changeless and neutral, has much dissipated since the discovery of electromagnetism, relativity, and quantum theory. As Whitehead has said, reigning philosophic doctrine is never dispatched with some formal ceremony accepted by all interested parties. What happens is that old propositions and attitudes gradually cease to be of interest as fresh and more viable propositions are gradually established. Yet the mindsets and language constructs of sensationalist-objectivism, in the face of accumulating scientific knowledge to the contrary, have persisted into this century. Mies Van der Rohe, whose "ideal" rectangles of glass and steel dominated American and European architecture in the 1950s and 'sixties, treated this form as an "essence" — an expression of supposed primary function and also of "ideal" beauty. Any unwanted associations or facts that accompany the experience of one of his buildings — that a stack of two-hundred apartments can appear visually and socially regimented through its uniform, flat grid of horizontals and verticals, or even inelegant as engineering science, or that an all-glass building in the 'fifties was susceptible to excessive solar gain and fading drapes — may be ignored. It is in the West that we have been convinced that abstract ideas — scientific, philosophical, and aesthetic — are realities that disdain embodied metaphoric as well as practical connections to the world. They require nothing but themselves to exist. We often defend these ideas with a militant energy that has no exact counterpart in the East, where both human concepts and natural phenomena are seen as manifestations of a unified one stuff or cosmic energy.

Whitehead has convinced me that the sensationalist inheritance that has been absorbed in the objectivism of "primary forms" in the work of logical positivists, many scientists, Bauhaus architects, and many modern artists has led them to misinterpret both the status and the results of their abstractions. Mark Rothko, the noted painter who was a younger contemporary of Mies, presented in his quest for essences soft-edged rectangles of near uniform color and texture as works of high-art. He, as other artists absorbed in sensationalist assumptions of our culture, transferred the status and values of "primary constant properties" to colors and preconceived objectivist linguistic channels of interpretation, in particular the notion that an art expression is more pure and thus more valuable if it refers to nothing but an ideal essence.

In the late twentieth century an artist who randomly places a load of dirt or even manure on a museum floor suggests that these materials and their displacement are as eligible for aesthetic judgment as configurations of traditional materials. With many postmodernists, I can accept that no material, even manure, given an appropriate scale and context (while, perhaps, moving the exhibition to the outdoors) should be excluded from aesthetic consideration. But the impositions of sensationalist legacy in European history as they have affected modern art should be better understood. Whitehead's point is that in the assumptions of seventeenth-century science that were woven into subsequent Western thought, we may perceive matter (read twentieth-century ideal form, including manure), reason about it, and even suffer over it, but we may not interfere with it, because the isolated bit of matter, informed by Greek, Medieval, and Cartesian notions of the ideal and the absolute, was considered to be ultimate bedrock.

For the Western scientist, or an economist such as Adam Smith who proffered his views on economics as given, iron laws of necessity built into nature, or certain artists in the twentieth century, the Cartesian attitude that one is expressing a primary and permanent characteristic or function rather than an impermanent characteristic or attribute is not merely an academic exercise. There is an accrued emotional and intellectual interest that descends from the Greek dramatists attached to this attitude. Whitehead shows how the Greek view of fate as remorseless and indifferent, urging a tragic incident to its inevitable conclusion, where the end is more important than either the beginning or the process of development, became the vision of science. That vision informed the sensationalist view of isolated bits of matter. Matter and, tacitly, ideal essences were obeying the laws of nature which, in the seventeenth and twentieth centuries, were equated to decrees of fate.

It may seem an exceptionally long stretch to credit this line of thought to the cultural background leading up to a museum exhibition of a random pile of dirt or bricks. Yet Whitehead, who was cognizant of unconscious belief systems at the springs of human action, shows how this view came to dominate science and to heavily influence economics and morality through the nineteenth and into the twentieth century. This, in turn, has convinced me of its applicability to aesthetics.

In the seventeenth century the scientific scheme and the sensationalist view had the effect of introducing a functionalist bias into thought. After Newton, structural and functionalist meanings of nouns gradually replaced others as preferred meanings. The bias,

conforming to the new world-view, devalued terms of feeling, spirit, and imagination because these were considered to be secondary and, consequently, impermanent aspects of the world.

In spite of the protests of many philosophers and artists such as Emerson and Frank Lloyd Wright against functionalist and idealist biases, the sensationalist treatment of experience had a powerful influence on everyday life. Whitehead talks about the blind eye of the industrial age as it created blight and dismissed beauty. Obviously, insensitivity to beauty was not the only cause of blight. Yet there is a parallel here with the simplistic functionalist and idealist biases in the architecture and city planning of many modernists who were influenced by the International Style. They minimized or ignored the social arrangements and customs of individuals and of whole cultures. Their boxlike housing blocks with neutral color schemes and grid-like plans proliferated around the world from the 1920s through the 'seventies. Their designers thought they were expressing supposedly universal ideas about form and technology that were free of atavistic patterns of social and functional use, and psychological associations. In the more affluent countries, many of these housing blocks have been torn down or extensively renovated because of their perceived negative impact upon the lives of their inhabitants.

Other factors enforcing the modern projection of neutrality into matter and the manner of seeing it are biases against religious and ethnic influences, and even of bonding with nature, that stem from Marxism and other materialist world views. Twentieth-century developments in aesthetics that favor the random, the automatic and the indeterminate in a rejection of predetermined order and values should also be mentioned. There are exciting and positive interpretations of the random and indeterminate, and I try to bring them to my discussion of indeterminacy and the seemingly random-access memory of neurobiology and the mental continuum. But to present events as being intrinsically neutral is one thing, while the basis on which the events are interpreted is another. We may enjoy a sense of an unbiased neutrality in the events captured in a photograph, but we inevitably choose our emphasis in making or evaluating an image based on scenarios directed by subjective aim. Further, some artists, for reasons ranging from social criticism to self promotion, have taken to shocking the bourgeoisie and various cultural establishments as operational policy. Hence, piling dirt on a museum floor may be motivated by these latter considerations. Yet the intellectual defense for the presentation, even if purported to be a post-modernist reaction against the limits of modernist ideal forms, depends on agreement among an art elite that the shape, or some other approved essence (even the artist's right to absolutely unfettered expression) can exist on a completely ideal plane.

According to Whitehead, modern philosophy has lost relevance for most non-academics and has nearly been ruined because so much philosophic effort is still contained by objective standards based on sensationalist-influenced logic. Juggling abstractions to separate the objective from the subjective, as in a logical positivist's struggle to express that there are three brown cows in a field without inconsistencies in logic, can never solve the problem of characterizing the cows as an actuality in their situation, which was the aim of Whitehead's philosophy. It seems to me that aesthetics in the mid-twentieth century, aside from the social issues of fashion and power on which Wolfe reports, reached apogees of confusion by trying to disconnect forms from their causes and by pursuing abstract essences because of fallout from the sensationalist tradition.

As for perception, creatures for their survival and development are not free to pick and choose from their perception of neutral matter. With Whitehead, evolution itself depends on a selection process that is based on subjective aim, which he traces back to the most primitive organisms and even to the elementary physical particles. In human affairs the enjoyment of consciousness and thought is not an outgrowth of value-free perceptions. Sunlight and warmth are more necessary for life than darkness and cold.

With the preceding commentary as background I want to consider Cartier-Bresson's photograph, *Aged Academic Entering a Cab*, included in my collage painting, figure 7. This extraordinary photograph initiates a sense of the sacred, of value, and of mystery behind the neutral aspect of events to which most acculturated people can respond. The decisive flat plane and larger scale of the aged man's profile, hat and cloak are seen in forceful contrast to the exaggerated perspective of the cab, onlooking men, and background

Figure 7. Herb Greene, *Epochal Time*

architecture. This geometrical contrast of flatness and depth, felt with my particular body-mind, has an impact something like the golden mean in the proportions of the Parthenon. It invokes an arresting conceptual prehension of valued order that allows me to feel the other prehensions of content in the perceived event as more positively unified contrasts. In other words, my attention and desire to continue my mental evaluation of Cartier-Bresson's photograph is stimulated and maintained by this geometrical set as I "map" it with references to concepts such as "suspension in time," "a distant future," "a distant past," and a changing socio-political situation.

The striking hat with honorific plume suggests privilege that possibly descends from the *Ancien Regime*. The man's feet are invisible, making his figure seem to float, in rewarding contrast to the hefty bystander in a beret whose feet are firmly planted on the pavement. This contrast enforces a sense of suspension or drifting, a sense that provides a reference frame in which the aged man becomes a symbol of the passage of time and of a social order. The cab, with its perspective overlapping of pipes, rack, braces, mirror, wheel and moldings, appears to me, in context with the aged man, as a symbol of technology about to speed humanity toward an unknown future. The vigorous depth and motion of the tire and the other parts of the cab produce strong tensions against the flat, stable, yet floating plane of the aged man. The contrasts in the images of cab and man produce the shock of collage. In the background, the mansard-topped urban architecture, with its eroded profile, looms like a ruin rising out of a distant mist. The sense of the past conveyed by this French architectural prototype enforces the sense of age symbolized by the man and his rather elegant "French" costume, and the sense of social change in the contrast of the older man with the younger onlookers in their street clothes.

To my eyes, the human transaction in the picture is probably initiated by the hat. In the context of the other data in the scene, the hat's arresting visual prominence and its rich symbolic possibilities direct the responses of the three onlooking bystanders, as well as the viewer of the photograph. The bystanders could be socialists musing over the passage of privilege into oblivion, the idea of mortality, or they could be feeling honorific sentiment. Most likely, in some degree, they may be subject to all these realizations.

The man, in the costume of cloak and hat which suggests authority, is an academic, not a famous political figure as several viewers have supposed. He conveys to me an expectation of respect. The cluster of window balcony railings and shutters look to me, in their shapes, like eight "badges" or "blinders" conveying vague notions of uniformity. The badge shapes, the sense of uniformity, and the authority we attribute to the hat prompted my initial painted response, a frontal "head-badge-authority" figure at the upper right, which looked to one viewer like a "tin God." I felt this was a near perfect response. Prehensions of authority based on class and institutional privilege, the "thinness" of a tin badge, and a blind but ritualized presiding presence through the metaphor of the "tin God" seemed accurate, while allowing the aged man to retain prehensions of respect and the span of human life.

The major stimulus for these notions of authority is the hat image, which I acknowledge and repeat below the "head-badge." Nascent fingers descend from the "head-badge," as if to make contact with the photographed hat and its significance. Below the painted hat is another set of larger fingers that touch the car door and hold a match to acknowledge incidents in the photo. The cigarette-match incident — possibly a sign of urban sophistication and, more recently, a health hazard — may seem outside the main closures of meaning, and yet add content to the context of the wider world.

The sacredness we find in the photograph lies in the way it allows us to map already deeply harmonized human interests into an incandescent concentration. As we view the photograph, we orchestrate notions such as civilization, French nationhood (in my case prompted by French elegance in the shape of the hat, the Parisian mansard roof which was originally conceived as a tax dodge, now seen as a "humanizing" visual stimulus, the beret, and the faces of the bystanders), mortality, destiny, and the passage of time into poignant human terms. This orchestration arises out of the contrasts in the photograph set up by its powerful design pattern. We may take pause at the passion that we feel in the face of information which appears so dispassionately before us. While the data in the photo may be theoretically neutral as mere phenomena, it is never neu-

trally entertained. Our response depends on our individual values, aspirations, and participation in an imagined history. It is Cartier-Bresson's genius as an artist and observer and his "knowledge of the world," as I once heard him tell a television interviewer, that enabled him to see the possibilities developing as he moved in to capture the moment.

In making this collage painting, I have attempted to picture something of my response to the hat and the potential movement of the cab, and to express as a reference frame the condition of thought where one idea slides into another and where associations contingent to every detail are latent for recognition. I am influenced by Whitehead and Aristotle, who both agreed that we see things in terms of potentialities and that we seek what is behind the actual to find what is possible. The vaguely differentiated area under the left side of the enlarged heads is intended to indicate an idea of the background and immanence of thought. The nascent fingers touching the pink painted image of the hat are intended to represent the "anthropomorphic tin God" touching the hat, as if to acknowledge its importance. In the context of my criticism of the sensationalist legacy, I am trying to give expression to the concept that a perceived object, processed in the mind of an individual, can never be fully disconnected from a pragmatic treatment of attributes, associations, and the framework of actual and imagined events in which it is constituted.

CHAPTER THREE

Immanence and Figure-Ground

I first began to form the notion of a mental continuum as an idea for expression in art and architecture when I experienced Frank Lloyd Wright's Unity Temple and his prairie-style Coonley House. In these seminal works, executed about 1906, there is an extension of space beyond what the viewer can see in one position. This suggests a sense of immanence in which the seen is charged with causality stemming from the unseen, as if the meaning of the forms in sight depends on continuity and elaboration from implied features in the extensive space beyond immediate view. Such elaboration, always subject to the complex neuronal and synaptic pathways of the mind, allows us to bridge, by feeling and imagination, unseen possibilities and causal connections that are set in motion by Wright's orchestration of the metaphoric individualities of his forms and materials; for example, that the interior space is extensive, and yet feels both protected and open. The body-mind, from a basic need for security, is led around corners and beyond. The sizes, multiplicities and scale of boards, blocks, patterns, textures and

openings suggest a gamut that refreshes and confirms our understanding of human scale and human order, with an appropriateness that we have learned from our reading of nature.

At almost the same time that I was able to experience Wright's architecture, I saw Rembrandt's paintings in the Metropolitan Museum of Art. I remember poring over *Lady with a Pink*, fascinated by the way in which inflections in the dark background of deep space around the lady gave incident and life to her face, eye, costume, pearls, and the flower in her hand. As I viewed the details of the figure and face, my eye was continually drawn into the background by vague designs resembling these same details. The lady seemed linked to a universe replete with causality. This feeling of the immanence of a causal universe is what I missed in the work of most artists of Rembrandt's era who also employed the dark, Caravaggio-like backgrounds then in fashion.

The expression of immanence as an idea is an outgrowth of the Renaissance. The Medieval mind accepted a universe with God at the top and all the physical elements ranged below Him in a spatial hierarchy, like ornaments on a Christmas tree. Reason was not free to question this hierarchy, nor to reflect on the nature of the various elements and their connections to one another and to the world. Renaissance philosophers and artists effected a transformation leading to our modern world-view. According to Ernst Cassirer, "Medieval spatial hierarchies were annihilated. . . . *In Renaissance philosophy* [italics mine] there is no longer any 'above' and 'below' but a single universe homogenized within itself. The difference we perceive in the various bodies in the world is not a specific difference of substance, but rather is due to the different proportion in the mixture of the basic elements that are everywhere the same and are disseminated throughout the entire world."[1]

Renaissance thinkers, including Leonardo, began to reason that all things are immanent in one another. One's perception of things fluctuates, so that at one time an object like a tree branch becomes the focus for immanent connection to other things, while at another time the tree branch merges with the background as another object comes into focus. Leonardo's advice to artists about using a "prepared mind" to imagine various objects in the ambiguous stains on a wall exemplifies these ideas. The objects found were often the battling horsemen of a mind prepared during the Italian Renaissance. The shadowy modeling known as *sfumato* in Leonardo's drawing and painting, where figures are sensed as emerging from a background, gives expression to this sensibility of immanence.

Rembrandt's deep but not empty space in which objects seem to emerge and retreat is another potent expression of the idea that objects and substances are not static but moving and energized by cause and effect. Frank Lloyd Wright's extensive space with its distinctive feeling of immanence and purpose descends from this inheritance.

Among the most compelling twentieth-century presentations of immanence is Tchelitchew's *Hide and Seek* (figure 8). This strange and somewhat scary work, executed with overpowering draftsmanship, is a consummate statement of figure-ground, the situation where an image on one side of its boundary can be reversed to become the background of a different image on the other side of the boundary. Tchelitchew seems to draw on an imaginative interpretation of scientific notions of relative position that are necessary to location and meaning for entities in space-time. Every visible object in the painting — tree, hand, child, artery, leaf and bird — is perceived in a state of change, reflecting the actual transformations that occur in nature. The painting presents ground and object in a vibrating pattern, a pattern in which the ground could be object and object could be ground. This representation disallows the presumption of empty space, which we habitually consider to surround objects like trees, birds and children. The fluctuating pattern of figure-ground in *Hide and Seek* echoes the vibrating diffraction patterns that appear in electron photographs of the atom, forging a link to that reality. Tchelitchew directs our attention to the relative

Figure 8. Pavel Tchelitchew, *Hide and Seek*

way we select one object from another from the myriad of sense impressions. I saw this painting as the most powerful and layered imaging of awe imaginable, and as a masterful expression of a new cosmological outlook of the continual change of scale and viewpoint that nature actually presents. Professor Victor Koshkin-Youritzin, in a fascinating catalogue on the work of Tchelitchew,[2] points out how the human figures that are drawn in multidirectional perspectives and small distortions in *Hide and Seek* are analogous to Michelangelo's figure groups in *The Last Judgement.* Koshkin-Youritzen includes Michelangelo's sketches showing human figures growing out of trees, and notes figure ground reversible images in Michelangelo's great work. Citing Edith Sitwell, he discusses the possible influence of *The Last Judgement* on Tchelitchew.

Artists often devise models that illustrate some principle or idea. The models need not literally look like the subject they represent, but they can help us to visualize conceptual and phenomenal aspects of that subject. Tchelitchew's figure-ground distinctions in *Hide and Seek* can illustrate a sense of an object's transformation in space-time. A hand becomes a tree and human figures diminish in perspective and are repeated at different scales and positions, as if to symbolize both passage and duration in space-time. At the same time the hand-tree image can appear flat, like some entirely different object, perhaps a satellite photograph of a river delta. These multiple readings can suggest a vast, scaleless yet interlocked universe.

In their impressive presentation of the embodied mind, Lakoff and Johnson[3] show how perception actually requires a figure-ground choice that is necessary to the formation of human concepts. This distinction is not often present in mind-independent, objective concepts done in the objectivist tradition, in which meaning is based on allegedly "objective" truth rather than the process of human cognition. For human concepts, figure-ground distinctions are crucial, as consciousness requires the exclusion of alternatives. It is "this" we perceive and not "that," and the "this" requires derivation from the unseen "that."

It would seem that all acts of perception are illustrations of an immanence-figure-ground paradigm that is necessary to understanding. Edward O. Wilson, in his optimistic book, *Consilience,* about the future of science, arts and the creative mind, says that

> Outside our heads there is a freestanding reality. Only madmen and a scattering of constructivist philosophers doubt its existence. Inside our heads is a reconstitution of reality based on sensory input and the self-assembly of concepts. Input and self-assembly, rather than an independent entity in the brain . . . constitute the mind.[4]

Wilson goes on to say that the alignment of outer existence with its inner representation has been distorted by the idiosyncrasies of human evolution. Natural selection built the brain to survive in the world and only incidentally to understand it at greater depth.

The task of science is to diagnose and correct the misalignment. The development of optical instruments, scientific relativity, and recent discoveries in neurobiology carry us toward this correction.

I see *Hide and Seek* as a landmark of mid-century art absorbing such scientific realignment. I also believe that a large proportion of the population, perhaps more than museum curators, sense something of the relevance of showing the interior of the body underlying its exterior appearance. I remember my first visit to the painting when a class of eighth graders was excitedly gesturing and wowing until repeatedly ordered by their teacher to move on. Now that one can watch surgeries all day on television and see computer-enhanced enlargements of tissues, cells and organs, and that we are becoming more aware of the workings of minute organisms on our well-being, I expect a heightened intimacy with our bodily interiors to become an increasingly expected and necessary fact of human experience. We are beginning to visualize the genetic code, hormonal flows, neuronal networks and the transmission of feelings that constitute our being. Once again art reflects and predicts how we actually live and what we pay attention to.

Picasso's *Portrait of Dora Maar* (figure 9) illustrates another dramatic treatment of figure-ground and the play of flatness and depth. Both the head and the body of Dora Maar open to merge with the field. As a diagram of a figure merging with the ground, the drawing acts as a metaphor. It suggests that there is a world of causality transferring information from extensive space to the figure, and from the figure to extensive space. The image seems like a shorthand notation of the third dimension creatively adapted by Picasso to link modernism's interest in painting as a flat surface to the Western tradition of modeling in perspective and deep space.

In their book, *Metaphors We Live By*, George Lakoff and Mark Johnson[5] give the name "image-schematas" to what I have called models in images. They show in detail how image-schematas are inherent in metaphors such as the body as a container, and represent a fundamental process by which we express our understanding of structure in the world. In figure 8, metaphors direct us toward a realization of what Whitehead calls conceptual feelings. These are thought-feeling constructs of causality, immanence, and the idea that more than one position in space-time is required to comprehend objects. Such is the power of the imagination in processing a few signs which link us to discourses of previously harmonized experience.

Lakoff and Johnson tell us that we remold our experience by metaphors as we experience the image in the first place. Thus image-schematas are mental organizations that we use to navigate between abstract propositions and the particularities of concrete images. Picasso's drawing allows us to find relations between the sense of the body as a container that is, nevertheless, open to the world, and an imagined sense of Maar's life history.

For example, while Maar is painted facing us, her left eye and left side of her mouth read in profile, and her hand is shown in two

Figure 9. Picasso, *Portrait of Dora Maar*

positions forming image-schematas in close proximity that imply the multiple positions of cubism. While Picasso avoids the illusion of homogeneous perspective space that characterized Renaissance painting, he achieves feelings of depth both of space and of human poignancy. The foreshortening of the arm and the tiny ear, in contrast to the larger scale of the face, suggest the third dimension and give a satisfactory and even forceful gestalt of the actual compactness of Maar's figure as we know it from photographs. The sensitive eyes and mouth, and the tensions and lyricism of the calligraphic strokes of the head, eyebrows and neckline all contribute to content via their metaphors. The pensive eyes and sensitively drawn mouth, their ambiguities reflecting perhaps an introspective sadness, pique our curiosity about the woman's state of mind. Picasso's decisive gesture of opening the figure has an abruptness that can be harmonized with the abruptness of the foreshortened arm and the spatially isolated right eye. The evocative power of these compressions and the economy of their powerful design demonstrates Picasso's genius as he creates possibilities for drawing upon already harmonized meanings of unseen experience through the reconstitution of a few potent cues. The abruptness forces our attention and recognition. A lesson to be drawn from this painting is that the parts are particularly effective as carriers of information, and that we continually formulate these parts into wholes based on our assembly of contexts. We remember this process from gestalt theory, while it finds fuller elaboration in Whitehead. Picasso's *Dora*

and Rembrandt's complex modeling in *Lady With a Pink,* and *The Jewish Bride,* for me, exemplify heights of the West's achievement in representing spatial depth as a metaphor of immanence and causality.

A few years after I became acquainted with cubism and *Hide and Seek*, I began reading Whitehead. His writing seemed to me to describe the probable view of how the unseen background, including the bodily experience, informs appearance. Whitehead's work suggested to me that the expression of the unseen background that contributes to the meaning of a perceived object represents an important aesthetic problem. In designing an image of the mental continuum and the contingent background of the meaning of our thoughts, one has to suggest a mental space that simultaneously symbolizes the many directions, contents, scales and overlappings that inform our ideas about objects, yet still satisfies our acculturated sense of ordered three-dimensional space. Our explanations of the objects of our world require such a synthesis.

A photograph may call our attention to multiple spatial dimensions, directions and sizes, and other, harder to picture relationships among objects. Occasionally the same photograph may initiate thoughts about immanence that especially inhabit the meanings we derive from the photograph. Cartier-Bresson's 1950's photograph (figure 10) of German workers in a large tavern is, for me, a vivid example. The workers form a tableau that expresses tiredness, resignation, class designation, possible ethnicity, and a certain civility. The facial types and the uniformity of grooming and attire suggest a German setting. My latent disposition, formed largely during the war years, to view much about German social and political culture in terms of authoritarian regimentation, fixes on the similarities of clothing, a beer hall gestalt which is not necessarily negative, and other cues to complete a closure of "vaguely negative German uniformity." If I were to view a photograph of four or five Portuguese fisherman wearing similar clothing while cleaning a catch, I doubt that I would feel "negative uniformity." This provides an example of how the mind utilizes stored overlays of already harmonized meaning, including time frames, to map cognitive outcomes as directed by the subjective aim or intentionality of the viewer.

The up-stretched arm over the cap of the worker who is face down makes a pointed and somewhat humorous contrast to the tired, down-turning body language of the workers in the fore-ground. This gesture illustrates Cartier-Bresson's penchant for catching the whimsical with the serious, suggesting a French rather than German attitude behind the camera. To the rear of the standing workers, out of focus, and fading into the spatial ambiguities of the background, are smaller, seated figures who add scope and contrast to the foreground figures.

I framed the photograph so that the viewer can focus on its contents and its boundary. The gray-green frame was left open at the corners to emphasize the vanishing perspective of the hall and the workers. The frame vaguely suggests a distended Iron Cross. I placed an image of a German helmet at the lower right corner of the "Iron Cross" frame to call attention to the way in which hats and clothing shape our response to the photograph and to give a sign of my subjective prehension of a latent militarism. My bias was directed by an oversimplified generalization that the uniformities of the workers — their clothing and expressions — reflect a German uniformity and obedience that contributed to two world wars. This bias led to my readiness to make an Iron Cross out of the frame and to add the helmet. Such associations are obviously subject to error and are subject to revision by adjustments in our thinking. I wish to show that they are inescapable to our mental life in fleshing out the emotional and intellectual content of meaning, and are part and parcel of the cognitive process.

A Nilsson photograph of a fetus is placed directly under the standing workers. The fetus appears to be clutching the choroid membrane that contains it. The sense of constriction in this fetus image has a counterpart in a sense of the workers as if they are held in thrall. To me, in this context, constriction connotes birth into a socioeconomic setting from which one is unlikely to escape. The inert face of the fetus, with its closed eyes, seems to be without volition and harmonizes with the expression of tiredness and resignation that we find in the face of the worker at our far right. At the far right of the canvas is an enlarged, hand-drawn image of a worker suspended as if he is without volition. The faint image of a

Figure 10. Herb Greene, *Ideation*

horse at the upper left of the worker derives from a "Leonardo stain." It offers a fuzzy interchangeability between horse and worker via the metaphor of "working like a horse." In this collage, as in others, I am trying to project an image of an object fading in and out of a background of possible meanings and associations, a symbol of the reality that underlies appearance in which an object requires other objects that are not present for its meaning.

As acculturated viewers we ask ourselves where the workers come from, and what their future holds. We compare ourselves to them, examine their clothing and other cues, and, perhaps unconsciously, act out or otherwise engage the up-stretched arm and their other body postures within our own bodies to arrive at answers to our questions. All this attests to the immanence of interrelationships among all things. That all things are immanent in each other is an idea that rests on a philosophic and experiential foundation. For most occasions in our lives we rarely examine the foundation's condition. Other cultures have developed their own treatment of immanence. Hinduism, with its notions of recycling life, seems more concerned with the idea than we are in the West. But it is the West, with its inheritance of Greek philosophic inquiry into all things, that has led to new conceptions and visualizations of matter and space-time, and whose arts produced Rembrandt, Wright, Picasso, and the sensibility of Cartier-Bresson. As artists, their expressions have captured and advanced our awareness of the role of immanence in our understanding of reality.

CHAPTER FOUR

Athena

The first time I saw the Athena profile included in my collage (figure 11) I sensed references to pronounced human intelligence and sensitivity, freedom, constraint, stony texture, aggressiveness and death. I felt that I was witness to a rare coordination of signs and symbols provided by the artist, the light and perspective introduced by the photographer, and by the changing circumstances of time and mind. The profile view emphasizes the forward thrust of the helmeted head and the streaming direction of Athena's free-flowing hair. Her eye lacks volition, allowing her to be seen as a symbol of the race unable to choose and driven inexorably towards war. The thrusting geometry of the helmet and face also allow us to prehend feelings of Athena being driven by forces beyond her control. The textured patina suggests an astral substance and scale, as well as weathered bronze or stone.

In context with prehensions of aggressiveness, lack of volition and death, I can infer that the impulse toward war is programmed into the stuff of the universe. I cannot imagine a frontal view of this sculpture making such an impact. Thus photographs of art allow us to find and select those compelling details that seem essential to our understanding and satisfaction. We are able to layer meanings that we might find through memories of photographs of stars and galaxies, our knowledge of testosterone and male domination over women in the light of twentieth-century feminism, and so on. The "astral" texture, which may not have been present in the original sculpture or in the artist's idea, together with the photographer's focus on the sensitive profile and thrusting helmet, both enlarge and restrict the references available for our interpretation.

The struggle between the intelligent and sensitive woman and the death-seeking warrior has its roots in the displacement of the Goddess of Neolithic times by the aggressive, male-dominated Gods of Bronze Age Greece. The feelings projected in the image of Athena are based on, perhaps, unconscious memories of the transformation of the Goddess culture of nurture, wisdom and partnership between men and women into male-dominated, warlike cultures, of which we

Figure 11. Herb Greene, *Athena*

are the heirs. While some scholars dispute the "displacement hypothesis," Riane Eisler[1] is among those who affirm it. She cites recent archaeological evidence that suggests developed and peaceable Neolithic cultures existed for several thousand years in southern Europe and around the Mediterranean. War-based societies gradually replaced these cultures between 4,000 and 1300 B.C.E. Eisler shows how she (Athena) retained her ancient emblem of the serpent, which symbolized wisdom, while she began to appear with helmet and spear, and with her chalice replaced by a shield. If we examine our direct, felt response to the actual cues in the image we can recognize this dichotomy.

A war helmet rides just possibly a little high over Athena's bountiful, free-flowing hair. If the goddess were only supposed to represent war, I would expect the helmet to be lower to her brow. To me, this positioning, in context with her flowing hair and my strong prehension that she is a symbol of intelligence, can suggest the possibility that she is uneasy with the warrior's role. Athena's eye, fixed in an impersonal stare, indicates her lack of control. These feelings are heightened by the angular, aggressive looking helmet, which frames the black abyss of the eye aperture to combine feelings of aggression and the ominous. There is deep irony in the contrasts of the eye-abyss — to me, a symbol of death — with life's possibilities expressed by Athena's intelligent profile and streaming hair. The confluence of cues in this superb head of the goddess conveys the idea that in spite of the sensitivity and mental power exhibited by the

race, mankind is driven by the impulses of war.

My first idea in designing the collage was to make a thrusting horizontal composition of lines and forms that emphasize the horizontal direction to convey my notion of "Athena being driven." A rush of spears becoming slabs of what look vaguely like weathered stones reinforce this horizontal theme. The base of a stony column, with its connotations of Greek architecture and a ruin, also suggests the fibrous tissue seen in photos of the brain taken with electron microscopes. My intention is that this "stony-tissue-column base" should act as a symbol of such notions forming within the mind. A prominent yet vague image of a stony raptor is positioned at center-right. Perhaps it is an owl, connoting wisdom — an allusion to the wisdom of Athena. It pounces on, or rides a spear-like "stony" slab. The bird is touched by the hand of an ideogram of a man at center-top. The man is reaching for and following the bird. Both bird and man are ambiguous — not clear like the head of Athena — but distinct enough to be grasped by the roving eye. The reference is to man aspiring to the predatory bird, which takes its prey with strength, speed and the advantage of flight. This theme is a response to the falcons on Athena's helmet. While one can read these particular falcons as pert, alert, and with possible tinges of humor, my closures of war, death, gravity and irony overpower such light-hearted readings as I map into my experience of war helmets throughout history that have been adorned with birds of prey.

To the lower right of the body of Athena is a large prong-like form with references to both helmet and spear. It is linked to Athena by a continuous band of writing, cartoonish forms that suggest heads, arms and hands extending up the prong as if emerging from the ground. This cluster of body images is a conscious reference to Gericault's *Raft of the Medusa.* The possibly human figures ride the prong-like doomed survivors on a raft heading for destruction. Among the less visible images are a serpent to the lower left of Athena's left shoulder, a shield between the left and right arms of the man following the raptor, and a vaguely terrified face which I see as a consciously made symbol of unconscious fear, to the right of the prong. Next to Athena's profile there is an image of a helmet that is perhaps more of Nordic origin than of Greek. As Whitehead points out, the first task of conscious perception is to recognize an object as being this rather than that, which is also the basis for the figure-ground duality of perception stressed by Lakoff and Johnson[2]. I have selected the "Nordic" or "other" helmet to express this aspect of perception, as well as to provide a modified repetition of Athena's fiercely aggressive armor.

What I am trying to accomplish in making an image of mind is to express our mentally "free" coordination of events in extensive space-time. During my perception of Athena, I take up a selection of cues such as the eye abyss in the helmet, thrusting geometry, and the "astral" texture of the bronze. In so doing, I try to image various contrasts, identities, associations and feelings, and the modeling of ideas such as that Athena appears to be "driven to destruction," and

present them as if they were emerging from a fluctuating yet continuous ground. In this way I attempt to symbolize the appropriation of meaning from references to other event-situations in space-time during the mental process. The process is dependent on what Whitehead calls the "extensive continuum," a concept that allows us to differentiate all perceived pieces of information in the universe and to make meaning from our combinations of their aspects by means of prehensions. Perhaps this sounds too ambitious for anyone to attempt and yet, inevitably, everybody does it. Advertisers who created the Energizer bunny, artists who work in collage, the jokes of comedians, and even teenagers who use terms such as "spaced-out" are examples. The term "spaced-out" is an example of collage thinking — in this instance a colorful and efficient way of saying that an individual's mind is way out in space and not attached to the body as a container in the here and now. The image, which juxtaposes space and the individual, has undoubtedly been informed by a background of popularized space exploration and demonstrates the human ability to create metaphors with ease and move them fluidly from one context to another. Gertrude Stein,[3] in her lecture *Composition as Explanation,* delivered at Oxford in 1926, described how everyone is involved in expressing the composition of their time.

According to Stein, who collaged words more masterfully than perhaps any other modern writer in her book of 1914, *Tender Buttons*, it would be no coincidence that in 1979, Bateson[4] would state that in every current of causation in our biology, physiology, thinking, neural process, and in the ecological and cultural systems of which we are parts — each circuit in each current conceals or proposes paradoxes and confusions that accompany errors and distortions. Such activity is endemic to nature's efforts to make appropriate transfers of information. This is the situation that underlies the process that is central to thought and evolution: two or more pieces of information or command working together or in opposition.

Collage thinking, or the controlled collision of ostensibly unrelated pieces of information to produce new meaning, has become possibly the most creative and energizing force affecting the composition of art and thought in our era. If true, this proposition would be a verification of Stein's insight that certain artists and, possibly, some of today's teenagers are merely the advance guard in expressing the composition of their time. Whitehead's postulates, which are based on a reunification of the body and mind, matter as energy and the origin of feeling, and the fluctuation between the objective and subjective, allow us to examine expressions such as "spaced-out" as transfers of information into a concrete reality.

I defy structuralists, with their presuppositions of determinism, and post-modernists, with their language-thought paradigms, to advance our understanding of the expression "spaced-out." Yet post-modernism is freeing us from presuppositions of separating the objective from the subjective and ranking the former over the latter, and may indicate that there is more public readiness for Whitehead's notions of our perception of interlocking and interacting events within the extensive continuum. In Part Two I suggest some reasons for the growth of interest and efficiency in collage thinking and how they connect to Whitehead's theory.

CHAPTER FIVE

Responding to Barocci

Barocci's *Head of the Virgin*, incorporated into figure 12, combines the beatific sweetness, selfless detachment and otherworld ideality projected by Medieval artists in the sculptured portals of Chartres with the image of a corporeal, natural, human persona attained in the Italian Renaissance. With disarming assurance, the drawing synthesizes cues of tenderness, grace and accessibility that Western culture has come to associate with the Virgin, abetted by images, such as the Barocci, in which there are no cues to distract from the drawing's message of sweetness and detachment. Compare Barocci's drawing with Leonardo's *Head of a Woman* from the Louvre (figure 13). The hair and ear of Leonardo's woman are formed into spirals that evoke his studies of water and energy. The chiaroscuro of the eye, lips and neck admit much ambiguity. These cues, suggesting brooding, intensity and mystery, are signs of Leonardo's genius and complexity, but would distract from Barocci's simplicity and directness. With the Barocci, we feel surprise, delight and freshness at his capture of grace within the countenance of a palpable person.

How does the artist achieve this response? He enforces a sense of the reality of his subject by the masterful anatomy of the head and the spontaneity and realism with which he renders the sash and hair. Spontaneity and realism suggest the here and now, which provides a contrast to the sense of detachment and to the spiritual. The broad forehead and the wide spacing between the eyes contribute to a feeling of calm. The narrowing chin and, particularly, the small mouth, slightly pursed, with lovable curves, contrast to the slightly plump face and contribute to the "sweetness" of the Holy Mother. The becalmed expression and immanent smile let us impute an objectification of the sacrament, defined by the *Anglican Book of Common Prayer* as the outward and visible sign of an inward and spiritual grace. The firm, ovoid outline of the head conveys a notion of geometric containment derived from classical Greece, while the face itself invites our gaze because of its projection of an unselfconscious state of being.

I have responded to the Barocci in my first drawn gesture by framing the head with winglike, oversized "hands" and "drapery" to help locate the head within the picture and to communicate both surprise and affirmation. These wing-hand forms encompass the head and touch the suggested body of the Virgin, as well as the surrounding background forms, as if to suggest that these forms are together in a continuum. Suggestions of fingers and feathers emerge from a background of curving, convoluted, whitish, gray-green shapes. The cues of feathers relate to the hand-wings-drapery that address the Virgin's head and the angel at the far right. The gray-green shades around the Virgin's face are extended to the surrounding areas. The intention is to suggest an image of particular thoughts coming into the mind — a necessary context for any object of perception.

I extend the imaged "continuum" into forms of fingers that are uplifted in a sign of prayer. This sign of prayer is not bounded by a concept of the virgin mother, but may also be understood as a sign of the idealized transfer of Mary's virtues to an homage to actual women, which the British historian W. E. H. Lecky[1] identified with the rise and influence of rationalism during the Renaissance. Located on the bottom right, these praying fingers are extensions of billowy, curving, cylindrical forms that frame a dark cleft under them. The cleft suggests an anatomical orifice, a cut, a wound, or the vertex of the painting's merging and emerging curving forms. There is allusion to female sexuality in the painted background. This refers to the sensual and sexual in human existence, somewhat in the sense of tenth-century Hindu sculpture, in which the sexual integrates in full and seamless forms expressing cosmic wholeness. The suggestion of the spiritual connected to the libidinal, as in western notions of Eros, is also intentional. Lakoff and Johnson[2] tell us that it is the body that makes spiritual experience passionate. The body brings intense desire, and pleasure, pain, delight and remorse. Without all these things in the background as contrasts, spirituality is bland.

I also wanted to suggest the infusion of an object with a sense of a particular memory of form. In this case I abstract or separate out an elliptical form, upper right, based on the outline of the head with its Greek overtones of containment, and show it being touched as if approached by extensions of the continuum representing fingers or feathers. The interior of this ellipsoid is rendered in such a way as to suggest that it is of stuff similar to the continuum. This detail signifies notions of a thought-entity separate from, but without complete detachment from the continuum. The ellipsoid is also symbolic of my subjective aim — the desire to understand, with the fingers that touch the ellipsoid as a sign of that desire — and of abstracting ideas during the rationalization process.

To fortify notions of religious iconography pertaining to the Bible and Greco-Judaic tradition, I have placed a smaller-scaled figure, robed, winged and haloed, emerging from the lower right of the picture — an angel bringing good news. To tie the Virgin's heavenly yet earthly face into the picture, simplified outlines of anatomical parts extend from the head to the body of the woman.

Figure 12. Herb Greene, *Spirit in the Body*

Figure 13. Leonardo, *Head of a Woman*

Breasts and an erotic swing of the hip are evident, but not too prominent, in the outline of the body, as is a pregnant belly in the background forms of the continuum. The curving, rounded forms surrounding the head suggest drapery, adumbrated angels' wings (in the upper left corner), the organic, the physiological and brain tissue. I am far from satisfied with the circling progressions of white lines as symbols. They are supposed to indicate energy, motion, spatial extension, representations of growth, pulses of life, and continua of serial time. The simplified surfaces and outlines are supposed to suggest the denotative and conceptual rather than literal nature of the wings and tissues that are referred to. But my progressions of white lines seem too weak for a graphic representation of such complexity. If anyone has a better idea I would appreciate them sending it to me.

The crudeness of the winglike hands and the ambiguous, unfinished outlines of the implied figure of the woman suggest that one's ideas are never complete, and that my treatment is a sign of thoughts in a state of transition.

Barocci's head elicits a strong feeling of the time and place in which it was created. The ideas that it communicates are so surely felt and expressed, and have so long since shifted, that no artist living today could create the equivalent. I want to place the head in an environment that encourages the viewer to rediscover the artist's achievement and to recognize the continuum of thought by which one takes up details to make meaningful closures of the head in a process of perception and of contemplation.

Figure 14. Herb Greene, *Plato's Receptacle*

CHAPTER SIX

The Denotative Form as Symbol

My Oxford Dictionary defines denotation as "an act of denoting; a sign denoting a thing; the meaning or signification of a term as distinct from its implications or connotations." Denotation also refers to the object or range of objects which a word or a drawing of an object denotes. My commentary is based on these definitions. I want to distance myself from the term as it commonly appears in semiotics and structuralism, where one struggles with ontologies of how shoe trees, family trees, and redwood trees come into consciousness, which causes me to feel that I am either in a house of mirrors or a prison trying to sort out signifiers from signifieds and connotations from denotations. I prefer Whitehead's house, where prehensions of experience and contexts can link us directly to various modes of thinking and feeling, as in my interpretation of Vermeer's shadow-hand, where cultural codes and habits and rules of language do not incarcerate meaning or lose us in a labyrinth of linguistic contingency. By denotative in this text, I mean the phase of recognition of a sign or symbol before connotations arise.

By repeating a few words, Gertrude Stein's famous line, "A rose is a rose is a rose," illustrates a modern predilection to minimize description in literature. The reader is encouraged to fill in appropriately placed outlines, or what I will call "denotative forms," with meaning. All poetry depends on this device, when words are considered as a collage of denotative outlines whose contents, drawn from myriads of information bits and connecting neurons, are linked to the colors, smells, delicacy, freshness and wilt of roses, and brought together in the mind by utilizing pre-organized reference frames. Shakespeare's line, "Tomorrow and tomorrow and tomorrow creeps in this petty pace from day to day, to the last syllable of recorded time," contains little description, and yet it is deeply evocative of Western reference frames about time, destiny and the futility in human affairs.

To give meaning to the examples cited above we seize on certain prehensions initiated by the words themselves and by their order. Prehension is, we remember, Whitehead's term for the first elements in sense reception to which we respond as we take up details of an object of perception in order to produce thoughts and feelings about it. In Stein's line, the words "a rose is a rose is a rose" may be grasped as a syllabic and euphonious construction in which the word "rose" becomes the longest emphasis. The rose becomes an object of contemplation. Connotations of a rose may or may not arise, but it is as if, in each repetition of the word "rose," we understand, by a modern interpretation of consciousness, that instead of conventional repetition there is some implied difference to savor. In order to understand Stein's intention it helps to be familiar with certain tenets. One was her belief that, after hundreds of years of sometimes marvelous descriptive English writing, the old adjectives and subject-predicate word order had become expected, familiar, and had lost immediacy and conviction. Another was the psychological emphasis on the interior life that shifted interest to the subjective response. Both artist and audience were seeking new ways of interpretation and participation in the world informed by this sensibility of subjectivity — a kind of "re-membering" of the world, to borrow Carl Frankel's recent phrase for the recovery of subjective values in sustainable economic development rather than limiting ourselves to "objective, materialist, cash-driven values."[1] Finally, a new cosmology based on scientific relativity and other factors affected the ordering of events. This change was reflected by a parallel change in art, in which homogeneous perspective gave way to multidirectional and nonlinear presentations such as the "stream of consciousness."

Alice Toklas made Stein's line of roses into a ring and reproduced it on Stein's stationery. The circular form of the inscription signified a sense of a whole, with its contents presented all at once. To Stein it symbolized a world in which compositional form should have no beginning and no ending: that is, it should be multidirectional and nonlinear. The line of roses was a compact expression of her "subjective-objective" treatment of phenomena, which emphasizes the reader's role in the completion of meaning, while at the same time concentrating the reader's attention on the phenomena under consideration. The power of the imagination is such that it can create denotative forms, including words and drawings, that enable us to tap into our reservoirs of embodied, emotional and intellectual experience with an incredible flexibility.

In my collage paintings, I signify thoughts issuing from cognitive and contemplative processes by showing a sampling of denotative forms that have been derived from the photographed events included in the collage, as well as from the resources and limits of my imagination. I utilize simplified outlines of a pearl, chair or breast in the painted ground. The denotative forms in the ground with their implied instructions, are derived from my reflections on the form's inflections and context. This process directs attention to ideas and meanings alluded to in the photographed events in the collage. For instance, in the collage *Plato's Receptacle* with Vermeer's *Woman Reading a Letter* (figure 14), the most prominent form within the ground is the twisting, off-white shape that is segmented into roughly defined, flowing rectangles. The flowing rectangles relate to the shapes of the letter, map, book and chair in the Vermeer, as if these forms were among the ingredients and modulators of the off-white shape. These progressions are intended to form a denotative visual metaphor of activity in the mental continuum in which the mind transfers relevant information from one idea to another.

For instance, we know that Vermeer's woman is pregnant contemporaneously with anything else that we know about her. In an attempt to suggest the activity involved in the awareness of this fact, I place a Nilsson photograph of a human fetus at upper right. The part of the background symbolizing the mental continuum in which the fetus is included should express the non-Euclidean world that seems relevant to our current understanding of geometry and the organic process of change. For harmony, the background representation should also appear to accommodate the shapes of the globe, book, table, map, fetus, woman and letter that are found elsewhere in the collage.

The denotative form is used to call attention to a thing so that the thing may take on two roles alternatively. It may take on the role of an object that can initiate creative action, or of a subject that initiates thoughts and feelings about how that subject arises from knowledge of the world. For example, the ghostly rug descending from the table can be considered to be denotative; it may be thought of as an object; one of the furnishings to complete the sense of the room in Vermeer's original painting. The rug may also be thought of as a subject, a reminder of how latent ideas about the rug arise from the world — for example, how the rug's vertical thrust harmonizes with and continues the vertical thrust of the standing woman, or how the rug, like the map, could be a symbol of Dutch trade. Other forms in the painting that I have designed to act denotatively and which, according to Whitehead, can fluctuate in meaning as either object or subject, are the simplified pattern of a window at the upper left, the globe-sun that is located next to the window, which is a response to the map and to the sunlight of Vermeer, and the oversized chair at the lower right that acts to complete one's memory of the chair in Vermeer's original painting. The large chair adds a sense of depth to the collage by contrasting with the smaller scale of the woman.

The woman glows in light. Her beauty and bloom, enhanced by her advanced pregnancy and her lips (splayed-back to an unnatural degree in a sign of breathy sentience), convey a subtle eroticism. In context with other messages in this painting — the uncanny verisimilitude given by Vermeer's precision in rendering light moving across the wall, the map, the sense of wholeness of a world ordered by benign cause and effect, the coolness of color and the sense of aesthetic distance — the erotic is downplayed, and yet it is unmistakable. Its deeply felt presence inhabits the sanctity of Vermeer's *mise-en-scene* to become what I would call an expression of sexual fulfillment as *natura naturans*. The subtlety and power of Vermeer's achievement here is probably unique in Western art.

In recognition of the erotic feeling in the Vermeer, I accent the twisting, off-white passage with breasts and other signs of female sexuality. The force of Nilsson's fetus image, the subtlety of the Vermeer, and the tact with which I hope I have incorporated the sexual images, all defer thoughts of overt sex in favor of sex and the erotic seen as teleological facts of nature.

The prominent map in back of the woman sets the sienna-gold tone for the surrounding ground color and is seen as an extension of the grid-like surfaces in the ground. The grid can be used to modulate the various forms in the composition so that first one form and then another can come into focus. The red outlines and washes within the picture signify blood, organs and bodily states of feeling. They refer to the physiological activity that underlies all our actions and states of being, including the calm that is expressed with such potency in *Woman Reading a Letter*.

In this collage I attempt to present symbols of ideas about the stream of consciousness in a perceptual response. One might rightfully argue that these attempts interfere with the existing character of Vermeer's painting. An apparent random composition of puzzling references and active surfaces would seem to conflict with a primary feeling in the Vermeer, which is an expression of concentrated calm and quiet. Vermeer conveys an overarching message, what the distinguished philosopher of aesthetics, Suzanne Langer,[2] called a "primary illusion." I would describe this illusion as ongoing life in a universe governed by benign cause and effect, including the feeling that the spiritual can be known through the material. While I am not satisfied with my collage, particularly as it disrupts Vermeer's wonderful calm, I include it because it at least partially expresses some of the meanings that are implicit in my response to the Vermeer painting. Because the woman's figure is cut off just below her blue jacket and the realism of the chairs and table

is diminished, the viewer may accept the figure as a fragment cut off from the original painting, and accept other fragments as well. In this collage, the ground gives up its objects of pearls, table, book, map and pole. All have harmonies, either of axis, color, texture or outline, with forms in Vermeer's painting. Yet we cannot entirely explain the complexities of feeling stimulated by *Woman Reading a Letter*. There is always fitting, forcing and crushing with language, as well as pointing to, lifting and elucidating.

Why do I choose the rare paintings of Vermeer when his best work is incomparable and his technique is so perfect that my additions can never live up to his work? With Vermeer we can feel that sensations, such as the coolness of his blues, represent deeply integrated thoughts reflecting both his original observation of light and a powerful intellectual sense of aesthetic distance. We can reflect on the painting with the engagement and equanimity that it reflects back to us. We sense that Vermeer's intuitions, such as placing the shadow hand in the headdress of *Woman With a Balance*, are also judgments. The studied expression in Vermeer's painting can suggest that volitions are cognitive. The depth of feeling reached by Vermeer seems inseparable from his acute intellectual distinctions. His work demonstrates the linking of perception, thought and feeling to the highest degree, and can inspire any effort to call attention to the process of such linkage. Further, it often takes me years to "complete" a painting, and I never tire of Vermeer's finest images.

CHAPTER SEVEN

The Shadow Hand in the Vermeer

The collage *The Shadow Hand in the Vermeer* (figure 15) combines a photograph of a Peruvian girl holding a sheep (from *National Geographic*) with a print of Vermeer's *Woman Holding a Balance*. My intent here is not to show that there are details found in one picture that are perfectly congruent with details in the other, but to suggest that making approximations and correspondences among things that we see, what Whitehead calls "events," are at the basis of the mind's ability to create meaning.

Both pictures contain human figures that appear to project thoughts onto objects held within their grasp. Both pictures depict garments, gestures of envelopment, and signs of sentience. We perceive these similarities and treat them with "fuzzy logic" to create associations and identities. This process enables us to compare the feelings of the "preciousness of life" that are communicated by each photo. Fuzzy logic, a term coined by computer technologists, is used in voice recognition and other computer programs that sort out similarities within variable data. It is related to the logic we probably use for most of our mental transactions, including the sorting of consistencies and inconsistencies among the disparate objects in collage.

The photograph of the Peruvian girl, described in *National Geographic* as "poetic," is distinguished, above all, by the sheep. It confronts us with feelings of the austere that help to dispel the sentimentality and cuteness that we might associate with a girl hugging a lamb. These feelings can be attributed to the surprising position of the sheep's head and prominent eye. The sheep seems to reluctantly accept the pressure of the girl's embrace, but its head, with our prehensions of its upward-thrusting, yearning inflection away from the girl, signals that it does not return her address. The sheep's eye — large, black and indicative of small intelligence — reinforces a feeling of distancing from the girl, and contributes to what is, for me, a feeling of austerity. This effect contrasts with the engagement and "love" that we read into the girl's embrace.

The girl, who seems to be both singing and musing as she

Figure 15. Herb Greene, *The Shadow Hand in the Vermeer*

embraces the sheep, seems centered in her own well-being. Vermeer's woman seems similarly centered. Her serene face provides us with not so much an overbearing warning about vanity — as art historians who focus on the scales, the painting of the Last Judgment behind the woman, and the seventeenth-century penchant for allegory usually attest — but with a sense of comfort and reassurance. We are reminded not of the constraints of life, but of its preciousness.[1] This sense of preciousness has correspondences with the sense of comfort and empathy projected by the girl hugging the sheep.

Vermeer's precise geometry, evident in the placement of the hand holding a balance at the corner of the picture frame and the leaning, rising, stable pyramid of the woman's figure, creates a sense of physical balance that acts in the collage as a counterpoint to the thrusting sheep. This harmony, and the others I have mentioned, can encourage us to meld aspects of the two situations. These harmonies can lift us to aesthetic and contemplative references, and possibly to Whitehead's notion that meaning resides in the co-dependency and relationships of all things in a world that is derived from a common past. This means that notions of comfort, embodied tactile understanding, geometric relationships, and other qualities inherent in realizations such as the woolly sheep and the fur trimmed jacket, are derived from in-some-way similar experiences in the space-time continuum that are common to events in both the sheep-girl and Vermeer's woman. Whitehead gives the term "eternal objects" to similar aspects of experiences that are recognized and used by the mind to negotiate consistencies among the diversity of perceptual forms, such as a white flower and a white wedding dress, or the tactile softness of sheep's wool and the fur-trimmed jacket worn by Vermeer's woman. These qualities are not literally eternal, but Whitehead retains the term as a deference to the language of traditional philosophy. More detailed explanations are presented in Part Two.

In response to the hidden hand in the woman's head cover and the prominent hands of both the woman and the girl, I designed large finger forms to frame, touch and reach out to the girl with the sheep and to the Vermeer. At first glance, one can see that the woman is pregnant. Below the two photos a tubular form connects the two sets of enfiladed fingers. An "umbilical cord" rises vertically at right. Tints of pink and rose accent the "organic" forms as signs of physiology and the sensual. To signify touching wool, "woolly" forms emerge from the fingers at the left.

Bernard Berenson, the famed expert on painting of the Italian Renaissance, placed the enhancement of tactile values among the primary aims of art. Among the imaginary motor sensations that we experience when we participate in the space, depth and distance in a picture, he would include our implicit urge to reach out and touch the woolly sheep or the fur-trimmed wrap. The sense of touch is the basis for our understanding of the substance and character of the world, and contributes to our sense of well-being. Most of us are familiar with how vital touching is to the development of human infants and to the young of other mammals.

The knowledge of touch, as distinct from the sense of touch, is given expression by the major finger touching a large embryonic eye shape. This finger links touch to vision and symbolizes an embodied synaesthetic connection that I am attempting to illuminate. Light, indicated by a yellow wash, extends from a pale disc, which could be a sun, at upper left, following the same direction taken by the light in the Vermeer.

The Renaissance philosopher Bernardino Telesio believed that to touch physical matter and to grasp the physical substrate of matter through the imagination was the basis for attaining knowledge of nature.[2] For Telesio, touch is the primary sense; it forms the basis for sight, thermesthesia, and all the other senses. The intellect is only a mediate and derivative "sense." It remains necessarily imperfect, in that it presents only an analog or simile of the impression. It is these functions of touch that I attempt to suggest in the symbol of the painted fingers.

The symbol of the overscaled fingers can take on other meanings. In context with Vermeer's hidden hand, the fingers can be "godlike," as if a greater presence, being or spirit were presenting the events in the photographs. In the context of appropriating meaning from the events in the collage, my painted fingers can be metaphors for the viewer's intention to approach the sheep and the pregnant woman as if to understand their implications. Light, and the act of touching itself, are woven into the symbolism of the fingers. There is also a suggestion that the fingers are of a mental order, because they are lacking in realism, as if they are largely denotative and not literally corporeal.

I have covered the girl's eyes with a veil extending from the background. Her eyes seemed too ordinary in contrast to the importance of the sheep's eye, and in this version of figure 15 they distracted from the immediacy and feelings of a certain dignity that we project into the image of the sheep's head. The veil, a piece of the ground shaped like a cloth with a hand-like appendage, slopes up to approach, touch, comfort and attach the girl's hair to the painted forms within the ground. This gesture reinforces the theme of touching, as well as serving to shield the girl's eyes. The painted background forms in this collage allude to the physical as well as to the spiritual. The allusion is to the mental continuum as conditioned by our bodily and mental life, and to a creaturehood and Eros to which we are irrevocably tied.

The process of assembling meaning that I have attempted to describe here may be likened to Derrida's "free search for meaning," rather than to a search for an ultimate source or interpretation of meaning. I have an implicit belief (my "prepared" mind) in accepting whatever may come from my design process, as illustrated by my finding a potential umbilical cord in the stains of my washes. With its metaphors of connection, the umbilical cord seems to add to my notion of the biological transference of life, while my subjective aim eliminates other choices with less pertinent potentiality. For example, I did not make the emergent curving tubular form into a snake, intestinal fragment or a neon light.

Whitehead's analysis of prehensions that allow the formation of fresh actual entities and concrescences of thought, and that can link aspects of all events within the extensive continuum (Whitehead's term for our sense of the entire world), provides a philosophic basis for post-modern freedom in the search for meaning.

CHAPTER EIGHT

Vermeer's *Head of a Young Girl*

In this essay I begin with a few paragraphs about concepts of modern physics — the quantum, the physical field, relativity and indeterminacy — that have been influential in recent descriptions of appearance and the unseen background of experience that informs appearance. My intention is to link the diffusion of these concepts into contemporary culture with my own presentation of the background of experience as a subject for art. I then use these remarks to lead into an analysis of a masterpiece by Vermeer in order to indicate how scientific and technological interests can support and energize the expression of some deeply harmonized and subtle feelings, ranging from erotic desire and relinquishment to imagined conceptions of time.

David Bohm, the noted physicist, has developed a world-view based on Quantum Theory. Bohm argues that the form of a physical object is not fixed, as Newton's laws would have it. Rather, an object is continually recreated in a form generally similar to its previous form, though different in detail. Bohm attempts to construct an order based on quantum fluctuations. He makes observations on the behavior of light, sound and electrons to show that physical objects, such as rocks and trees, are explicit manifestations of an implicit order, the order of the entire physical field. He calls this implicit order the "holomovement," after the hologram, which he uses to help describe his theory. He likens the holomovement to a ground from which all objects and thoughts emerge:

> When we look into the depths of the clear sky; what we actually see is an unspecifiable total ground of movement from which objects emerge. Particular ideas or thoughts or ideas coming to the mind may similarly be perceived as being like particular objects that arrive from an unspecifiable ground of deeper movement. What we call "mind" may be this deeper ground of movement, but if we think of particular thoughts as the basic reality, we miss this.
>
> Such a way of looking at everything fits in rather well with our general experience. Thus, while

any statement may give an explicit expression to our thoughts and feelings, the meaning or significance of this statement is in a vast and unspecifiable implicit background of response. Unless we share most of this implicit background, the explicit statement will communicate little or nothing. So one may propose that, also in the mind, the explicit order arises out of the implicit, and that the basic movement is one in which the content of each of these continually passes into the other.[1]

According to Michael Talbot in *The Holographic Universe*,[2] Bohm seems to hold that determinations of consciousness, life and all things we call "objects" are ensembles enfolded throughout the universe. If we knew how to access it, we could find the Andromeda galaxy in our left thumbnail, for in principle, the whole past and implications for the whole future are also enfolded in each small region of space-time. I can accept Whitehead's theory of prehensions, where aspects of any phenomena within the extensive physical field can be seen in terms of contrasts and identities by an apperceptive mind, but I don't know enough about physics or holograms to support Bohm's theory or Talbot's explanations. My intuition is much against the latter, which I find dependent on "logical mysticism" rather than evidence, but with thin knowledge, I have learned to leave an opening when it comes to scientific theories.

To get back to the excerpt from Bohm, this excerpt raises three points that bear on my attempt to image the mental continuum, with its implicit background and its indeterminate aspects, as an art symbol. First, Bohm's emphasis on an implicit background from which thought and objects arise is consonant with Whitehead's theory, in which the shapes, colors and ideas we experience during perception draw upon similar shapes, colors and ideas coded from past experience, and are then synthesized into fresh realizations that are directed by our subjective aim. Second, Bohm, like Whitehead, requires that the mind be interactive with a perceived event. The quantum physicist realizes that the instrument with which he observes events modifies those events. The cognitive mind, qualified by the enduring personality with its particular aptitudes and limitations, selects and emphasizes and, thus, also modifies events. Third, Bohm, like Whitehead, sees classical physics as being limited to special cases. He shows how the order of Cartesian coordinates, useful in locating points in Newtonian dynamics, is superceded by new models based on holograms and other spatial configurations — models that can often obtain a more fundamental description of physical and mental reality in space-time.

Bohm's search for new models to describe reality has parallels in the work of twentieth-century painters as diverse as Picasso, Matta, Pollack and Bacon, not to mention the thousands of others who have moved beyond naturalistic representation, Renaissance perspective and Cartesian coordinates, and who have employed chance and indeterminacy in their search for more fundamental expressions of reality. Science influences art. We are taught that light rays bend as they travel through gravitational fields. This probably has influenced Matta's painted presentation of warping planes, forms and spaces. Vermeer used instruments to discover that we have adjusted to optical illusions in our everyday perception, such as the appearance of warped straight lines at the perimeter of our cone of vision. Yet I am unsure of how either set of facts effect my observations of the furniture in my studio. Is it possible that the knowledge that light rays bend could influence one's perception of furniture, just as knowledge of the foveal shift influenced the breaks and shifts utilized by Cezanne in his painting of apples? The point I am making of all this is that what we think we know comes to influence what we feel, how we see and what we choose to think about and to express.

The art of Vermeer, perhaps, cannot be fully appreciated without knowledge of the development of lenses and optics, as well as the idea of time stopped at an instant, a presupposition of Newton's laws of physics. For example, developments in optics and lenses parallel Vermeer's possible use of imaging devices, such as the *camera obscura.* Kenneth Clark[3] suggests that Vermeer probably looked at a scene through a sheet of ground glass in a dark box, which would account for his unique way of rendering highlights as small globular dots of paint and his rendition of tones. In painting furniture, figures and rooms, Vermeer sometimes simplified the tones without any indication that emphasized one object over another as to the object's position in perspective. This resulted in

Vermeer's peculiar flattening of adjoining objects, and our sense that he balanced human optical expectations, such as perspectival vanishing, with his observations of pointillist dots of light that were obtained from optical instruments.

In the detail of *The Love Letter* (figure 16), notice how Vermeer emphasizes the flatness of pattern in the wall ornamentation and moldings of the room as they abut the doorway through which we view the scene. There is no halo of light, which artists often use to separate overlapping planes. The column and entablature seem to frame a doorway that would be too low for the ladies to pass through without stooping. Yet each tile seen through this door appears about eight inches high, which suggests a sufficient height for passage. Daniel Arasse[4] suggests that Vermeer changed perspectives and vanishing points within a single painting to disallow the viewer's mental and bodily "easy access" to the painting and to a "simple" meaning. Finally, the right side of the maid's jacket has been painted in dark shade and conforms to the picture frame on the wall in a close harmony of shape and proportion. Notice how the maid's breast has been unnaturally flattened to further Vermeer's decisive geometric pattern, and how we process the resulting "thinness" of the maid into a positive prehensive contrast to the relative amplitude of the matron.

But while these details point to techniques that Vermeer used to give the objects in his paintings a sense of impartiality amidst his magical realism and fine harmonies, it does not explain other

Figure 16. Vermeer, *The Love Letter* (Detail)

qualities that we admire in his work. For example, in his painting of a standing woman reading a letter (figure 14), we are fascinated by a sense of "time stopped at an instant," quiet and sanctity. I believe that Vermeer's ability to see pattern and depth simultaneously — possibly an outcome of his use of an optical device — helps to create this effect. One responds to Vermeer's precision in delineating objects as if they are fully comprehended in three-dimensional space. At the same time, one responds to the strength of their design as a flat pattern — a pattern that initiates a conceptual life of its own and that sometimes reminds us of an abstract painting by Mondrian, in which we read a similar duality. This duality of depth and flatness produces readings of action and stasis in Vermeer's painting. The immanent action of events seems frozen in time. Vermeer, with his intelligence directed toward both the poetic and the accurate rendering of visual fact, could have reflected the notion of discrete instants of time, a notion that seemed necessary to seventeenth-century explanations of nature.

The feeling of stopped or frozen time has perhaps never been realized more poetically than in Vermeer's *Little Street in Delft* (figure 17). In this picture the facade of bricks and windows is rendered with wonderful accuracy and liveliness, yet it is as flat as a cardboard cutout. This flat facade, so easy to retain in the mind, is contrasted with the adjoining alley, partly obscured by vegetation yet plunging into the depth of the space beyond. The figures of women attending to domestic chores and children playing are rendered with

no more partiality than are the bricks in the wall. One is fascinated by the "neutral realism," as immanent action is halted by the flatness, and by the "fixed," Mondrian-like pattern of rectangles that qualifies the scene.

Vermeer's exploration of certain subtleties of human feeling is perhaps without equal. I have chosen his *Head of a Young Girl* (figure 18), as a subject for analysis because his expression of feelings is interwoven with his acute optical concerns, as well as correlations to seventeenth-century notions of time. While in the Mauritshuis, I moved aside to let a man in his thirties with a sleeping baby on his back get a close look at the portrait. He stood not taking his eyes off the painting, for more than twenty minutes. Before turning to leave the painting he blew a kiss. I took this gesture as a sign of his pleasure and respect. He may have felt some of the feelings described by Edward Snow,[5] which give something of the density of feeling and richness of thought that are communicated by this single small portrait:

> It is always the beauty of this portrait head — its purity, freshness, radiance, sensuality — that is singled out for comment. . . . The experience of *Head of a Young Girl*, for all its sensuousness and singleness of impact, is one of unresolved, almost viscerally enforced contradictions. An intimate mirroring that is also a painful, disturbing estrangement. An all engulfing (yet patient, gentle) yearning

Figure 17. Vermeer, *Little Street in Delft*

composed equally of desire and renunciation. . . .

Yet everything that cuts so quickly is at the same time softened, eased, on the threshold of a strangely sensual letting-go. A startled expression mingles pain, apprehension, and bewilderment (it might almost have been wonder), dissolves, in virtually the same moment it registers, into a wistful, languishing, seductively acceptant look of comprehension and relinquishment.

Head of a Young Girl is the rarest of masterpieces in expressing immanent action, complex and yet determinate feelings of subtlety and strength, and a sense of optical accuracy. The head, seen against a background of deep yet flat, black space, is treated with a subtle flatness and selected omissions (notice the suppressed nose and missing eyebrows) that act to isolate vivid details such as the eyes and lips. The effect allows for a more powerful expression of the information imparted by these details — something like the isolation and power of the details in Picasso's portrait of Dora Maar (figure 9).

The best color photograph of *Head of a Young Girl* cannot prepare the viewer for the impact of the original. The face color was constructed as if part of the finest Impressionist painting ever made. A thousand tiny dots of ever so slightly varied color fuse to lead the eye in a never static, iridescent, optical experience that contributes massively to the feeling of freshness that Snow mentions. I saw this

painting in The Hague in 1969, and again in the 1995-6 Vermeer exhibition in the National Gallery. I was disturbed to see less color in the face than I had remembered. I could not find the "Impressionist" dots of color. Had the recent high-tech cleaning changed the painting? My friends told me that others have thought so. Had low lighting and protective glass altered my perception? At any rate, I decided to stick with my original impression because I had spent several hours examining this face from a number of close up positions with 20-20 vision, and had formed a distinct and much-thought-over impression of magical dots of color that could appear as smooth and continuous as enamel while at the same time retaining the most subtle vibrating iridescence imaginable.

The contradictions of feeling described by Snow result from a number of discrete contrasts in the details of the head. The eyes and mouth are designed with full curves and slightly exaggerated "piercing" points. Notice the right corner of the girl's mouth. The upper lip has been extended beyond the lower lip so that its design into a curving, down-turned, pointed shape is seen in contrast with the full curve of the lower lip. The feelings produced by these shapes are determined by the qualitative associations that they carry. They are initiated by what Whitehead calls "strain feelings," which I discuss in detail in Chapter 20. Strains are our encoded felt responses to the topological aspects of form: soft, sharp, stretched, compressed, and so forth. It is largely through strain feelings that memory, with its ability to link all modes of bodily and mental

Figure 18. Vermeer, *Head of a Young Girl*

experience, gives qualitative character to events in which we partici-pate. In the case of the Vermeer, the feeling of poignancy derives partly from the piercing, pointed forms contrasted with the full, relaxed, sensual curves in the design, which form part of a matrix of harmonized cues and contexts stemming from the tear-like pearl, the assertive eyes, the withdrawing gesture of the head, and the knot of tension at the top of the turban — tension that is released in the turban's vertical tail.

When I began work on *The Evolution of a Mouth* (figure 19), I decided that references stemming from the mouth, eyes and turban would be prominent in the ground. The first problem was to place the portrait within the canvas. I devised a rectangular frame that partially surrounds the head. This alludes to the heavy frames of Baroque painting, and acts to stabilize the head within the "shifting" ground. I reiterated the frame shape in perspective, leading into the girl's turning head and following her glance. This gesture acknowl-edges spatial depth in the flattened portrait and responds to our bodily (implied strain feelings) and conceptual feelings (that she may be turning toward or away from the viewer) of her turn and glance.

Next, at the upper left, I placed a large photograph of an animal orifice made by an electron microscope. I planned to modify this photo so that its forms would relate to the lips of the girl. To rein-force this relationship, I drew lips that are more easily recognized emerging from the frame, directed toward the large orifice. My

purpose here was to present the two ends of a symbolic gamut — from the beautiful human lips, to me a sign of sentience and Eros, to the arresting primordial orifice of unknown scale — as if to say that out of this "organic" history suggested by the gamut of orifices, even if our individual associations may differ, has come the domains and associations of content that both males and females of many cultures will know as a beautiful feminine mouth.

To further associate the magnified orifice with creaturehood, I work a couple of roughly elliptical forms (which are latent eye and pearl shapes) into simplified "sheep-like creatures" with plaintive bleating mouths. "Instructions" given by the suggestions of dividing cells in other parts of the collage enforce the idea of organic trans-formation and suggest the potentiality of recognizing "eye-sheep" shapes. Whitehead characterizes geometry as the science of interme-diaries. It is easier in a painting to design intermediary geometric forms pertaining to the shapes of lips, eyes and pearls than it is to design forms reflecting the taboos and conflicts that are called up by the erotic sensuality and the retreat and advance of the adolescent girl. By repeating shapes and textures, a gamut of lips can be sug-gested.

In calling attention to the functions of orifices opening and closing, in subjects ranging from flowers to humans, one touches on oral-genital functions that have largely remained unspeakable taboos in Western culture, at least until the modern interest in the subconscious. Antonio Gaudi, whose architecture is, in my view,

Figure 19. Herb Greene, *The Evolution of a Mouth*

sometimes questionably associated with the irrationalities and subversions of surrealism, has shown in the windows of the Chapel of Colonia Guell, that references to the orifices of animals and plants can elicit feelings of joy, radiance and mystery. Deeply-buried memories of these forms, with their ties to primordial origins, can provide contrasts to aspirations and spirit. How showing the orifices in the parts and functions of animals, plants and humans, enlarged and in brilliant color on television, will effect this persistent mystery remains to be seen.

In his sculptures, such as the *Standing Figure* in the Museum of Modern Art, Dubuffet presents ideograms of eyes, mouths and other facial features in a seemingly random intertwining of black lines on a white ground. It is as if the subconscious recognizes these familiar parts emerging from the surrounding ground. Object and ground become arbitrary distinctions and the viewer's eye bumps into recognizable objects as if by chance. In my collage, I want the ground to project unconscious selection and also conscious decision, as if the one state were continually passing into the other. There is a sense of random overlapping and unexpected juxtaposition, as in the photo of a fetal hand touching the lip shape at the lower left. The hand is a sign of touching and or reaching out. It suggests an inborn necessity for direction and comprehension that transcends random-ness. Likewise the stabilizing horizontal alignment of the major orifice (left), the girl's head, and the large pearl (right) suggests a planned axis. The unfurling knot (lower right) indicates release

following the direction of the girl's glance. I want certain objects in the ground — for example, the magnified orifice with its unique texture — to be more clearly determined than are Dubuffet's linear ideograms of eyes and noses. Such determination is required to obtain more complex associative potentialities, such as the thoughts and feelings about what the texture's magnified scale and cracked surface has to do with human lips — for example, in an imaginative comparison to a magnification of the texture of human lips.

The pearl worn by the girl hangs like a teardrop, suggesting sadness. It is also, as critics have said, an orb reflecting and absorb-ing the world. I reiterate the pearl in the large, tear-shaped form (right) surrounded by red shapes that relate to lips and orifices. Close to this form are bright, white, elliptical shapes placed to lead into the girl and shaped to refer to droplets (the moisture implicit in the breath) and to the shape of the tongue tip. Thus certain features of objects are made more specific to direct more content into the response.

Finally I would mention the arresting white shapes of the girl's eyes. The forward moving whites contrast with the recessive blacks of the pupils to enforce the visceral contradictions of which Snow speaks. I reiterate large, elliptical, white shapes at the center bottom. The left ellipse is enveloped by a coiled form, a sign of physically and mentally engaging these shapes. Above the right ellipse are blue shapes that suggest cell divisions, to enforce the biological and evolutionary theme. They also suggest the shapes of immanent teardrops, pearls and eyes.

In perusing the collage, the viewer is not asked to follow a specific route or analysis. There is an intentional redundancy that can be taken for eye and cell shapes — forms that are generally similar, but different in detail, and which may not all be utilized in pondering the eyes of the girl. Redundancy is a requirement of neuronal action, reinforcing the decision that this is the form I seek and not others. The redundancy also suggests a labyrinth in which viewers find their way. I have provided visual "instructions" as guides for the viewer. For example, the unfurling knot has a bright, white, gull-winged band, reiterated in white highlights on the lips around the major orifice. This loose echelon of wing shapes moves the eye along the progression of lips. It is a reminder of the poetic impulse of longing and freedom associated with bird flight. It also provides a reference to the sensuality of curving shapes, and to

characteristics of longing and release in the Vermeer.

In this essay I have described a sampling of thoughts chosen from among the actual complexities of "taking up" the cues in *Head of a Young Girl*. My aim in the collage is to present a range of forms derived from the painting and from my imagination of longing, Eros, and the organic. I want to suggest possibilities of interpretation that can be connected and an environment in which any recognized form can assume a temporary preeminence. I have emphasized lip shapes to imply a gamut of orifices, beginning with a suggested "primordial form," from which the complex meanings of human lips have evolved. My painted ground constitutes an attempt to visualize the changing implicit background necessary to project meaning into objects, and to trace the derivation of thoughts about them. In this sense, there is correspondence with both Bohm's and Whitehead's theories.

CHAPTER NINE

Hitler

Occasionally we are presented with an image that intensifies our beliefs and leaves us with the feeling that our knowledge would be limited if we had not seen it. Analysis of such an image is always subject to error, yet as curious creatures we cannot resist. That is the way I feel about this photo of Hitler incorporated in the detail of my collage (figure 20). I am still fascinated by the films of Hitler that are repeatedly shown on television. During his speeches, which often became rants, I expect the staccato thrusting arm, his down-pointing gestures with their negative metaphor of "down is bad," and his body communicating the authoritarian "up," but I never get used to the occasional gelatinous trembling of his face and a walleyed pike blankness to his eyes, which suggest to me a rage that is mechanical, as if disembodied from the human. The simplifications of black and white films have a power different than hand-drawn caricature, because they let us focus on exaggerations as we realize that the events shown are not actual distortions.

I have long thought that Hitler's potential for evil was unusu-ally manifested in his face and body language, as seen in his photo-graphs and films: his pasty complexion, his severe Teutonic haircut suggestive of a desire to appear as military leader with a monk's dedication to his cause, and his terse, little mustache, which, in black-and-white photos and films, seems a black void punctuating a face altogether devoid of strong features. One can read something of the obsequious German-Austrian stereotype (One remembers Churchill's remark about Germans being either at one's feet or one's throat.) into this bland physiognomy, and remember other instances where Hitler is shown with a pinched and timorous smile, giving an ironic twist to the fierceness of his political persona. Stalin turned out to be a paranoid monster who killed more people than Hitler, yet during the war, American editorial cartoonists exaggerated Stalin's Mona Lisa smile and his curving handlebar mustache. He could be portrayed as a kindly, if enigmatic, Uncle Joe. I can't imagine a softened portrayal of Hitler that would not appear false to me, because of the inescapable negative peculiarities of his face, cold

Figure 20. Herb Greene, *Hitler* (Detail)

eyes, body language and hair style.

In his study of human destructiveness, Erich Fromm[1] makes an interesting case that Hitler was a necrophiliac. Regardless of whether he was or not, many of us can concur with Fromm's observation:

> Hitler's face betrayed the sniffing expression mentioned in the discussion of necrophilia, as if he were constantly smelling a bad odor; this is quite apparent from a large number of photographs. . . . [H]is laugh was never free, but was a kind of smirk. . . . [A]ll reports agree that Hitler had cold eyes, that his whole facial expression was cold, that there was an absence of any warmth or compassion.

Hitler's obsequious and fierce face and behavior allow us to attribute to him the repellent characteristics of both worm and wolverine, which we can match from our repertoire of associations about the behavior of Nazis. The very blandness of his face imparts something to the imagination that allows us to coordinate a group of his negative features (intense cold stare, pasty complexion, tight mouth) into greater potency. We seize on this coordinated group of negatives to gain concentration for the build up and continuance of our negative feelings. Yet we are all aware of how symbol-making human animals, with different experiences, strategies and aims, found positives to replace negatives in Hitler's features, as instanced

by the thousands of swooning women who adorned Hitler's parades.

In figure 20, the camera has caught Hitler in a pose that suggests both German Romantic longing and Teutonic will. Hitler looks out, his gaze directed not toward the audience at hand, but as if toward imagined, Wagnerian heroes whose approval he seeks. Mussolini looks taken aback, as if withdrawing from the intensity of his colleague, whose appearance allows us to confirm our ideas of him as a mystic consumed by an inner vision and an inner rage. As we experience this image, we feel a heightening of emotional intensity that is produced by a creative valuation of conceptual feelings. According to Whitehead, a conceptual feeling combines a sense of an object's definiteness and exclusiveness (Hitler's cold eyes, his intensity and detachment in front of the Italian dictator) with emotional feeling (feelings of threat and fear from his lack of compassion) derived from qualitative characteristics of the object.

For example, in figure 21 I attempt to heighten a conceptual feeling of subjugation that I associate with Nazis, and with Hitler's authoritarian body language and grim facial expressions. I include a Cartier-Bresson photograph of Russian gymnasts. The pyramid of crouched figures and the audience in uniforms produces a tableau that suggests mass subjugation and awe. It presents a challenge for evaluation in context with the photograph of Hitler, with its possibilities of including mystic vision and ominousness into our scenarios of his power in Germany and his plan for the world. The photo showing the piled-up gymnasts suggests subservience to the

Figure 21. Herb Greene, *Hitler*

state. The mass of figures can be associated with the burned and agonized forms around Hitler to produce ominous feelings about human suffering caused by Hitler. Another photograph by Cartier-Bresson, upper left, shows a parade line of youthful Russian boxers. Their white gloves suggest controlled aggression and harmonize graphically with the bald dome of Mussolini's head. The feet of the boxers, not quite in step, inject a note of dishevelment that can be associated with things Russian. For example, the tails of Russian jet fighters with welds left rough because this saves money and does not interfere with aerodynamics, or scarves flailing out of heavy winter coats. A gray band makes the marching boxers faceless and harmonizes with the stadium rail.

The mind coordinates various centers in the brain that store information about scarves, shapes, colors, language, cultural codes, bodily experience, and all other sensory experience. By enlisting the cooperation and parallel functioning of these centers, the mind arrives at efficient reconstitutions or mappings to produce meaning via subjective aim. What follows is a rough gloss of my mental processing of Hitler amid his collaged surroundings. The background forms around Hitler and Mussolini suggest torn and blackened animal and human creatures about to be either engulfed or revealed by a great wave. Black caves or, more likely because of the context of the surrounding burnt creature-like forms, black grave stones are indicated. An ominous curving band leads from the stadium, continues around Hitler's table, and ends as a frizzled

exclamation point derived from Hitler's mustache in the middle of a mechanical looking "dome-head." The dome-head is my response to Mussolini's bald pate with its curved outline, flatness and bluntness. The rounded, solid-appearing dome-head with extended tongue is without eyes — a blind, screaming, stretched, creature-like form that responds to the rounded, solid boxing gloves and the mechanical feeling of the stacked gymnasts.

In designing the dome-head I am directed by Whitehead's insight from *Process and Reality* ". . . that each fact is more than its forms and each form participates throughout the world of facts. The definiteness of fact is due to its forms but the individual fact is a creature and creativity is the ultimate behind all forms, inexplicable by forms, and conditioned by its creatures." [2]

Whitehead's statement applies to all forms, from the realization of the equation $1+1=2$ to a realization of the ominous in a picture of Hitler. Rather than finding a world of neutral and objective forms, Whitehead finds a world of overlapping events in which the viewer's intellectual activity, with its origination in the bodily life, is synthesized into concepts bearing traces of the viewer's sense of being a creature. My intention in designing the dome-head is to build a metaphor of the mechanical and the mindless, combined with a sense of animal creaturehood.

The human mind-body can be likened to an instrument, but one that is subject to complex directives, often subconscious, that project feelings of experience. By alluding to nervous energy and bodily forms in the painting, I am trying to express a sense of "being a creature" recognizable as an idea. A number of modern painters have taken pains to project similar conceptual feelings into their work. In my opinion, the most exciting and successful is the Chilean painter Matta. His images, with their cosmological, psychological and physiological allusions, often appear as if they are a visual metaphor for the body-mind as it conditions forms. Matta also seems able to express an anxiety that ranges from our concerns for life security to our social conflicts. The human baby is born anxious and usually does not smile for a number of weeks. This fact is among many that have influenced artistic projections of human anxiety. Matta's most successful work remains a unique achievement of modern painting, and I wish I could be more influenced by certain of his works in designing the forms that surround the photo of Hitler. I also remember being aware of my response to Matta's expression of anxiety while thinking about designing the image of the Prairie House (figure 32). One problem for art has been to express particulars about anxiety as a contrast of being, while giving expression to energy, compassion, heroism, love, hope, awe and other positive views of life.

Figure 22. Herb Greene, *Texas Mother*

CHAPTER TEN

Texas Mother and Vermeer's *The Love Letter*

My collage detail (figure 22) includes a photograph by Russell Lee from the Farm Security Administration Archives. An apparent young mother and her son look out of an opening framed by unpainted boards. Probably the most compelling quality of the photograph is the way in which it captures a moment of unselfconscious pleasure in human existence. The mild face of the mother, her body leaning lightly in graceful concordance with her head, imparts this feeling. Her face and hand are much enhanced by the arrangement of her white garments as they appear against the black window opening, and by the textures of the boards and curtain. The rough cloth of the mother's dress, the safety pin that holds it closed and the unpainted boards, together with the mother's expression, convey honesty and openness as well as poverty. There is a mildly lyric concentration here that reminds me of James Agee who, with photographer Walker Evans, could find poetry in the unpainted boards of Southern tenant farmers' houses.

I have been told that the woman grew old and fat and sued the government for invasion of privacy. Whether true or not, this brings us to another message conveyed by the picture. The boy's eyes (which I have slightly obscured) look intently at the photographer, suggesting the candid situation of the picture. This prehension provides a contrast to the mother's lack of self-consciousness, but it also can make us uneasy because we sense that we are participating in an intrusion.

Intrusion is a feeling that some have recognized in looking at Vermeer's *The Love Letter,* calling the incident of a maid transmitting a letter to her richly-appointed mistress contrived while placing the viewer in the role of a voyeur. The two shoes and the leaning broom in the foreground (which I have painted over for simplification) are considered to be fussy and a piling on of domestic incident. I find much in the picture to allay these criticisms. First, the face of the maid with pert nose and unassuming, smiling brightness, and the face of the mistress with her overlong horse-nose, and indecisive, rather mooning expression are described with the sharp characterization worthy of a fine novelist. Second, the harmony of geometric shapes, the contrasts of spatial depth and flatness, and the colors and tonalities are controlled, complex and compelling. The two shoes repeat the rhythm of pairs of pictures on the wall, ladies and floor tiles — like an orchestration by Mozart — to override any excessive storytelling set up by the objects and furnishings in the room. Further, the women framed by the doorway can read as being in a private volume, actually protected by the barriers of shoes and broom in the doorway, which suppress the sense of intrusion. Finally, the frontal perspective as viewed through the foreground doorway could only have been realized by a master. The placement of the mistress at near center of the picture is the kind of optical puzzle with which Vermeer sometimes challenged himself, as, for example, with the abrupt and surprising back of the artist that occurs in the celebrated *Artist in His Studio*. While *The Love Letter* may not move us with the sense of love and the continuity of life found in *Woman Holding a Balance*, it is a fascinating masterpiece, and it conveys with the reserve and detachment peculiar to Vermeer a sense of good feeling about human existence. The quality of light that he creates as it falls on garments, laundry and lute, and his tensioned yet calm and balanced harmonies are outstanding.

In my collage (figure 22), the most obvious analogies between the photograph and the Vermeer are that each image shows a sympathetic human pair, prominent white garments, and rectangles that suggest rooms. There is a drapery at the upper right of each image. There is a sense of well-being in each picture. The bright yellow and white costume of Vermeer's lady projects joy, and sets off her lute with its implications of play, spirit, pleasure and, as I have been educated by art historians to believe, sex. Among the visual releasers that encourage the viewer to draw analogies between the Vermeer and the photograph are the white head wraps of the maid and the mother. The curved, soft yet crisp and arresting shapes of the wraps encourage us to seek other analogies, such as the affinities of texture between the shirts worn by the maid and mother, and the contrasts of the architecture surrounding the two pairs, which in each case presents an archetype of its class.

The principal addition I have made is the passage of white and yellow forms extending across the bottom and up the right side of the picture signifying the mind playing with ideas. This passage extends to the viewer's left to become a vague but recognizable "hand" or "fingers," designed as if to pull back the draperies and boards to reveal that picture and its implications. The passage as a whole is left purposefully vague, allowing the viewer to find denotative figures and shapes derived from other events in the two pictures. Wholes and parts of simplified lutes appear at various positions and scales. There are suggestions of bodily forms, sensual curves and birds, all seemingly arising out of garments, laundry and draperies. A piece of a rectangular frame obtrudes, colored rose, white and yellow. The rose color refers to blood, arousal and bodily tissue, while the yellow and white, in direct response to the lady's costume, signifies good feeling and, in context, seems consonant with the implicit enjoyment of music. White also suggests purity. The larger, rose-colored forms at far right hint at creatures, wing tips, fingers and sexual parts. The passage containing these indications suggests metaphors of extension, aspiration and bodily mass. As in other collages in this presentation, expression of the ideas of femininity and sex as facts of embodied sensuality and of natural necessity is intended. The mind can thus include the subject of sex in an expression of spirit by associating symbols of sex with forms that rise and project a sense of aspiration, differentiation and unification in mental processing, images of bird flight, music, balanced proportions and other cues.

Since I have previously mentioned the idea of spirit connected with sex, the reader may feel that I am obsessed with this concern. Most of us have persistent thoughts about sex. The depth and complexity of our associations concerning our reproductive process confirms that for us, sex is among nature's most salient facts. Expressing our conscious and unconscious feelings about sex consumes much of our energy in life as in art. While the collage I am discussing may lack expressive clarity in regard to this theme, I can explain something of my concern by describing a familiar masterpiece by Rembrandt that treats sexual themes with great power and tact. Because the painting is also a particularly rich study of the cross-referencing of cues and contexts, I have taken my analysis into some detail.

I remember viewing Rembrandt's *The Jewish Bride* (figure 23) while overhearing a man who commented that by placing the husband's hand on his wife's breast, Rembrandt had violated all public propriety. This man evidently missed the nonsexual meanings that Rembrandt brings to focus in this painting. The husband touches the breast with decision, but without pressure. The wife's fingers overlap the husband's fingers, forming an important focal point of a picture that projects feelings of extreme tenderness and trust. The husband's other arm embraces, protects and comforts the wife. The swelling proportions of his richly-textured robe impart fullness, power and grandeur, while the robe's color exudes warmth. The radiant sleeve is perhaps the most powerful of all Rembrandt's painted statements that utilize chiaroscuro. This sleeve is like some glorious cosmic event in which the amalgamation of golden light, golden substance and golden bits of impasto — carefully organized yet freely composed — suggests the idea of an infinity. The deep background space contributes to the illusion that the expanding sleeve emerges into being before our eyes. We can be reminded of an orbiting galaxy. I have a feeling that manifests as a proposition. It is as if from within this vast, spatialized universe all of the previously-mentioned human values have emerged. Plato characterized Eros as the powerful drive toward union of our selves with objects and ideas that are bearers of values — forms of nature and culture — directed toward the good and the true, and yet connected to the libidinal, sexual quality of love as it moves toward the higher form of *agape*.

This wider context of Eros is I believe, a subject of expression in *The Jewish Bride,* and the archetype I attempt to touch upon in my collage (figure 22).

Rembrandt never saw a photograph of a galaxy, nor are there literal celestial images in the sleeve. But it is indisputable that he has developed a symbol of many in one and one in many that we can process into an infinity symbolizing a universe. Both the awe we feel from the scale and depth of the sleeve and the good feeling from the golden substance, red warmth and light can be processed into thoughts that we use to qualify other elements throughout the painting. In like manner, amplitude in the bulges of the man's sleeve, his doublet under the sleeve, and the woman's bustle can be felt as they contribute to positive feelings of swelling, power and fullness. It is these effects that expand into our other feelings — for example, the feelings of tenderness and trust.

The robes and hairstyles of husband and wife seem redolent of both Biblical and contemporary references. Their faces look like the faces of real people, a possible composite of Dutch and Jewish features softened by a temperance drawn from Rembrandt's imagination. They could be faces of Rembrandt's contemporaries, except that the eyes are passive, staring unfocused into space, linking the personas behind them to the ideal. Their feet do not show, enabling their bodies to emerge from deep space as figures that are both iconic and corporeal. This allows the mind to integrate a sense of the physical, of ideality, warmth, infinity, tenderness, Judaic-Christian

overtones, and Rembrandt's famous projection of psychological character into a multidirectional but consistent gestalt.

In *The Jewish Bride,* Rembrandt's knowledge, imagination and technical prowess reach a level that is rarely achieved. One detail — the two hands touching — underscores the power and subtlety of Rembrandt's imagination and the potential of the symbol-making mind. The thumb and forefinger of the wife's hand touching the husband's play several roles. The slenderness and relatively relaxed position of the wife's fingers express feminine receptivity and tenderness in contrast to the size and thrusting assertiveness of the husband's thumb. The orchestration of tenderness in the woman's fingers and the firm but restrained hand of the man contributes to a feeling of responsibility that we recognize in the couple's relationship. The contours of the wife's fingers fall within canons of European painting that provide a link to Raphael and the classical tradition. The husband's extended thumb seems forceful and erect, but Rembrandt has glazed over its longest front increment with a warm, subdued red, which markedly shortens its length and masks its assertiveness. In this way it can be read as a unit partly submerged in a class of less-defined objects included in the background. The shortened thumb, shaped and highlighted to harmonize with the bold highlights of the sleeve, becomes less forceful and more in harmony with the gentle fingers of the woman.

In *The Jewish Bride,* we take in enough information from the painting itself to determine the artist's complex intentions. White-

Figure 23. Rembrandt, *The Jewish Bride*

head uses the term "superject" to refer to the process by which we utilize already deeply harmonized meanings to direct our synthesis of diverse information. In the case of Rembrandt, the sexual is qualified by tenderness, trust and the other references that I have pointed out. Kenneth Clark calls *The Jewish Bride* an image of "grownup love."[1] That could be a term for the pervading superject, although "grownup love" does not account for Rembrandt's handling of deep space and the multiplicity of suggestive objects in the robes and beads. To me this handling has something to do with the cosmos and infinity. I would say the overview, or superject, is a composite of tenderness, trust, married love and responsibility emerging from an ordered and beneficent universe.

Returning to my collage detail (figure 22), the sexual cues in the photographs that I have incorporated into the collage are more ambiguous than in the Rembrandt; where our attention is powerfully directed to the subject of sex by the bold gesture of the man's hand on his wife's breast. I have attempted to express thoughts linking sex imposed by nature to sex qualified by thoughts and inventions of culture. In this case, the sexual must be tempered by the photos of the young mother and Vermeer's matron holding the "love letter." In these photos sex is limited to tacit and subtle implications of the feminine, motherhood and the absent male. I use curving, somewhat sensuous contours to define ambiguous forms that suggest composites of laundry, lutes and creatures — forms that rise up in aspiring and unifying gestures. My intention is to signify

freeing the spirit from the earth. The buildup of white masses is punctuated with allusions to birds, boards, floor tiles and letter pages, and signifies the changes that underlie physical organic transformations and the energetic mind moving from one piece of data or idea to another.

This collage also contains metaphoric gestures of longing. As an architect, I have given expression to longing in several houses. The rising aspiring lines and the outreaching roof in figure 24 express longing. In figure 26, the sentient yet baleful "face" can impart ideas of poignant expectation and longing. The patterns of boards and the tapered form of the house compliment the face image to suggest a wounded creature tied to the earth, longing to be free. The expression of longing and aspiration as design aims has occupied me since I studied architecture with Bruce Goff. His lectures on aspiration as a necessary ingredient of human experience made a lasting impression. He thought architecture, in addition to expressing ethical building techniques, the nature of materials, and responses to site and clients, should also express human striving for expressions of sensitivity, feeling, longing and aspiration. Rousseau stressed the necessity of longing. He was afraid that longing would be lost to culture as the growing bourgeois society focused on security and material satisfaction. As an architect, I have accepted many bourgeois attributes: comfort, the collection and display of material possessions, cautious roof designs to avoid leaks, and the aesthetic taste of actual clients. I have wondered how to

Figure 24. Herb Greene, *Cunningham House*

Figure 25. Herb Greene, *Cunningham House*

Figure 26. Herb Greene, *Prairie House*

express longing because comfort, security and taste are not adequate to satisfy human curiosity, the expression of spirit, and the lure to attain more abundant understanding.

Getting back to my collage (figure 22), creating an expression of longing is driven by the generic need to understand. This idea is expressed in the gesture of the painted fingers lifting back the painted surround around the Vermeer to better "understand" what is revealed. There is also the longing to understand how perception can be expressed, as in the recess, upper right, where a curving, white bird silhouette reiterates the head-wrap shapes of maid and mother that initiated my process of cross-classification. The extending, white forms that are building, reaching and transforming also indicate longing. They indicate how the forms of our cognition fade in and out of focus during any act of perception, and are expressed by acknowledging the form of sea shells, which stem from the shapes of the white coifs. During this writing I have painted in the large, flat-white bird in flight at upper right. The bird shape can be read in perspective, alluding to the play of flatness and depth that dominate both the photographs of the mother and Vermeer's ladies. I was displeased with the previous forms in the recess, which looked vaguely like tadpoles, as well as lutes. This is at least the sixth version that I have attempted and I still long to improve it, but for the moment I am at a loss to do so. The sense of longing is perhaps more clearly visualized in the forms of the architectural examples, figures 24 and 26, but it appears in this and other collage paintings as an intention to express the sentient, mindful being as it tries to understand.

CHAPTER ELEVEN

Crying Frenchman

The first time I saw the photograph of a Frenchman fighting back tears included in the detail of my collage (figure 27), I remember thinking with unguarded naiveté, that in the long term, photographs like this would reduce the human inclination to make war because the image elicits such powerful feelings and thoughts of visceral and intellectual strength about personal and national tragedy. This photograph sometimes initiates shock. Some observers give start to a laugh when first confronting the image, as if in uncontrolled mimicry of the man's lips, and possibly the feeling of relief at being the viewer and not the viewed. Damasio[1] tells us that deep grief and smiles are executed by brain structures located deep in the brain stem. We have no means of exerting direct voluntary control over the neural processes in those regions. Such smiles and grimaces cannot be faked, the illusions of actors notwithstanding. At any rate, I believed that the photograph possessed an organized pattern that produced more intense feelings than that found in most art, making it of exceptional historic and aesthetic interest.

Years later, while watching a television documentary, I saw the same unforgettable image forming before my eyes. The photo had been edited from a filmstrip showing the surrender of French flags at Marseilles after capitulation to the Nazis. Kenneth Clark calls such images moments of vision.[2]

> It is the sudden awareness of the inexplicable. The flow of accepted associations in which the mind, like a manatee, maintains a healthy torpor — what we gratuitously call the law of nature — is sometimes interrupted and we are shocked to recognize, for a second, how odd things really are.

In the photograph, the man is about to weep and the woman is not. The man's face conveys a sense of grief so profound as to transcend our expectations. The surprising angle of the camera suggests that physical events exist in geometrical relationships beyond our habitual assumptions. These factors sharpen our appetite to find supporting incidents. For example, to feel the background architecture with its stark, black, void windows as

Figure 27. Herb Greene, *Crying Frenchman*

threatening is to support the dread that we feel. I have almost obliterated the windows to concentrate attention on the faces, even though the windows contributed to my sense of the oddness of things, and of a "moment of vision."

We respond to details in the perceptual world that trigger already harmonized experiences of similar occasions. Although clear and visible details usually initiate our response, it is the rich, invisible background elicited by these cues that gives depth and quality to our experience. For example, it is this background that leads me to conclude that the man and woman are probably French. The particular shapes of the faces direct me to think so, just as past experience leads us to recognize the Slavic "ski slope" of a Krushchev nose. Of course, I may be wrong about the faces being French, but the point is that I am able to supply a mass of already harmonized experience about French culture and history to flesh out my reality of the image. The man's straight, stiffened posture and his "French" face suggest Gallic pride, which can become a context for the intense grief that I read into the trembling mouth and eyes. It is French liberty and honor that is being lost, with all the connotations that information brings to the viewer. During a university seminar discussion of this photo, one student insisted the man could be upset over the prospective loss of his business, perhaps making uniforms for the French army, and that his grief might have nothing to do with patriotism. There is no practical way to disprove this assessment, but the fact that the editors of *Life* gave the image a full page in their large format *Picture History of World War Two* indicates

that, to them, the man's body-language and facial expression communicated not mere personal self interest, but a reverie involving self and nationhood — a transcending idea involving histories of French and other people, living, dead, and imagined. That is the meaning they recognized and believed appropriate to the context of their book and to the interest of potential readers.

To further elaborate on how we determine meaning from cues in the photograph, we note that an erect or stiff posture is codified in experience. The mind decides how to process a code by using strategies appropriate to the overriding context. For example, we interpret the smile of a Dracula to be evil and threatening by the exposed teeth, turn of lips and eyes, body language and costume (which also relieves us of seriously worrying about it). Interpretation arises from selecting from various learned rules or codes and using strategies appropriate to the context. The dominant impression, or closure, of the crying Frenchman is formed by cross-referencing the cues given by the man's face, his posture, business suit, the woman, and background architecture, all informing and directing one another via our subjective aim. Clues are selected from the given data and are processed in synthesis and in parallel with one another, rather like a string quartet where each musician responds to the others to produce a total gestalt.

That the man weeps and the woman does not inverts our habitual assumptions about the emotional expressions of the sexes. The woman's face is set off by dark clothing. She is spatially receding from the man. He is posed almost frontally, but is turned enough to continue the sense of receding space and emphasize an upthrusting posture. This subtle but strong twist in perspective harmonizes with the direction of his posture. We respond physically to this orchestration of movement. We follow the movement until we are stopped by the frame that freezes the event for our attention. The moving camera, of which we are unaware, has injected a dynamic that also contradicts and surprises our habitual assumption that the man and woman should be more frontally posed. These surprises — the receding spatial dynamic with its implication of movement in space-time and the poignant face of the man — help place the event beyond stereotypes of patriotism or posing. We process them to feel a sense of reality that no painting of this event could have established.

Because the man's arms are not visible in the photograph, he seems even more vulnerable. To emphasize the prehension of vulnerability and to stabilize the photograph within the painted ground, I frame it with primitive, arm-like appendages, which hang stiff, weak, unable to act. At the left is a photograph of a crocodile. The creature is behaving normally, yet it can suggest an armored menace hundreds of millions of years in the making, implying that predation is here to stay. The fleeing stork and the log, which looks a bit like an animal form fleeing or stalking, enforce the predatory message. The writhing grass seems compatible with the messages of menace and fright. I repeat vaguely reptilian shapes in the ground, and rely on elements common to both photographs, such as the thrusting perspectives and associations of the crocodile to the tank.

The German troops riding the tank appear as if they are pieces of the machine, without volition and possibly as inured to predation as is the crocodile.

According to the caption of this picture, later republished in *Life Goes to War*, volunteer researchers variously identified the crying Frenchman as a black marketeer, a uniform manufacturer, and an emotional Italian visitor. The volunteers may have been determined to debunk the patriotic implications of the picture. It doesn't matter to my point because we are unable to fake the rush of embodied experience brought forth by the appearance of events, even though further analysis or information may change our evaluations. Humankind responded to the sight of the cool, pale moon before they realized it might have had a hot interior. At the moment I can't quite remember if the moon's core is both molten and solid like that of the earth or is of some other form. Sometimes I have misguided responses to the appearance of the moon, or to my wife. According to Whitehead, for human progress in mental development and in science, it is actually more important for a proposition to possess interest rather than truth, although truth can add to the interest. Of course, the camera can be manipulated to make propaganda and to serve many intentions, but an image such as the crying Frenchman reminds us of how the photograph has enlarged the repertoire of our factual experience. We study this face and posture to bring forth our embodied experience, to establish and verify our beliefs, to learn, and to make fresh meaning.

CHAPTER TWELVE

Ships and the Feminine Gender: Michelangelo's *Sybil*

Sewall Wright, a distinguished geneticist, describes the kind of knowledge that is provided by one's own stream of consciousness:

> At any moment this (stream) has a focus, but one which shifts continually, now on perception of the outside world, now on a memory which has somehow been stored out of mind (perhaps for many decades), now an emotional state, now on a toothache, now on a construction of an abstract pattern of thought, now on communication with others, but again and again on the often painful process of choosing among courses of action, and then of acting.[1]

I use this statement to direct my discussion of choosing and taking action in making a collage (figure 28). This collage includes photographs of the aged Churchills and Turner's watercolor, *First Rate Taking on Stores*. I have placed the Churchills and the Turner some distance apart because I thought that each piece needed quiet space surrounding it to be read clearly. I want to acknowledge thoughts that connect events in the photos, doing so in a way that suggests that these thoughts are being realized in a state of meditation, rather than in the shock of collision.

Mrs. Churchill's gaze, which suggests feelings of concern and possible reverie, directs my response. Colliding forms could conflict with the soft gradations that express my idea of "a liminal, rising awareness" intended to symbolize a meditative state. Among the experiential domains that connect the Churchill photos with the image of the Man of War is the convention that ships are usually referred to as "she." Graceful feminine shapes and objects that are directed by, or dependent upon, males are among the roots of this metaphor. We know of Churchill's connection to British naval history, but we are not as likely to pick up on connections among ships, the feminine and Mrs. Churchill. Here we proceed by acknowledging Whitehead's dictum that we establish meaningful unities among diverse realizations such as ships, the feminine and

Figure 28. Herb Greene, *Ships and the Feminine Gender*

Mrs. Churchill through the variety of their prehensions. Further, the airiness and delicacy of Turner's rendering can be linked both to an idea of the feminine, and to the intricacy of Mrs. Churchill's garments, as well as her hair and hands.

There are other connections as well. The surprisingly high hull of the ship (to accommodate tiers of cannon) and its huge masts remind us of a technology long perished. We may feel that both the aged Churchills and the ship are being carried away in an historic time stream. The steps in back of the Churchills make me think of the stripes worn by English seamen in the eighteenth century. (A thought stored out of mind for years — or was it the nineteenth?)

In assessing all these ideas, however, I find them scattered. While they can be connected, the connections are loose. Influenced by the effect of Mrs. Churchill's gaze with its dreamy component and the airiness of Turner's watercolor, I decided that the expressions within the ground should be loose, lightly-indicated and somewhat lyrical, with passages of waves and graded transitions of color. Mrs. Churchill's gaze, expressing concern, together with the aged prime minister's failing ability, is the impetus for the gradations of white to rose — a symbol of the spreading and projection of bodily feelings such as empathy and concern.

To organize the graphic expression of the entire composition, the painting is structured by a lightly defined matrix of horizontal and vertical divisions that respond to the photo sizes. The painted passages faintly indicate sails, ship's hulls, hands and body tissue.

They overlap one another without reaching an accumulative buildup. They fade in and out of focus within the field which, in addition to sails, ships and masts, contains vaguely-delineated waves, horizontal planes that define the steps, the surface of the ocean, and the playing field for the imperturbable English lawn bowlers seen in a small photograph near the Churchills.

The sails, hulls, hands and other forms in the painted field around the photographs, seen in context with the events illustrated there, are foci for consciousness. These forms represent not so much literal repetitions of the sails and hulls of Turner's ship, as denotations or image-schematas, such as ship hulls that appear in different scales and perspectives. They are constructs that extend thought beyond the forms in the photograph that initiated my response. For example, the gradations of rose color that spread over the forms of hands, tissue and planes to the left of Mrs. Churchill form a construct that alludes to the sentience, reverie and concern that I feel are present in Mrs. Churchill's gaze.

The eugenicist Karl Pearson has given in his writings a more refined description of the process that I am attempting to describe. According to Pearson, immediate sense impressions form lasting impressions in the brain. These impressions form the physical components of memory. The synthesis of immediate sense impressions with these stored physical components leads to the formation of constructs which we "project" outside ourselves. We call these constructs "phenomena." For us, such constructs constitute the real world. It is as if the things we actually see as objects of perception are as shadows.

Sentience, airiness, the feminine attributes of ships, and the imperturbable are projections of constructs that we term "phenomena." In this painting one can let the eye travel from one photo to another, from the rounded ship hull at the far right to the squarish hull on the lower right of Mrs. Churchill's image. The hulls form a set linking the notion of ships with Mrs. Churchill and Turner's ship. Verbal explanations can be obvious and banal. One can let the eye lead the mind and gradually form notions, such as sentience, concern, the passage of time, and so forth. Such constructs are based on our ability to think metaphorically and to form image-schematas to route our responses.

Figure 29 is an excursion into my perception of a photograph of a fertilized human egg attached to the uterine wall eight days after conception. Initially I am drawn into a representation of cells and transformations into animals, insects, and fetal and human images. I have an urge to see profundity in the mass and complexity of the fertilized egg.

I build a discursive yet anchored mental construction — a realization that out of such amorphous and tiny beginnings will come the panorama of a human being. I adhere a print of Michelangelo's *Sybil* from the Sistine ceiling at upper far right. It is an indescribable revelation of an androgynous authority figure that I will nonetheless attempt to describe. The head implies wisdom and a premonition of death. The hair is tightly woven, suggesting binding, strength, and male as well as female hair. The eye is extremely sensitive in handling, almost closed in a sign of resignation. The mouth has both male and female contours, as does the nose and chin. All this within a head that is compact, classically contained, and yet heroic in scale and ready to expand. This input merges and emerges from the already mentioned tissue of cross-referenced domains. Not lastly, one can feel an additional presence, a harbinger of a fateful yet unknown future for the race.

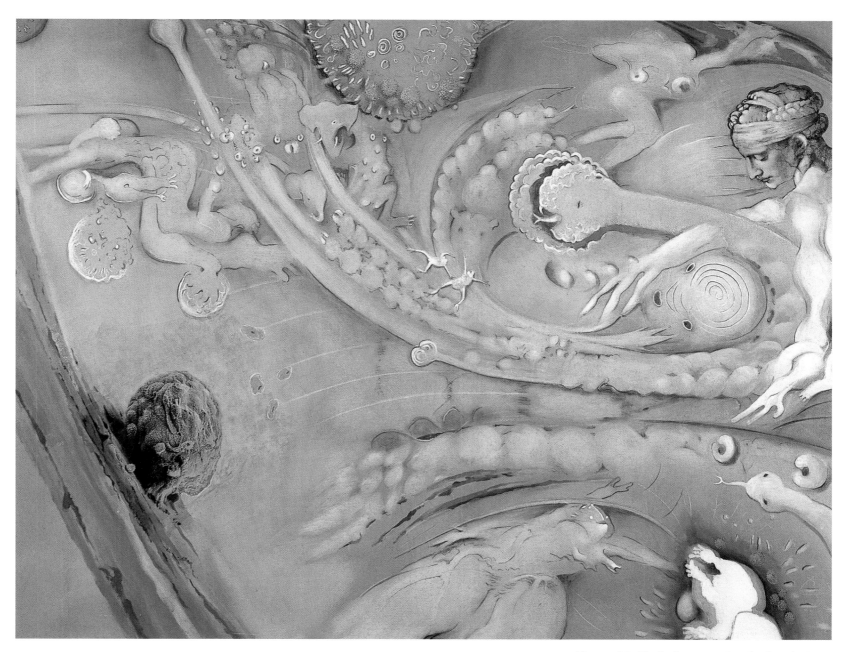

Figure 29. Herb Greene, *Beginning to End*

CHAPTER THIRTEEN

Konorak / Giselbertius / Vermeer

The three photographs in figure 30 express seminal concepts about human sexuality. The carved stone goddesses at the far left from the Hindu temple at Konorak (about 1000 B.C.E.) display anatomy that has been modeled to represent a great swelling, a symbol of suksuma, the one stuff of the universe out of which the multitudinous diversity of all nature is differentiated. In this work of art sex — symbolized by the full hips, breasts and sensuous curves — is a manifestation of life force integrated with cosmic energy.

On the other hand, the sculptured portrait of Eve by the Romanesque master Giselbertius, from the portal of Autun, shows the sexual conflicts that have dogged the European mind for over two thousand years. The artist's virtuosity is dedicated to Eve's head, her shoulders, and the exuberant vegetation. Eve's hips are masked by a sinuous branch, and her hand touching her face possibly suggests a gesture of shame.

Vermeer's *The Procuress*, at far right, deals with a theme common to his European contemporaries, but with results that are highly original. The woman is shown pressing her shoulder to the man while withdrawing her head. Her face suggests untroubled self-contentment. She gives herself and yet maintains her independence. The man touches her breast without pressure. His attitude seems not prurient, but of warm familiarity with something held in reserve. His expression, like hers, is sensual but wholesome. Each one expresses communion with self. The result is what Snow has described as "what may be the most unsentimental, guilt-free, spiritually-satisfying representation of shared erotic experience in all of Western Art."[1] Vermeer contrasts this message with the prurience and sexual unease expressed by the face of the androgynous voyeur to the left, and the bon vivant cavalier, whose head I have painted out but whose hand, directly to the left of the woman's hand that accepts the coin, holds a mandolin in what is probably a symbol of masturbation.

The grouping of these works allows us to study them together, looking for an integrative interpretation of the facts that they contain and for our response to these facts. Whatever we know about the cultural histories they represent, these images are masterful,

Figure 30. Herb Greene, *Konorak*

dense poetic statements — sure, complete and full of life. Through them the historic past becomes a part of a living present. By comparing them, they can help us to feel how the present has come into existence.

The main task of my composition is to suggest merging and emerging aspects of the events, in all three photographs, to form an image of a mental space-time in which aspects of the events can coexist. The sculptures of Konorak and Giselbertius are placed in close proximity to contrast their spatial perspectives, and to compare their textures and forms within a single glance. The sleek form of Eve seems to move horizontally (an effect created by the camera angle), yet still retains frontal position with the picture plane. This frontal motion is contrasted with the swiftly receding perspective of the two Hindu goddesses, suggesting that they and Eve inhabit different streams of space-time. The theme of textured stone is carried over to the hand-painted stone frames around each of the three photos, leading the eye from one to the next and suggesting a unifying texture and structure for the painted ground.

Making meaning out of a perceived event, which always involves decisions that an event is this and not that, entails terrific unconscious mental activity. I have attempted to suggest something of this process by selecting the swelling thigh of the Hindu goddess. It is a form that seizes my attention, not only because of its more obvious connotations, but probably because I have been disposed to develop a curving mass as an organizing form in architecture, as well as in painting. For me it has become a symbol of power, the sensual, and of non-Euclidean form. Just below the center of the collage I made a large curving form from pieces that might be sections of the great hip and leg, or of a stone column from the background architecture, or of the stone drum placed prominently over the pubic area of the goddess. A pubic shadow is reiterated behind the knee of the large, hand-painted leg. This carries the eye to the dark V-shape above Eve's knees. The large, white rectangular form positioned to the right of the shadow is partially determined as a sheet or drapery, slipped or pulled from covering the hips. It is an allusion to possible meanings drawn from art history that involve drapery and modesty.

Eve's feet are hidden behind the tree and the snake. In response, feet at different scales appear prominently in twisted positions in the ground. The rhythm of feet, including the superbly formed feet of the Hindu goddess, reflect the multiple positions of hands and feet in so much Hindu sculpture, and can be associated with the multiple spatial perspectives of cubism that are suggested by the painting. In making meaning from the data in the collage, one can only be moved by the power and flexibility of the mind in creating contexts and interpretations. I have tried to project an awareness of time, to make us think of time as an idea so that we can meditate on what in the photos might be transitory and what might be lasting in our experience. While adequate descriptions of psychological time, as well as physical time, so far, are beyond our grasp, the aesthetic expression of both aspects of time remains a compelling objective of twentieth-century art.

Part Two

Whitehead and the Painted Ground

CHAPTER FOURTEEN

Terminology

Rather than listing Whitehead's terms alphabetically in a more conventional glossary at the back of the book, I have placed them here as an introduction to the text of Part Two. Readers of the work have found this position preferable, and the sequence of presentation traces a logical development of ideas related to the book.

Whitehead's theory parallels gestalt theory in that both are concerned with the formation of perceived parts into closures, or wholes. But Whitehead goes beyond the goal of that ever-present gestalt diagram: the recognition of a profiled human face in the outline of a vase, made visible by reversing our attention to the light-colored background bordering the black-colored vase. Theoretically, Whitehead accounts for anything that can be felt and thought during the process of such recognition; for example, when I see the profile of the vase reminding me of a poorly-designed Roman urn in so many texts that I become bored with it. During the act of perception such conceptually or emotionally based feelings exist on the same level as other determinations of the face/vase, such as its black color or its appearance as a human face rather than that of a baboon, even though we may screen out such ideation in favor of accepting the concept of the reversible face/vase as a fact of theoretical importance to perception and thought.

Whitehead finds all the above realizations individualizing themselves in a plurality of modes that are interlocked by our subjective aims. He had to deal with recognition as a process occurring in time, where feelings are integral with thoughts and often seemingly in dialogue with them. Both neuro and cognitive scientists have found feelings and thoughts to be much more dependent on a base of embodied experience derived from the body and the mind acting together than we have allowed for in our habitual objectivist determinations. For example, a baby's learning (involving depth perception and knowledge of objects) that he or she cannot touch the moon or an adult's conjectures about what the crust and rocks of the moon are made of rely on such networks of embodied experience. Classical thinking confines the explanation of a baby's and adult's learning experiences to fixed instants, conventional subject-predicate propositions, the erroneous structure based on "primary" and "secondary" forms, and a misleading emphasis on logical relations, as if they are disembodied from nature. Whitehead's explanation of the actions of baby and adult includes human purposes, goals, "four-dimensional event structure," physio-biological mental functioning, intentions and interpretations that amend and enlarge conventional notions of causation. Intentionality informs every human interpretation of fact, from the law of gravity to the recognition of calm in a Vermeer and the realization that the evolving universe is indifferent to the human predicaments of suffering and fear, and yet is instrumental in the evolution of the human spirit and mind.

Consider again Shakespeare's familiar lines,

Tomorrow and tomorrow and tomorrow creeps in
this petty place from day to day
To the last syllable of recorded time,
And all our yesterdays have lighted
fools the way to dusty death.

Can a logic of phonemes, the logical-linguistic definitions used by Wittgenstein or Derrida's proposition that "there is nothing but the text" (mere words and linguistic forms) take us to a full-blown realization of Shakespeare's lines? Not unless they can recognize the

Western ethos which, for over two thousand years, has striven to define human purpose, individuality, futility, fate and existential meaninglessness; or understand appropriate metaphoric contexts for "yesterdays," "creeps" and "petty" in context with the line "from day to day"; or the appropriate reading of "fools" *in situ*.

Presentational Immediacy and Causal Efficacy. For Whitehead, there are two modes involved in every act of perception. One is presentational immediacy, which is the initial reception of bare sense data of experience, including the shapes, colors, sounds, tactile sensations and smells that are directly and immediately perceived before further acts of interpretation. The other is causal efficacy, which is the transfer of the embodied experience of our body-mind that fills the bare sense of presentational immediacy with meaning. When a baby learns that it cannot touch the moon he or she is learning about space, color, distance, form and "being in the world" with the moon. This is embodied experience, which is the ground for causal efficacy, to be reconstituted in new situations as bare sense data are presented. Adults contemplating what the moon is made of undergo the same transfer in their imaginations.

Actual Entity. I see the texture, buff pink color, and outline of my thumb. I also see an imperfectly manicured thumbnail and the wine-colored mouse pad beyond my thumb. An actual entity is an experiential closure of several of these factors into a unity. Such an actual entity, having attained its individuality, adds a determinate condition to the evolving satisfaction or concrescence, and yet this composite entity becoming in the mind exists only to perish. I have to keep renewing my closure of the thumb in a living, evolving, time-consuming world. I have to reconstitute another closure within the space-time continuum and my memory, which are always changing, however imperceptibly, to my perception. Whitehead's actual entity that must be composed as a composite of other actual entities is, for me, the philosophical basis of metaphor that cognitive scientists Lakoff and Johnson find fundamental to cognition.

The realization of the unseen bone in my thumb is an actual entity. A glacier, the texture of a pear, the straightness of a picture frame, or a particular emotion felt in a work of art are actual entities. Through their variations of importance and diversities of function, actual entities are recognized as the ultimate drops of experience — complex and dependent on their relationships to other things that we have experienced in the extensive world.

Whitehead tells us that his conception of an actual entity is little more than an expansion of Plato's *Timaeus*, in which Plato characterizes, "That which is conceived by opinion with the help of sensation and without reason, is always in the process of becoming and perishing and never really is."

Prehension. Prehension refers to apprehension that is not necessarily conscious. To prehend is to grasp a component of an event on its way to becoming an actual entity. For instance, I prehend the gradation of blue sky as it darkens toward the horizon, or an anxious feeling when, as an eight-year-old, I see the local bully approaching me. Prehensions are the only means of penetrating events to advance thought and feeling about their contents.

Event. An event is a discernible or an imagined happening. The term applies to our perception of things such as an apple, a planet, a unicorn, or of an identifiable emotion, such as a particular joy by which we know the actual or imagined world. Events are known through the medium of prehensions and actual entities, which are our initial closures of experience. Actual entities are produced by mental concrescences during the early stages of perception. Our notions of the moon or a particular joy are derived from such constructs and grasped into unities. Events are to be conceived as four-dimensional happenings having relationship to other events in the extended physical field of space-time. By feeling, recognizing contrasts and identities, and by thinking both logically and metaphorically, aspects of one event are harmonized with aspects of other events to create meaning.

Writing on Whitehead, Professor Albert Levi[1] tells us that an event can also be described as a unity of causal process instead of an enduring assumed substance with material identity. An enduring object, such as a stone, is actually the repetition of pattern sustained through changes in its character. A stone loses atoms and molecules as we view it, although we do not notice this because of the scale and duration of our observation.

Actual Occasion. In my studio I look through a window to a deck and trees beyond. The wall surrounding the window, the window, trees and patches of sky are events that are extensive and overlapping, with some ambiguous boundaries. The window frame is an actual occasion, a spatialized set of cues, which is a limited event itself enabling me to focus on it within the environment of events previously noted. For human perception, the world is built up out of actual occasions. Events, actual entities and actual occasions represent different foci upon which to grasp and process the objects and thoughts of perception.

Concrescence. All actual entities are composed of other entities brought together by a mental act. As I perceive the blue sky I form an actual entity bringing together a selection of my past experiences of blue, atmosphere, light, space, the horizon, sunsets, and so forth. I may also bring in a component of anticipation, for example, whether the sky suggests a good day for a picnic or not. This is a process of concrescence. As Whitehead explains, the concrescence solves the problem of how several components of objectified content are to be unified in one felt realization.

Negative Prehension. In a concrescence of blue sky, I ignore the dirt specks on my eyeglasses to focus on the sky's brightness and blueness. The process of concrescence involves the exclusion of prehensions that do not fit its primary focus. I have dismissed the dirt specks as a negative prehension. Certain negative prehensions can be included as contrasts within the realization of an actual entity. For example, my closure of blue sky includes the view of dense, polluting smoke from a chimney that I have chosen not to dismiss.

Nexus. A nexus is a set of actual entities felt in the unity of their prehensions. The nexus of calm in Vermeer's *Woman Reading a Letter* (figure 14), where proportions of the colored shapes are calm, the light is calm, the body language of the woman is calm, and the sense of her interior life is calm, provides an illustration.

Duration. A duration is a sensed simultaneity within events. It is a limited natural entity of perception happening in time, and is necessary to form gestalt wholes. For instance, I discern the branch, foliage and tree shapes to recognize a redwood tree.

Datum. The datum acts as both a limitation to, and a provider of meaning as we organize our responses to events. A real component, like the particular deep blue sky over the Aegean Sea seen on a clear day, assumes the role of directing my concrescence of light on Greek ruins at Delos. The moon acts as the principal feature of a datum directing a concrescence of the nighttime sky, or perhaps the datum is the gaze of a fair companion with the moon in the sky beyond.

The datum is rather like a gateway directing me as I shape additional elements of feeling and ideation into determinate linkages attaining the unity of my particular satisfaction.

Eternal Object. An eternal object is a form of definiteness that can occur in diverse actual entities, such as a particular shade of white that occurs in a white flower, white paper or white wedding dress. Events, actual entities and concrescences are unique. Eternal objects provide the grounds of continuity and unification among these diverse entities. No character belongs to the actual, apart from its determination by eternal objects. Directed by subjective aim, the mind processes a shade of white, a notion of poverty, or the arresting profile line of the head of Vermeer's woman reading a letter, by mapping and cross-referencing from appropriate, selected experiential domains and contexts out of a vast number of remembered potentialities. Our ability to map these potentialities into feelings and thoughts holds together our world of meaning.

Whitehead[2] tells us that if one objects to the term "eternal object," the term "potential" would be suitable. The eternal objects are the pure potentials of the universe, and actual entities differ from each other in their particular realizations, as in the orange color of a fruit or the orange color of the jacket worn by Vermeer's milkmaid.

Extensive Continuum. The extensive continuum is a mental concept necessary to explain the connections and associations among events, actual occasions and actual entities in the physical universe outside our heads. The embodied experience harbored in the body-mind provides the source for making connections and associations within the extensive continuum. Meaning always involves human understanding of a world that we can make sense of. Thus understanding depends on our ability to see entities in terms of other entities in this world. Thus understanding requires imagination. The bread looks and smells fresh. Thus the color, texture and smells of the bread, and our associations with freshness and staleness, become paramount to understanding. The extensive continuum supplies the vehicle for this understanding.

Feeling. Each actual entity includes a process of "feeling" the many data associated with it, so as to absorb them into the unity of one individual satisfaction. For example, I feel the outline, wrinkles, skin, curves and light reflections of my hand as I lift them out of the event in which they are situated to create an actual entity such as "graceful proportions" or "reptilian quality." "Feeling" is the term for the basic operation of passing from the objectivity of the selected hand data to the subjectivity of the actual entity in question. Considering that my hand appears as a rather pallid, somewhat reptilian object, surprisingly I can still feel my hand as an aesthetically pleasing satisfaction because I have focused on what I see as its good proportions and my knowledge of its good uses. All data are potentials for feeling.

Conformal Feelings. In a concrescence of the sharpness of a spear point or the roundness of a beach ball, I feel the qualitative character of the sharp angles of the spear as piercing, or the roundness of the ball as soft, taut or expanding. These are **physical feelings,** resulting from my processing of **strain feelings,** Whitehead's term for our feelings as we respond to the piercing of the spear point or stretched tautness of the beach ball. As I realize the definite distinctions of the spear or the ball, I have felt the limitation that is imposed by my past experience by physically and mentally conforming to that experience. Such feelings are **conformal feelings.**

Strain Feelings. Strain feelings are our body-mind responses to the topographies of forms and their textures. The taut roundness of a beach ball is a strain feeling. Our sense of merging with fog or snow evokes strain feelings.

Conceptual Feeling. A conceptual feeling involves a conscious limitation allowing an entity to be realized as this particular and not some other. This exclusiveness requires the recognition of eternal objects, such as sharpness and straightness in feeling the spear point, or of roundness and tautness in feeling the ball. Thus to be conscious of the spear point or the ball requires conceptual feelings, even though familiarity with the object, "beach ball," may allow us to short circuit "taut roundness" and skip ahead to other closures and concerns.

Propositional Feeling. A propositional feeling refers to comparisons and inferences derived from logical subjects. Hamlet's speech, "To be or not to be . . .," contrasts propositional feelings. Such feelings can only arise in a late stage of the cognitive process, after subjects such as "being" and contexts such as "not being" have been sorted through by subjective aim.

Object. An object is any actual entity that can be felt. Objects range from the continuity of a spherical surface to the particular sentience expressed in the face of a young woman in a Vermeer.

Object and Subject. An actual entity is an object in that it is able to initiate and fashion creative actions. For example, a creative action is my processing the sight of chewed fingernails into a sign of nervousness. An actual entity is also a subject arising from prehensions of the universe. For example, I have prehensions of life situations (prehensions of the universe) that lead to chewed fingernails. Objects can become subjects and subjects can become objects. A thumbnail or a notion of sentience is either an object or a subject, depending on which emphasis is acted upon.

Superject. The overview that shapes the concrescence and directs the subject. The first light of dawn as a subject conditioned by the overview of one who has been frightened by the dark would be an example. The blue sky directed as a sign of comfort and joy or, in contrast, as a sign of drought would be another.

Subjective Aim. Subjective aim is the agent that lies behind all purposive adaptation to the environment. In human experience, subjective aim is expressed in our actions upon our imagined future. It is the influence of the future on the present as it directs the completion of concrescences and satisfactory closures. Subjective aim is the element effecting creativity in the perception of an event, for it determines which possibilities are selected for its completion. Neuroscientist Antonio Damasio,[3] in a carefully crafted treatment, explains the neural basis of the self. He envisions how ensembles of neurons receive signals from the representation of both the perceived object and the self as qualified by the object. This information is then utilized in a third kind of image that initiates a subjective perspective. Subjective aim becomes an interpretive scheme of which we may or may not be aware.

Appetition. The urge — conscious or, more often, subconscious — to continue or to withdraw the feelings and thoughts that arise in a concrescence. Appetition is characterized by the self-interest of the enduring personality as it accepts, rejects and transforms fresh experience.

Whitehead and Heidegger. I wish to note several similarities and differences between Whitehead and Heidegger. Currently the more influential philosopher in the academy appears to be Heidegger, who in the 'twenties and 'thirties produced writings on what Whitehead terms "subjective aim." Heidegger[4] discusses at length the introduction of "prehensive drive," and "appetition" by Leibniz, as a foreground to his own concept of *Dasein*, his German term for the existential conditions of "being in the world." This drive, and its ordering of thought and experience in coming to meaning, is approximate to Whitehead's subjective aim, in which a synthesis of knowing, feeling and appetition overtakes a concrescence "in advance," as in my oft-repeated example of the profile of Athena's "Greek" nose and forehead, which I process as a sign of intelligence.

Heidegger identifies conditions of being in time and situations of knowing that refer to a perceiving "I" and the self. These categories may be linked to Damasio's[5] recognition of the proto, core and autobiographical selves within the brain structure and states of consciousness. These differentiations suggest refinements in recognizing the conditions of the self. Speaking for myself, the ontological expeditions that Heidegger demands in order to recognize and understand these conditions through "logical propositions" about the essence of being, transcendence and time lose me in linguistic and conceptual ambiguity. For instance, Heidegger insists on absolute logic at the same time he denigrates rational thought to investigate "being." Heidegger assumes that an ideal clarity of language obtains to explain "essence," "freedom," "lawfulness" and the "ground" (the latter being equivalent to Whitehead's causal efficacy). The "neutrality" of Dasein is stressed, as if the formation of content in the mind and the roots of behavior are structurally outside of nature and open to neutral and objective investigation by the "independent" self. While Heidegger brings awareness of necessary existential process into philosophy, his structuralism and "nature-free" logic reflect the sensationalist-objectivist-rationalist traditions that I have been contrasting to Whitehead's theory of organism.

Whitehead starts with a modern physical explanation of the world and the universe as an extended physical field of energy with all its evolving complexities; for instance, that the calcium in human bones is literally made of the dust from exploding stars. This physical world, including the self as body-mind, is the product of interacting events within the physical field. The human mind and thought evolve as part of this vast event structure. There is neutrality in the operations of the physical universe, but a completely neutral, objective understanding of the entire physical field remains forever inaccessible to mind, which has evolved into both a repository and a creative agency for processing emotional, embodied, moral and aesthetic experience. This makes "perfect objective neutrality" beyond the reach of a "being in the world." Whitehead's scheme shows how we create unities of thought and feeling by the recognition and creation of contrasts and identities among prehensions of any and all interacting events that we experience, and by recognizing emotion and feeling as objects capable of analysis. Damasio suggests much the same from the standpoint of neurobiology.

I close with my rendition of Whitehead's "enduring personal-ity" and Heidegger's "being in time." As previously noted, in youth I felt pomposity in some passages of Beethoven's symphonies. Now I feel, as well as sensual pleasure, historic and artistic importance in the same music. I realigned and perhaps developed my socio-political, moral and aesthetic maps to my gain as a mindful being. With the music of Wagner, no such luck. I cannot put a positive spin on what I hear as romantically-bloated passages with images of overfed, horn-helmeted warriors emoting about death and the warrior's life in Valhalla as the goal of the afterlife. Further, I cannot overcome my negative prehensions of racial superiority in Wagner implicit in my understanding of German culture and some of its expressive forms. In the language of Heidegger, "to free oneself for the total essence peculiar to that which reveals itself as time," and to "proceed to analyze the structure of time" as if the mind is up to these tasks as existential exercises, is to suggest a Germanic love of order and of the absolute, which I see as excesses in certain of their expressive forms, such as Heidegger's idealism in our ability to reach "essences of being" by ontological constructions. I agree with Iris Murdoch,[6] who says that Heidegger's "essences" suffer from optimistic romancing, and that we cannot expect much practical utility from such over-generalized claims.

For Whitehead, in the tradition of English empiricism as contrasted with German idealism, the problem is to understand the complexity of feeling and belief initiated by one's participation with events. Neither emotions, nor embodied experience, nor moral and aesthetic feelings can be ultimately excluded from concrescences of the feelings and thoughts of objectivity as indicated by recent observations in neurobiology. Neither can one finally limit prehensions to those of imposed order, love of the absolute, and to thinking and being that stand "outside of nature." Currently, I have negative prehensions of Heidegger's "pedestal of logic" at the center of being and negative feelings about his identification with Nazi ideals. Accused of desiring to be the Führer of German philosophy, it is interesting that Heidegger often appeared for his philosophy classes in tailored Tyrolean shorts, jacket and cap, attesting to the German and Nazi elevation of the hardy peasant as a preferred archetype — pure in blood, emphasizing an aggressive spirit, tradition and patriarchy against rationality, democracy and a disinterested scientific inquiry. These characteristics keep me from much sympathy with his approach. I know this is to my detriment, as his concepts of being in the world and being in time have been of great interest to French existentialists, even if I, in the grip of biases toward American pragmatism within my enduring personality, am unable to make a "Beethoven shift."

CHAPTER FIFTEEN

Process

Whitehead's project in explaining process was concerned with how the energetic activity considered in physics becomes the emotional intensity of life. To this end he utilized traditional philosophic terms with terms and explanations derived from modern physics, such as "vectors" and "quanta," from life sciences, such as "bodily feelings," and from mathematics, such as "coordinate division" to develop his explanations. We continually accept new terms such as "nanosecond" and "megabyte" and should not be put off because some of Whitehead's terms seem unfamiliar. At the same time Whitehead points out how an old, established metaphysical system gains a false air of adequacy and precision from the fact that its words and phrases have passed into current literature and remain widely accepted. Lakoff and Johnson, throughout their book *Philosophy in the Flesh: The Embodied Mind and its Challenge to Western Thought* (1999),[1] mount overpowering arguments that delineate biases and errors concerning "static" matter and "separate" mind that have been absorbed in the language of scientific materialism and classical rationalism, and that currently abuse notions of common sense. To give just one of dozens of their examples, Kantian morality, with its tenet of an autonomous intellectual will that is free of emotion and based on pure reason, must be qualified by current neuroscience, in which Damasio[2] has reported on patients with damage to certain cerebral connective tissues. The patient's ability to reason cannot function when it is cut off from emotional centers in the brain.

To get back to Whitehead, his description remains for me the most apt philosophic explanation of how process works in forming mental concepts. I want to comment on his system as an influence in how I think about and make images. Whitehead's idea of process requires familiarity with his understanding and use of potentiality; for example, how potentiality might be actualized during my realization of chopping a tomato.

Imagine that I see in front of me a ripe tomato, knife, cutting board, chile powder and bowl. I grip the tomato and chop off a piece. Potentiality refers to both the physical elements and the mental activity of making linkages involved in the act right down to considering the atomic. Considering the tomato, my hand, knife and board as Whitehead's actual occasions, I have prehensions of them and their representations, both actual and immanent, within my conscious-unconscious gradient. There is a certain firmness and gentleness in my fingers holding the tomato, a lack of enthusiasm in hoping for a good tomato taste in a California tomato, a recognition of the separate piece, the hazard of the knife, the anticipation of adding spices to my proven recipe, and so on. In this instance I have to force myself to consider the atomic, but it is within the realm of potentialities. This process has involved a span of actualizations of potentialities. The actualizations become only to perish, with some of their antecedents being actualized in some new form as I proceed to think about making my renowned guacamole. Potentialities of the tomato alone could include its edibility, nutritive value, soil enrich-ment, spoilage, climate for growing, a petrified, Runyonesque metaphor of a ripe tomato as a beautiful young woman, and more. According to Damasio, consciousness only arises when the chopped tomato as object, myself as the organism, and their relationships can be re-represented.

This process of re-representation is enlightened by Professor Wallach's interpretation[3] of Whitehead's definition of potentiality. Potentiality is not actuality, but neither is it nothing at all. It is the aim for achieving a new definite actuality; it is reaching for the togetherness of feelings that form a novel being. Our own attitude shapes what we see at least as much as what we see effects us. Percep-tion consists of prehensions of what we see, hear, touch, taste and recall made conscious. A large dose of chile pepper may be unbear-able to some and zestful to others. An appearing dog may hearten some and discourage others. It is how a subject prehends or feels its antecedents that causes it to be what it is. In humans and, to a surprising extent, in chimps and dogs, Whitehead says there are notable feelings of sympathy, that is, conforming to and with another within a range of positive and negative feelings to continue or to break off the interchange.

During this process the enduring object of the chopped piece of tomato may also be likened to a space-time system entering into a plurality of space-time systems given by the knife-blade, chile, tomato and bowl. Time is no more an enduring substance than is the mental or physical actualization of the chopped tomato. The Whiteheadian unit of time within process is the "epoch". The epoch embraces the potentialities of the linkages in space-time among the cross section of various prehensions of bland tomato, blade, bowl and seasonings that are being actualized.

With this foreground I take up the analysis of a collage paint-ing. The photograph included in figure 31 is by Cartier-Bresson. It shows an interrogation at a deportation camp in Dessau, Germany in 1945. The most arresting event is probably the angered woman striking or gesticulating toward the shamed woman, who appears to be a camp functionary, perhaps a guard. According to the caption accompanying the photograph, this functionary informed the Gestapo about the angry woman. Teeth bared in a snarl, the angry woman has her large, sturdy chest thrust out and her neck stiffened so that her body-gestalt can be read as combining strong aggression and repulsion at the same time. I also have positive prehensions of French national character enforced by other occasions, such as the face of the angry woman, the sitting man, the standing man in prison stripes with cap, the thin-faced man with beret directly in back of the angry woman's gesticulating arm (Could he have been a member of the resistance?), and the shamed woman, who all appear to me to be French. I am feeling positive prehensions of "Frenchness" that I wish to continue. I can't verify my prehensions of "Frenchness," but with the information at hand I am unable to suppress them.

The apparently well-fed, shamed woman appears to be sorry for herself. Her eyes, mouth and head are down-turned, and her gaze is averted. I have a propositional feeling that her remorseful look is personal, not symbolic of the larger group as with Athena's volition-less stare in figure 11. The angry woman also appears to be reasonably fed and in civilian clothes. One scenario is that she is a deported person whose wrath is based on her disdain for the Nazis, detention camps, and perceiving a *collaborateur*. The sitting man seen in profile in a posture of attention seems to show disgust with the human situation, and/or discomfort at having to preside over the confrontation of the two women.

Considered as a mingling of prehensions of the components of the photograph, like the activities in my making salsa, I experience a protean creative process that reproduces itself anew as I proceed to satisfactions that are directed by my subjective aim, which includes trying to understand my feelings about why I think the photo is so very interesting and why it is yet another example of Cartier-Bresson's genius, although not as rich and satisfying with potential meaning or as powerful to me as his *Aged Academician Entering a Cab*.

Designing a Collage

After adhering the photograph to canvas my first tangible move was to make a white-tipped cross, positioned so that one of the onlookers in the crowd could be carrying the cross. I felt both negative and positive prehensions at the impulse and my results. Negatively, the cross seemed too obvious and patronizing a symbol for Christian history and morality. Yet I chose to keep it on several counts. I liked the arresting white geometric shape as a contrast to the rather amorphous human figures. I felt that it was inescapable to think of Western moral determinations without the saturated history and many domains of reference that are provided by the cross, which, for me, includes the irony of the Christian role in the historic persecution of the Jews that I associate with the camp scene.

Figure 31. Herb Greene, *Collaborateur*

By including the cross as an occasion overlapping with the prehensive epochs of the camp and human figures, I thought that I could stimulate and challenge the viewer's responses.

One reason that I am so attracted to photographs is because of a concrete, embodied sense of epochal time that they can create by giving us actual representations and symbols of human situations, emotions, and of eras in which their events are happening. A component of my fascination with the photograph has a scientific side. I can examine the stilled forms with exacting care to determine the components of my response. Damasio[4] describes how an actual scene external to the brain is remade or recalled in the mind internally. The power of the mind to make neural patterns for something to be known, such as my prehension of disgust or primal anger, is preserved even when consciousness of that something is no longer being made. Further, I can notice how my prehension of disgust in the face of the seated man can be held in the mind by a detail that ostensibly has but a secondary role in my gestalt of disgust, such as the man's sunglasses, which in this instance can be felt as partly shielding his participation in the scene.

My next move was to introduce a large, horizontal black cross that would form a strong upper boundary to the photograph and enable me to orchestrate potential imaged ideas within its black region. Implicit in the choice of black is its sheer physical sensation of deadening and void, and cultural coding of the unseen, severity, mystery, and more. I believe my following move was to seize upon the squarish table surface as a repeatable form to give a loose geometric order and perspectival direction to the collage. These repeated planes could locate some of the metaphoric figures, which are attempts to image some of my concepts and feelings as I respond to the photograph. The table itself is an actual occasion that, as a space-time system, is coordinated with the systems of the human figures. It sets up notions of juridical restraint toward the angry woman and of the accused's subordination before the community. The table, with its prehensions of the abrupt and the impromptu, is important to the aesthetic and intellectual impact of the photo.

Notions of the abrupt and the impromptu contribute to feelings of immediacy and spontaneity in the photograph. The table's size, edges and plane also contribute to feelings of a mathematical order that can act to stimulate our coordinations of valued experience from the causal past. If that statement seems wanting, I would say that the process is approximate to the experience of viewing the famous photograph of four marines raising the flag at Iwo Jima. The progressive rhythm or mathematical order of the Marines and their archetypal body positions at different points along the sloping flagpole is necessary for us to infuse that memorable tableau with a heightened sense of formal order, patriotism and determination. The abstract pattern of the table in figure 31 helps us to strengthen our conceptual satisfactions in feeling the anger, shame and disgust that we recognize.

At the top of the black cross arm is a cluster of "head-dots" that are supposed to signify a group acting as one with two arms thrust upward. At top center is a supine, pink-white (female?) figure that reaches down to touch or grasp a red nipple or eye that is located a blob-brain-head image with bared teeth, in which I try to express something of a Freudian id. At far left is a figure seen from the back that is pointing toward both crosses. At bottom left is a white figure clutching its slumping head, as if a variation of some of my prehensions of the accused and her situation.

A single sunglass appears at far right worn by a twice-profiled head, with which I try to capture something of my prehensions of disengagement and disgust that I feel in the seated official. A small photo of a young chimpanzee playing with its image in a mirror is placed at the center of the black cross. Barely visible in the reduced size of the illustration, it is a reminder of our remote anthropological roots connecting to origins of conscience, communal roles, aggression and cooperation. The active passages of stripes call attention to prison garb. These passages are intended to arrest the eye and mind as vibrating topographies repeating key information in determining our associations with concentration and detention camps, and as signs of the "electric" speed of our mental transactions. This later analogy is qualified by my habit of using lines as a preferred means of expression in my work. I am looking for a handy metaphor (electric speed) consistent with my subjective aim.

Once again, prehensions are the concrete facts in relatedness. Let us take the use of the color red in the collage. I want viewers to experience prehensions of anger, blood, cuts, wounds and the interior body. I want viewers to experience some degree of physical and mental shock. Lakoff and Johnson[5] tell us that, as pure physical sensation, the red color is not merely the external reality of reflectance properties of the painted surface, nor is it a thing or substance out there in the world. The color red is the consequence of electromagnetic radiation, lighting conditions, color cones and neural processing. Color interpretation may vary among cultures, for it is a function of the world and our biology. We have the color concepts we do because the physical limitations constraining evolution gave evolutionary advantages to beings with a color system that enabled them to function well in crucial respects. I would say to recognize blood as red, to recognize green as restful and important to plant life, and to recognize black void as possibly dangerous are such functions.

What Whitehead's scheme has done for me that other schemes have not done is to reinforce my incentive to compose, superimpose and collage forms as representations of any thought or feeling that stems from my processing the color red in context with the photographs on the canvas. In so doing I am trying to make a symbol of the seeming infinity of the world. I am ready to respond to any paintable linkage of the color red, as subject or object, directed by my subjective aim. Of course, I also narrow my choices with that same subjective aim that shrouds every phenomenology.

CHAPTER SIXTEEN

Metaphor

A thing, such as a coat or an idea of radiance, can be thought of as being made up of other things. The coat may be in a painting, made visible by the energetic brush strokes of van Gogh. The coat may appear rumpled or pressed. We may assume that the coat is made of cloth and thread. An idea of radiance may be informed by the expression of a human face, heat energy moving through distance, and so on. Yet, the original thing does not wholly contain these other things. This concept, which provides an embodied, experiential basis for metaphor (which I define simply as seeing things in terms of other things), is fundamental to process philosophy. It has motivated my efforts to give the idea expression in the painted ground of my collages. I have touched upon the concept in previous chapters on figure-ground, immanence, denotative forms and process. In this chapter I want to extend my discussion as a preface to chapters that follow, in which I apply more of Whitehead's explanations to an analysis of the metaphoric nature of images.

While Whitehead rarely used the term metaphor, present-day cognitive scientists have determined that metaphor is not merely a literary device, but is a prerequisite of all thought. Of course, metaphors can be inappropriate and even disastrous. Flat-Earthers and Augustine's perpetuation of menstruation as a symbol of carnality come to mind. Yet metaphor cannot be avoided even in mathematics. Understanding space, dimensions, distance and geometric forms depend on understanding the body as located — as a container with a back, a front, as the perceiver of extension, and so on. The conception of four-dimensional happenings, groupings, sets and loci all depend on Whitehead's requirements of the body-mind's transposition of embodied experience into metaphors of thought. Lakoff and Johnson[1] tell us that conceptual metaphors ground abstract concepts through cross-domain mappings.

Mapping the body as container with the concept of loci informs the teenagers coinage of the term "spaced-out." This is not a liability — a means of obscuring fact with peripheral externalities — as would have been held by classical rationalists, but a gift — a

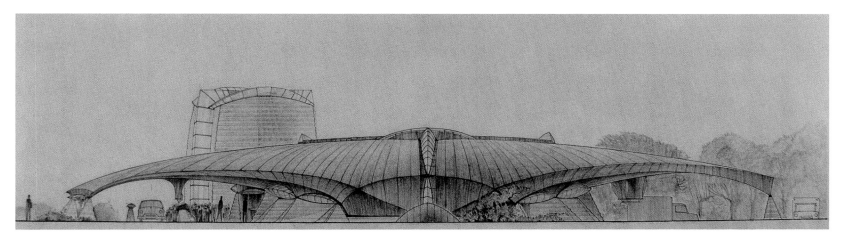

Figure 32. Herb Greene, *Post Office*

Figure 33. Herb Greene,
 Prairie House

tool for understanding things in a way that is tied to embodied, lived experience. "To be or not to be" is an expression of conceptual mapping. Existence is mapped onto implicit categories of lived experience: time, destiny, possibly a morally-based life, death, and so on. This mapping is not a slow, careful, conscious process, but happens on the scale of our observations, seemingly at once, via neural connections.

Let us go back to Whitehead's famous argument against the presupposition of simple location advocated by Descartes and Newton. For Whitehead and modern physics, the physical things which we term "stars," "rocks," "molecules" and "cities" are each to be thought of as changing situations within space-time. There is a focal region that we describe as where the thing is. Yet its influence can stream away to the various reaches of space-time. Intergalactic cosmic rays interacting with human genes and the historical influence of the city of Rome are ready examples. For physics, the thing, mutating gene or Rome, is what it does and what it does includes its stream of influence. The focal region of the thing cannot be separated from its external stream. Thus if we attempt to conceive a complete instance of the thing in question, we cannot confine ourselves to one part of space or one moment of time. The physical thing has to be conceived as a coordination of spaces and times, and of conditions in those spaces at those times. Thus with the denial of simple location we must admit that, within any region of space-time conceived as a thing such as a rock, an innumerable multitude of

contingent things is, in a sense, superimposed.[2]

Here is a technical explanation that nourishes the deepest root of metaphor from which all other analysis must proceed. Classical philosophy, without the ever-increasing evidence of modern neurobiology to show us how the body-mind actually works, held that objects had fixed properties and that metaphor was merely an unscientific verbal elaboration of language. Whitehead goes on to say that the coordinations of space-time described above illustrate a rule that lies open to mathematical interpretation. Such an interpretation lies far beyond my imagination, but I can accept his statement that, for an object conceived as a region of space-time, the innumerable multitude of potential things within its purview can be sensed as superimposed. When we come to prehensions of rocks, ducks and cabbages, and our processing their images into actual entities, the mental act of cognition requires the same conditions of expression: the potentiality to see these objects in terms of other objects.

The house (figure 33) built on an undomesticated Oklahoma prairie was conceived as a sort of Rorschach blot directed by my Whiteheadian influence, in which one could find references to emotion and feeling in the forms of the house. There are scary and tragic references, as well as references of comfort, security, regional landscape and history. I want to briefly discuss this house and its metaphors, including metaphoric observations of others that did not occur to me.

The plan shape of the house is an asymmetrical ellipsoid, to

Figure 34. Herb Greene, *Energy, Mass and Air*

create curving, enveloping and "comforting" interior wall shapes and to deny mainstream architecture's preferences for Euclidean forms during the 'fifties and 'sixties. The west-facing window points in the direction of oncoming wind storms. The window and its surround present an image of an eye and a face. There are suggestions of a wounded creature tied to the Earth yet attempting to free itself from Earth's bounds. Suggestions of barns, buffaloes and birds are intentional. The mass of the house suggests substance, while the irregular and broken, feather-patterned wood siding suggests something of a ruin. In context with the prairie horizon one can think of an animal, shack, or technological object with an aluminum carport swooping up to a never-finished, rooftop teepee, which was to function as an aluminum screened porch. During the tail end of an Oklahoma thunderstorm a bus load of people pulled into the driveway. One man came to the door to ask if this was where the tornado had struck. I responded bemusedly that I was not aware of a tornado in the vicinity only to have the cedarwood screen door pull loose from its hinges and fly about twenty feet in a gust of wind. At any rate, some people in the bus, with tornado damage on their minds, evidently experienced prehensions of wind-riven wreckage in the house image.

Responding to the exterior forms, English author John Farmer[3] found negative allusions in a positive light. He saw a poetic expres-sion of both fears of a nuclear apocalypse and the vanishing prairie, which suggests how one mixes and matches data to preestablished contexts. I was always curious how little sarcasm I found in the wide press coverage of this small house. For me there were unsuccessful passages, awkward perspectives, and rough and expedient details; for example, the somewhat crude finishing of a metal carport by a modestly-paid, past-his-prime, imbibing welder.

Figure 33 shows an elevation of a post office designed while I was a student at University of Oklahoma, eight years before the Prairie House. In this sculptured building, I was interested in expressing mass as a form that was simultaneously heavy and light in feeling, that would tie the mass to the earth and yet suggest that the form seemed to be rising up and away from the earth. I was trying to dramatize feelings of gravity and pulling free of gravity. These metaphors, immanent in our bodily experience, are present in the Prairie House.

This recent painted image, *Energy, Mass and Air* (figure 34), without any photographs, is included to show how certain meta-phors of the body — rising up, turning down, power, softness, mass and lightness of being — continue to dominate my imagination. It is as if these metaphors became the primary ground for my expression of bodily feelings.

CHAPTER SEVENTEEN

Events

An event sets a limit on perceived experience. It enables us to think about the contents of the experience as a happening selected out of the profusion of sense presentation. Events have particulars such as forms, colors, sounds and tastes that we process into objects, feelings and ideas. While an event is a perceptual demarcation of entities, the content and meaning of these entities stems from a synthesis of feelings and ideas that we process into various scenarios of meaning. The way in which the contents and meanings of an event become representations in the mind, and how these features maintain self-continuity and pass into other states, has increasingly received scientific and philosophic study, which can inform us as we reflect on our everyday experiences.

For example, take a pencil held in my hand as a perceived event. I find it situated with other events in the same visual field, such as the yellow pad on which I write and the part of the room that I see beyond my hand and pad. Perceived details of the pencil could include its shape, the material of which it is made, its weight and its logo. Each detail discloses its own connections to the world, connections that we use to form a particular closure of the whole, as in a chewed, #2 yellow pencil, or an expensive gift pencil that I am afraid to lose.

Our concept of the details, which can be considered as events, such as the logo on the pencil, and the ensuing closures of meaning that we use in processing the meaning of the pencil, depend on an unseen ground of memory and a propensity for anticipation and learning that we develop over a lifetime. A baby reaches for the moon and will only gradually bring new memories to that image to know that the moon is out of reach. For Buddhists, the circle serves as a symbol of endlessness and hence of aimless change. In the West it is often a symbol of an ideal limit and perfection. The neurologist R. L. Gregory[1] documents the case of a fifty-year-old man, blind from birth, who recovered his sight through a surgical procedure. At first this man, who had successfully adapted to an unsighted world, was enthralled over the buzzing plenitude of newly-visible shapes.

As time went on, however, these visible shapes seemed empty to him. He also had great difficulty with depth perception. For instance, he would stumble over the chairs in a room. His drawing of a bus was much less coherent than that of a four-year-old. He began to feel disadvantaged competing with sighted people, even though his other perceptive senses were adequate to his needs. What he lacked was the accumulated background or embodied experience necessary to inform visual perception. According to Gregory, the man became overwhelmed by his deficiency, lost interest in life, and died several years later.

The complex issues effecting perception and mind that are suggested by the examples above can be made more tractable with Whitehead's theory. To begin, Whitehead starts with the rough, unformulated world where the immediate actual events of life are made apparent by sight, touch, taste, smell, sound, and our more inchoate feelings. This radically untidy field of activity is the only place where our intellectual derivations can begin. Whitehead, with his unerring instinct of the body as receptor and generator of experience, repeatedly stresses how this fact has been hidden by the "exact" language of classical science. It is as if the "exact" abstractions can represent the immediate deliverances of sense experience, which is both incurably vague and complex. A particular shade of color, a taste or sound is never a smooth, sharp demarcation of fact.

It is because sense data seem so distinct and vivid to us that civilization since the Greeks has imputed a preeminent clarity to these data. With modern studies in psychology, perception and cognition, and through the insights of philosophers including Telesio, Whitehead and Merleau-Ponty, we now understand that the clarity of sense perception arises from a background of bodily experience and a complex network of memory and association. The discrimination of a particular shade of blue sky or the ability to perceive depth are dependent on these dimly-perceived backgrounds.

A particular shade of blue sky in Whitehead's system is already a complex unity based on an integration of many factors, such as a sense of light and atmosphere, the possible contexts of adjoining landscape, an awareness that the sky is this shade of blue and not some other, and the thought habits of the viewer. The selection and synthesis of these factors represents the formation of what Whitehead calls "actual entities," a realization of a particular atmosphere, color shade, contrasts with clouds, and other factors, so that the actual entity can be identified and thought about. Here he is speaking about matter conceived as process, but the concept applies to perception as process as well.

> The older point of view expressed in classical dynamics enables us to abstract from change and to conceive of the full reality of nature at an instant, in abstraction from any temporal duration and characterized . . . solely by the instantaneous distribution of matter in space. . . . [F]or the mod-

ern view, process, activity and change are the matter of fact, at an instant there is nothing. Each instant is only a way of grouping matters of fact. Thus there are no instants, conceived as simple primary entities. There is no nature at an instant.[2]

To get at perception in which there is no instant but only a process happening in time, we have to consider the terminus of sense awareness to have two aspects. Take the example of a yellow writing pad. The first aspect consists of directly perceived individualities, such as its shape, yellow color and green lines. The second aspect consists of facts attending the individualities, the facts that I know the page of the yellow pad is made of cheap paper, that I know that it has a reverse side, or that I know the green lines will help me to organize my writing. Whitehead terms the first aspect "presentational immediacy." Presentational immediacy is the immediate sensory registration of the data. Whitehead terms the second aspect "causal efficacy," which is the derivative background of ideas, intuitions, feelings and propositions that are initiated by the mind acting on the data given in presentational immediacy. Thought objects of perception, like the page of the yellow pad, are almost wholly hypothetical. The universe is largely a concept of the imagination resting on a slender basis of direct sense presentation.

Even though causal efficacy provides the massive background with which we interpret presentational immediacy, it is difficult to give as clear an example of the former as the latter. This is because, as

in the case of the reverse side of the paper, the knowledge has to be inferred. Appearances are entirely dependent on the reality of this inferred background. Most of the depth, power and necessity of this background comes to us through what Whitehead calls "non-sensuous perception." Non-sensuous perception is the inheritance of our embodied past expressed in the present; the intuition of the past half-second that informs the present moment of experience. He illustrates the point by having a speaker pronounce the proper name "United States" followed by the name "United Fruit Company." The speaker is carried from "United" to "States" or to "Fruit Company." The immediate past of each "United" survives to be lived through in a present that is energized by prehensions of its following term. In my case, negative associations — big business using influence with the United States government to exploit local populations, the questionable use of pesticides, changing the company name to the catchy Chiquita Banana partly to obscure the company's negative political history from public view — accompany United Fruit Company. Thus each actual entity of an event draws from an unspoken background as we "collage" actual entities with their contrasts and identities into scenarios of meaning.

We can use a similar analysis to describe the role of non-sensuous perception in the viewer's response to Picasso's *Baboon and Young* (figure 35). We can say that closures of (a) the stance of the baboon mother with her oversized and splayed feet , (b) the potbellied bulk of the mother, (c) the clinging, "praying" baby, and

(d) the mother's toy car head with its somewhat leering and ambiguous expression, are brought together in the same way as the word closures "United" and either "States" or "Fruit Company". Each term (a, b, c, d) lives in the present by our making closures among the various terms in the mode of non-sensuous perception. Our selection of certain aspects of a, b, c and d as they coalesce in the closures produces particular feelings of humor, audacity, profundity and irony that I describe in more detail at the end of the chapter.

C. H. Waddington, the English geneticist and Nobel laureate, has commented on Whitehead's events as follows:

> "We [scientists] start by accepting the real existence of certain scientific objects such as atoms, electrons, gravitation, light, etc. . . . Whitehead stated that we start somewhere else; not with objects, but with "events" which are four-dimensional happenings, i.e. processes. All knowledge, and all talk, is derived from experiences of events. Scientific objects — atoms, etc. — are not basic, but are derivative, intellectual constructs invented to assist us to understand events. . . . For Whitehead real existents were events. Each event has a definite character, but this results from the "concrescence" of an infinite number of objects, which are essentially relations with other events, through their "prehensions"' into a unity. . . . In doing science we have, on the one hand, to try to formulate simple objects which express the most important causal relations between events, but at the same time we have to ensure that these objects include (as sub-objects) as many as possible of all those involved in the event. The thrust of Whitehead's thought is not to simplify unduly; every time you reduce you leave something out, and scientific ideas are richer and nearer to nature the less that has had to be omitted in order to reach them. . . . [E]very event reacts with every other, but not with all aspects of every other."[3]

This concept of events as four-dimensional happenings with potential connections via their prehensions is the seminal concept behind Whitehead's philosophy and probably all collage paintings. Indeed, it is a concept with which we can begin to explain the coordination found among all physical and imagined events — including the coordination of collage juxtapositions — from Picasso's toy car-baboon mother, to the ubiquitous television commercials for Energizer batteries. In an example of the latter, the battery-driven, toy pink bunny beating a drum incongruously marches across a scene in which two well-dressed, thirty-something women, languorously seated in Ethan Allen "French provincial" furniture, are assiduously praising a brand of French roast coffee. Among other references the collage makes a comparison between the somewhat languorous gestures and fashionable pomp of the women and the disarming herky-jerky motions of the animated toy, which express a certain energy, gaiety and determination. If we consider the battery ad in terms of events, certain prehensions and actual entities of the toy bunny gestures and those of the stereotyped women are compared by similarities and contrasts. We may enjoy the ad, which, among its other meanings, can be read as a lightly humorous comment on social pretensions while impressing us with the name recognition and "longevity" of Energizer batteries, leaving us with feelings of good-natured humor and self-approval at recognizing the airs projected by the women.

A couple of other comments about events before I apply Whitehead's concepts to the analysis of an art image. Events are spread out. This means, first, that we do not visually perceive a theoretical point. The point of a pencil or a needle has size. Second, an occurrence of events extends through a duration of time. Thus we never perceive instants of time. Looking at the tip end of the pencil with which I write, I perceive a glinty, reflecting highlight, a tapered shape, a quarter-inch of exposed lead, and a grey-black color. Each cue is a response by my brain to different signals in the visual field. These cues are processed into events that extend over other events. The highlight extends up the wood cone of the pencil tip. The grey-black lead extends over the yellow pad in view. Events have vague, shifting boundaries. Where does the highlight on the pencil lead leave off to become the gray black lead? But if events have shifting boundaries, the event is nonetheless the locus for the ingression of our memories of similar experiences of highlights, conical shapes, lead and gray-black color, which we reconstitute in the present moment.

An event, however shifting our responses to it may be, is nonetheless simply there. It is the many characteristics ingressing (Whitehead's term for incoming-merging) into the event that have an imagined and hypothetical character. Whitehead calls these ingressing characteristics "objects" when the mind recognizes them as actual entities. Actual entities are recognized within a gradient of conscious to unconscious awareness. For instance, the glinty highlight of the pencil becomes an object — an actual entity reconstituted from my previous mental experience of related situations — that helps me to process the pencil as a form in the round. I am not usually conscious of the process because the directed and experienced mind shortcuts the loop of connecting circuits and reference frames that link pencil, roundness, highlights, and other relevant categories. Otherwise I would be overwhelmed with detail and could not think at all.

When we perceive an event, we select certain groups of objects that give the event important or useful properties. Whitehead uses the term "eternal objects" to refer to the seemingly consistent characteristics that can be recognized in actual entities and that can occur in more than one event. For example, the particular blueness of a patch of sky can ingress into other events, such as a sky-blue ceramic tea cup or a surface of reflecting ocean. We can also compare contrasting objects, such as the bodily gestures of the women and the jerky gestures of the toy bunny. Eternal objects are the forms of definiteness in actual entities that enable us to hold our world of perceptual objects together by comparisons with embodied experience.

An Analysis of Picasso's Baboon and Young *Using Whitehead's Theory of Events*

A perceptual event is best envisioned as a matrix of cues within the visual field. We act on the cues with apparent simultaneity. What really happens is that some cues act as instructions for the interpretation of others. A perceptual event is always a process; it is never a fixed totality given at an instant. Any verbal presentation of the perceptual event has to be somewhat linear, and thus somewhat arbitrary in assigning emphasis and order. As Whitehead characterized the event of "Humpty Dumpty seated on a wall," the wall is not actually antecedent to Humpty Dumpty. Bearing this qualification in mind, I turn to figure 35. My eye is drawn first to the car-head of the baboon mother, her girth and to the baby on her chest. These closures and the recognition of a tail, an ear, and a leer are near simultaneous perceptions. I could as well have included the mother's feet and the baby's arms. All these features can be considered as events. I shall describe what I believe to be important useful properties initiated by the ingression of selected objects that qualify these events.

The mother's head is fashioned from a toy automobile and her body is made out of a potbellied stove. The idea of a toy car as a baboon head is made convincing partly by the addition of outsized ears, which contribute forcefully to our recognition of a baboon. Spherical, staring eyeballs in the windshield, and the use of the front fender and bumper to create both a leering grin and a closed, neutral mouth help to define the baboon mother's ambiguous expression. The round head of the baby on the mother's chest resembles a human head. The baby's longish arms are as human as they are apelike. The clinging, outstretched arms can be taken as a symbol of humankind propitiating the frontally-staring car, which can be read as an icon of the machine. These features engender intra-subjective links among our feelings of mother, machine, humankind and praying that are haunting and paradoxical.

Consider the baby's head. Its form admits to several possibilities. It could be a baby baboon, a human head or even a planet-world. In his expression of these possibilities, Picasso utilizes the negative prehension. This is Whitehead's term for the initial mental process of taking up any perceptual object, a process that includes the recognition that the object is this and not that. The negative prehension excludes possibilities, yet it enables us to feel the contrast of an excluded possibility together with the selected possibility, which can give art ambiguity, depth and complexity of meaning, as in Picasso's baboon-mother. This comparative process can be a component of a propositional feeling, which is a latter phase of the perceptual process. The feeling that the baby's head could also be a human head, and its near spherical shape also a symbol of the world, are propositional feelings.

Figure 35. Picasso, *Baboon and Young*

Paraphrasing Rudolph Arnheim, who describes the process in simpler terms,[4] memory concepts are flexible. As we search for a suitable closure or concept — this toy Volkswagen is a baboon head or this baby head is a planet — we call upon various aspects of such concepts until an appropriate one presents itself. Continuing our analysis we notice that the baboon mother's arms do not comfort and support the baby but extend out into space. The mother's eyes also stare into space; they do not engage the baby. These cues offer instructions that we use to form certain propositional feelings. They contradict the idea of mother caring for infant. They allow alternatives such as disengagement or indifference. I call attention to the baby's outstretched arms on the mother's chest. Along with the baby's arms, I recognize the mother's shoulder, biceps, extended forearm and hand as events. The arms are long, consistent with my experience of baboons or other simians. The gesture of both arms reads not only as "clinging to mother," but also as an act of obeisance. Picasso's genius is evident in the economy with which he recalls simian and human anatomy and spans meanings from clinging to praying. He has left much unfinished texture and detail. This provides an ambiguous ground, encouraging us to impute meaning and to find harmony in the more defined details.

There is a pronounced sense of audacity in Picasso's sculpture. Among the instructions which direct us to audacity as a reference frame are the outsized feet, planted as if to forcefully present the "outrageous" aggregation of pot-bellied stove body and outsized leering car head with even more exaggerated ears. Another instruction is provided by the material itself. The bronze surface of the sculpture has connotations of age, permanence and costliness, and is redolent with associations from art history. Picasso is probably aware of shocking conventional taste here, just as Degas was when he presented a bronzed ballerina wearing a tutu made of real cloth to a Victorian audience conditioned to figures of homogeneous marble or bronze. Picasso is making a statement, qualified by audacity, humor and confidence, that his ad hoc assemblage of discarded objects is in the same class as preceding high art bronzes. At every level, my description involves a complex meld of feelings induced by shapes, subjects, contexts, propositions and associations that are directed by my subjective aims or ideals as I survey the events in Picasso's sculpture.

This discursive analysis may leave the impression that perception is a linear interpretation of individual cues. This is not usually the case. Perception is much more a networking matrix in which random and simultaneous cues are evaluated on both conscious and subconscious levels. The mind is comparing shapes, forms, textures, associations, and other stored knowledge to intensify and control the relationships between toy car and baboon mother. The process calls attention to likenesses and narrows down alternatives. We make new meaning out of analogies between forms and ideas not usually associated with each other. By making associations, displacements and new combinations, we create symbols that unify the dissimilar

at a level of deep feeling or highly-interesting intellectual significance. For instance, Picasso's audacious ensemble evokes irony. Is the baboon-car mocking humankind as if it worships technology? Or does Picasso's sculpture mean that we have come to recognize that the universe is constituted so that some aspects of any of its events, no matter how disjunctive the events may appear to us, can mingle? The most likely answer is that Picasso's decisive design devices intend to project the importance of both meanings.

The most fascinating property of the human mind, unlikely to be duplicated by computers, is its ability to anticipate and reconstitute the briefest shorthand notations and to place them within appropriate, rapidly changing, highly complex contexts that can link events throughout our known continuum of space-time. The spherical head of the baby is presented as if it were included in a class of similar events: the spherical eyes of the mother, the spherical headlights, and the spherical midsection of the mother, which supports a second baby with a spherical head at lower left. This is the familiar artistic device of repetition. It creates rhythm, and it is a means of separating while linking the forms within the class. As Suzanne Langer puts it, "The explicit image is of two or more particulars, but the whole gamut is implicitly presented, so that they seem like selective realizations springing out of a matrix or body of potentialities."[5] A selective realization can be powerful, as in the head of the baby. Is this the head of a baby or a planet-world, or a symbol of "Technological Man and Woman" objectified within the gamut? Langer goes on to say, "The appearance of partial realizations within the gamut makes elements emerge and submerge like transient aspects of its inward being." Langer's partial realizations and transient aspects are another way of describing the inter-subjective feelings engendered by Whitehead's negative prehensions.

To sum up: visually perceived things, such as stones, pencils and artworks, are best considered as a matrix of cues that are processed as Whiteheadian actual entities whose meanings have come to realization out of our experiences in the continuum of space-time. The body-mind, conceptualized as a changing yet continuing stream of actual occasions that form the individual personality, governs the process of synthesizing meaning. Visually perceived things are not single, permanent entities, nor can any part of an entity remain contained within one limiting focus of meaning. All entities extend to the world beyond themselves. Gregory Bateson comes to a similar, common sense conclusion about the extensive world.

> I see a redwood tree standing up out of the ground, and I know from this perception that underneath the ground at that point I shall find roots, or I hear a sentence and may know at once from that beginning the grammatical structure of the rest of the sentence and may very well know many of the words and ideas contained in it. We live in a life in which our percepts are perhaps always the perception of parts and our guesses about wholes are continually being verified or contradicted by the later presentation of other parts. It is perhaps so that wholes can never be presented.[6]

Bateson's direct observation is consonant with both Whitehead's theory of perception and the deconstruction of wholes that many post-modernists advocate. The intimacy of scientific theory and direct observation continually surfaces in the art of the West. Among great artists, Leonardo is famous for his contributions in returning the Western mind to the direct observation of nature as the foundation of knowledge and of understanding. Leonardo believed that there could be no true experience without the analysis of phenomena. In the experience of concrete being, rational principles are infinitely and multifariously interconnected and superimposed on one another. Only the power of thought can separate them and show their individual significance and validity. In this tradition, Whitehead's theory of events can enlarge our understanding of the process by which the mind creates contrasts and identities in order to produce meaning in our thinking and our creativity.

CHAPTER EIGHTEEN

Visual Patterns and Structured Societies

Whitehead uses the term "structured societies" in his explanations of how we unify contrasts during perception. The recognition of groups of cells, the Milky Way and the bulges of the over-muscled physique of Eve (figure 36) are examples of the endless variety of structured societies. Whitehead calls attention to how we recognize patterns to sort through the complexity of perceptual data. We sort to recognize already harmonized unities that are directed by the viewer's subjective aim. Our formation of such societies indicates that there is a purpose pervading nature in which the mere complexity of the given, which produces incompatibilities, is superseded by complexities that produce harmonized unities.

The process by which thought is organized to produce harmonized contrasts can be illustrated in the formal patterns of art with both power and subtlety, as in the head of Eve from the Sistine Chapel incorporated in the detail of my collage, *The Evolution of Eve* (figure 36). In Michelangelo's original, Eve's upper body turns toward the apple that she reaches to grasp from the hand of an androgynous human figure that transforms from the hips down into a serpent coiled around a tree. We recognize the swell of Eve's great biceps and forearm and the long, beautiful curve of her neck. These bulging forms and their bounding lines act to our perception as a structured society in which the experiences signified by these forms can gather strength. For instance, the great swelling of the anatomical forms indicates, to acculturated viewers, the heroic, often striving quality that Michelangelo added to the lexicon of Western art. There is a super-intensity in Eve's directed, curious and fearful glance. Her nostrils flare as if in anger or fear, in harmony with the feelings of her swelling, powerful neck and her thrusting, bulging eyes.

The head of Eve is among Michelangelo's remarkable expressions of *terribilita*, in which the artist evokes feelings of determination, intellectual arousal, and animal and sexual energy, and projects a force directed by or toward terror and the possibility of imminent destruction. Finally, we are left with a feeling of humankind's unquenchable curiosity in spite of fear. Even a detail like the inner

Figure 36. Herb Greene, *The Evolution of Eve* (Detail)

folds of Eve's ear, an example of the artist's accurate grasp of anatomy that enables him to modify accepted norms, is drawn in the image of a simplified serpent, with a gaping jaw to reinforce feelings of fear and danger. This detail also suggests the serpent's seductive voice in Eve's ear, which would support the theme found in the human-serpent that offers the apple to Eve in Michelangelo's original painting. Wilson[1] explains the tendency to react with both fear and fascination toward snakes as an epigenetic rule. He describes how culture draws on that fear and fascination to create metaphors and narratives. I also feel prehensions of the wrathful God of Judeo-Christian tradition. But above all else, it is Michelangelo's ability to express the heroic within and beyond the fabric of Renaissance thought that impresses me. Kenneth Clark[2] has aptly described the values that are expressed by Michelangelo's Eve.

> This quality, which I may call heroic, is not part of most people's idea of civilization. It involves a contempt for convenience and a sacrifice of all those pleasures that contribute to what we call civilized life. It is the enemy of happiness. And yet we recognize that to despise material obstacles, and even to defy the blind forces of fate, is man's supreme achievement, and since, in the end, civilization depends on man extending his powers of mind and spirit to the utmost, we must reckon the emergence of Michelangelo as one of the great events in the history of man.

To put us in touch with despising material obstacles, and even with defying the blind forces of fate, are among the messages of this painting. While it seems presumptuous to dissect one of Michelangelo's great accomplishments by using abstractions such as the notion of structured societies, whatever we call them, and however discursive our verbalizations of abstractions must be, our mind relies on such schemes to process meaning. One way to think of the head of Eve is to realize it as an unusually powerful organization of structured societies that allow us access to the intensity and depth of feeling and meaning that are present in Eve's features.

A remarkable example of a structured society in Eve's head is found in the design of her eyes (figure 37). Michelangelo gives Eve's left eye facing us an arresting quality and a thrust toward the apple by incorporating two distinct adjoining forms. One form is the large white area of the left eye swelling outward, as if in response to bodily energy, fear and desire. The second form is the pupil of the eye narrowing and projecting, like the pyramidal lens enclosure of an early camera, to point directly at the apple. The eye to our right is unusually small compared to the left eye, yet it is equally intense, with a white area like one flat side of another pyramid projecting outward. The contrasts in scale and shape between the two eyes add dynamism and heighten the look of curiosity, fear and intensity in Eve's face.

The pupil of the left eye is formed into a vertical slit, pointed and elliptical. This is not possible in a human eye, but it is charac-teristic of a cat's eye and of a snake's eye. This shape opens a reference frame for the imagination to cross-classify our notions of Eve with the attributes of curiosity and myth that can be associated with cats, and possibly form a link between Eve and human fear of, and fascination with, snakes. Our response to the thoughts and feelings evoked by such details as the bulging, projecting, "human-cat-snake eye" enables us to understand these details as Whitehead's "atomic bricks," with which we build our higher experiences. Although these bricks are only remembered traces within the elaborations of consciousness and thought, the fact that we can recognize them gives credence to Whitehead's claim that the feelings that they evoke are determinate.

Structured societies enable us to deal with complexity. At the same time they are unspecialized. This allows the powerful forms of Eve, with their gestalt of the heroic, her eyes with their expression of curiosity and fear, and other harmonized closures, such as her aroused nipples, to overwhelm unwanted details, such as the cracks and stains in the paint, as well as the anatomical improbability of Eve's oversized arms. Our interest in the heroic gestalt can be maintained as long as unwanted detail can be ignored. Thus structured societies enable intensity of feeling to be mated with survival of feeling.

In describing the superb curve of the left boundary of Eve's neck, which continues on to divide her hair from her face, we sense power and swelling in the curve that we associate with the heroic

limbs. We also feel a component of sensuality, a component of bodily extension, and at the same time the contrast of bodily contraction, or pulling back from extension. There is a sense of advancing and withdrawal that we feel while perusing the whole of Eve's body. But we also recognize the beauty and grace of the curve as an entity, without attachment to advance, withdrawal, bulging, animal and sexual energy, or to the heroic.

In Whitehead's system this intrusion does not destroy meaning because, as we shift our focus onto the sheer beauty of the curve, we subject this focus to what he calls "graded envisagement," allowing us to shape the actual and include what can be felt positively, but which has been excluded from the original gestalt of *terribilita*. Thus every event, including Michelangelo's Eve with her over-muscled physique recognized as a Whiteheadian structured society, is a limitation imposed on possibility, but one that can accommodate other gestalts.

One could discuss additional structured societies in the design of other features in the head and figure of Eve, like her muscular underarm, shaded to form a vague but potent image. Is it a giant nipple and breast? Is it something else or nothing else? There is more to discuss and more that lies beyond our reach. Studying the many contrasts in the portrait of Eve, with their depth and gravity of interest and the miraculous expression of their unity amidst the individuality of their details, encourages me to go along with what a number of experienced observers have written: that Michelangelo

Figure 37. Herb Greene, *The Evolution of Eve*

remains the greatest artistic genius who ever lived. When I lose myself in the communicative power of Eve I feel impervious to deconstructionist arguments against elevating Michelangelo's art above Bernini's, or the sculpture found on Easter Island. One might as well argue that elephant "art," interesting as it is to our contemporary sensibility, exists on the same plane. To argue that there is no "progress" in making or interpreting art from standpoints of understanding, history, intentionality, the evolution of culture, civilization, values, the expression of power, nuance of feeling, and complexity must end in sophistry.

In my treatment of Eve (figure 37), I have her twisting and rising up, appearing amidst veils and draperies as an allusion to draperies in Greek sculpture and Renaissance art. The emerging cat refers to Eve's cat's-eye pupil. The bird links the subject of cats to Eve and her wing. Eve's winglike appendage refers to the nudes seen flying about Renaissance and Baroque paintings, as well as humankind's longing to soar. A fishlike head at the lower right corner extends the suggestion of a gamut of animals embedded in a mass from which Eve, with her body metaphors of rising up and out, is shown reaching for the apple. To me this arrangement is a metaphor of "upward" evolution in human complexity and value.

The bright red area suggests, among other things, Eve's birth out of a female body, a wound, and a female fear of snakes, with a snake image emerging from the wound-vagina. The context of the red area acts to constrain, as well as suggest, possibilities of interpretation. As Johnson[3] tells us, metaphorical systems are like channels in which a subject can move with limited, relative freedom. Meaningful inferences will depend on the metaphorical background against which the phenomena appear. Thus the bulging outlines of Eve's limbs and the metaphoric elaborations of their prehensions within selected contexts of birth, rising up, fear, curiosity, red wound and emergent snake constitute a vital part of the process by which we build our participation in, and our understanding of, the image.

CHAPTER NINETEEN

The Act of Perception

In this chapter I apply Whitehead's analysis of perception to photographs selected from my collage paintings and other art works. In Whitehead's scheme a perceptual object is determined through an animal's utilization of its prehensions of that object. For human beings, with their complex resources of language, billions of neurons, and their maps to many provinces of meaning, the perception of a Ming vase, for example, excludes and unifies prehensions. As I prehend aspects of the vase — its shapes, patina, incisions, the silhouette, the condition of the bronze surface, and my being a collector who doubts the authenticity of the vase — I have processed dispositions for continuing or avoiding the integration of these aspects. The products of integration are called "concrescences." Subsumed in the process of concrescence are stages designated by the terms "nexus," "duration," "datum," "negative prehensions," and "purpose" or "subjective aim," which will also be discussed. Finally, I take up the notion of harmony in the act of perception.

Concrescence is the Becoming of Actual Entities

An actual entity is a mental construct made by uniting several prehended factors into a unity. In figure 11, in context with other cues, I prehend the profile of Athena's nose as an ideal type, a symbol of wisdom, or a boundary between void and Athena's body. These are all examples of actual entities. The straightness of a picture frame and a conception of a star can be actual entities. Intersubjective thought-objects rising to consciousness via prehensions can become actual entities. For example, I am aware of a type of guilt, shame or anger of one person toward another. Actual entities differ among themselves, but through their gradations of importance and diversities of function they are all, first, closures of experience, complex and interdependent. An actual entity, once realized, may perish or it may merge into the unconscious. It may also become a component in further processing, as in a concrescence, or last in memory. Whitehead defines "concrescence" in its most general form.

"Concrescence" is the name for the process in which the universe of many things acquires an individual unity. . . . [The process is] a determinate relegation of each item of the "many" to its subordination in the constitution of the novel "one" (the particular actual entity of the concrescence).[1]

Gerald Edelman's work[2] on how the brain processes perceptions, which would include a Whiteheadian concrescence (including a concrescence of Vermeer's "subliminal" shadow-hand), offers a helpful model to visualize the process. Edelman finds that the brain responds to the information given by our sense organs by creating "maps." There follows a selective strengthening of those mappings that are the most useful and promising for building a closure of meaning. The perception of a chair depends on the harmonization (Whitehead's formation of many into one) of a number of scattered mappings throughout the visual cortex. These mappings connect many varied aspects of the chair: its proportions, its material, its color, the disposition of its legs, and its relation to rocking chairs and stools. Probably, in other parts of the cortex, the feel of sitting in a chair and the bodily actions needed to do so are also connected.

This process is always dynamic and depends on the active and incessant orchestration of countless details. Such a correlation, which is never the same twice, is accomplished by the connections that are reciprocal between the brain's maps. These connections may contain millions of fibers. The continuous transfer, selection and

reevaluation between activated maps enables a "concept" or "picture" of a particular chair to be realized. Christopher Wills, in his book *The Runaway Brain,*[3] tells us that during the evolutionary process of absorbing and juggling information, it has not been possible simply to add to the complexity of a single map in only one part of the brain, making it more and more detailed in the process. Instead, the brain distributes information into many different, less-detailed maps in different regions.

Thus by Edelman's description, during a Whiteheadian concrescence, we select from the diversity of possibilities in the data and our experience to produce an actual entity. As mentioned above, the profile line of the nose of Athena, together with other contextual cues (my feelings for classical Greek, "forehead-nose" profiles as signs of intelligence) and knowledge of Athena's association with wisdom, produces my cognitive mapping of a novel actual entity that, in my mind, denotes acute intelligence.

Damasio[4] explains why cognitive maps are more likely to be of a superimposed, rather than blended, construction. A cognitive map for the feelings of particular face shapes may be superimposed on the face of Vermeer's woman holding a balance, on maps of clothing types, of Dutch history, and so forth. Remember: Whiteheadian events include every possible category of entities. "Dutch history" can mingle with, or be superimposed on, "female hair styles" or any other event. Connections among maps are selected and acted upon by our subjective aim (interpretive scheme), which directs a particular outcome. To me, such a view of mental process seems consonant with both the collage thinking that produces meaning for the teenager's term "spaced-out" and for Whitehead's theory of concrescence.

For Whitehead there is only one genus of actual entities. This means that he can derive notions from any species of actual entities in order to interpret other species. Accordingly, if an electron and a human psyche are both considered examples of actualities, he could use ideas (unification, indeterminacy, feeling, extension, existence in space-time) derived from each one to interpret the other. The proposition that all actual entities are derived from the prehensive process of organisms within the extended physical field leads to Whitehead's doctrine that the determination of fact in a concrescence is similar to that of an aesthetic experience. All aesthetic experience is feeling arising out of the realization of contrast amidst identity. Even animals show evidence of a rudimentary awareness of this situation. Among bower birds in New Guinea, to attract the female, the male of one species builds a well-crafted, arched teepee-dome of twigs and leaves about two feet high. Under a wide-arched entrance to this structure he then arranges eight very near rectangular shapes of shells, pebbles, leaves, feathers and other small objects in two approximately parallel rows. He makes each rectangle with a distinct type, shape, color and size of object. Whitehead mentions the "excess" of energy in the universe that extends beyond the mere function and immediate survival of organisms. The tendency to play, the development of extravagant mating costumes and rituals, a readiness to adventure, and the development of pattern recognition can be seen in the evolution of mammals and birds. The tendency to form patterns is also a prerequisite of mind. Human art and aesthetics can be seen as having evolved from these precedents.

Concrescence Into Unity and Self-Consistency

> The perceptive constitution of the actual entity presents the problem: How can the other actual entities, each with its own formal existence, also enter objectively into the perceptive constitution of the actual entity in question?[5]

This is like asking how, in my previous example, my thoughts about the Energizer bunny and the "sophisticated coffee drinkers" enter into each other, or how my intersubjective feelings about the aged academic and the three urban onlookers in figure 7 are established. Classical doctrines' insistence on separate universals, attributes, subjects, predicates, substances and systems of relations are incapable of a solution. Whitehead's answer lies in the theory of prehensions and concrescences that terminate in definite unities of feeling in which we manage, by utilizing brain maps and connections, to find contrasts and identities among seemingly limitless groupings of information found in billions of storage neurons.

Figure 38. Herb Greene, *The Becoming of Consciousness* (Detail)

Whitehead tells us that creative action always exemplifies the universe becoming one in particular unities of experience realized by the self. These unities add to the multiplicity of things by which we know the universe as many. For example, the invention of blues music, with its unity of meaning in acts of self-experience for many Americans, adds to the multiplicity of the world, so that the word "blues" takes on new connotations. The association of a state of being that can be expressed or assuaged by a particular form of music with its particular associations adds to the repertoire of usable (objective) information in the world. This process of unification becomes the basis of objectivity. Whitehead says that concrescence into unity depends on the self-identity of each actual entity. No actual entity in such a realization can play disjoined roles. Self-identity means that the entity must have one self-consistent function, whatever the complexity of that function.[6]

Thus I experience a self-identity of function in my concrescence of Athena's nose. In my case it contributes to my realization of acute intelligence connected to classical Greece, and to other reference frames, such as a male urge to war and destruction, that I feel are harbored and projected by other event-cues in Athena.

Actual Occasions

Whitehead uses the term "actual occasion" in place of "actual entity" when he wants to emphasize the notion that objects are derived by abstraction from perceived events that we interrelate in some determinate fashion, as when I recognize a door frame while also seeing portions of the adjoining wall. The spherical heads of the baby baboons in Picasso's *Baboon and Young* (figure 35) are an actual occasion when they are recognized as a set of forms, and when their prehensions are unified as a concrescence of a particular character or type, such as babies' heads, spheres or planets.

Actual occasions and groupings of events are the final real things of which the world is composed, and there is no "reality" behind actual entities by which we describe actual occasions. The ultimate facts of immediate actual experience are actual entities, prehensions and nexus (which are effective groupings of events and actual occasions). All else is, for our experience, derivative abstraction.

Let us consider Vermeer's *Milkmaid* (figure 38), in my collage, *The Becoming of Consciousness*. Limiting our attention to the face considered as an actual occasion within the events of the painting, the process of concrescence is the subordination of the many individual characteristics of this face, all recognized as actual entities. The downcast eyes and open mouth can be read, with other possibilities, as signs of obeisance and sentience. The coarse texture and broad proportions of the face take on peasant connotations, and the face's mask-like quality suggests the hieratic and deified. All of these characteristics, and more, are woven into the constitution of a novel unity conditioned by my subjective aim and the vivid aesthetic pattern of the painting. My attention has been shifted from cultural stereotypes to a vivid creative unity. Further, there is not my concrescence and the face. My concrescence is itself the novel individual thing in question. For Whitehead, "actuality" means nothing else than this ultimate entry into the concrete. The synthesis of the components that go to make up the feeling of novel unity can only be described discursively. For this reason, the feeling may be difficult to express, but it is open to analysis and this is what makes Whitehead's scheme valuable.

Thus Whitehead's actual occasion is analyzable. Its separate entities, with their distinctions, are integrated into a complex entity of one. The term "feeling" is used as the generic term for the process. An actual occasion is the concrescence effected by the process that entails Whitehead's categories: (1) the actual occasions felt (chasm-like shadow separating face from coif); (2) the eternal objects felt (blackness and void of the shadow); (3) the feelings felt (mystery, "framing" of an entity, such as a gap or a mask-face sign of sanctity); and (4) its own subjective forms of intensity (the power of great art to channel my thought process and heighten my satisfaction).[7]

Responding to Whitehead's categories, my feeling of the dark shadow in figure 38 involves a concrescence of the actual occasions felt (1). Among these felt occasions are the chasm-like shadow, luminous coif, downcast eyes, powerful figure and thick jacket. Responding to category 2, the eternal objects felt (qualities transferred from the past), these could include the three-dimensional depth of the coif shadow and jacket cleft, the wholesome golden-orange color (which, in context with the deep, shadowed cleft, can remind me of a "wholesome" harvest field by Breughel.), and the face realized as a mask receptive to, or projecting, a "deified peasant anima." Responding to category 3, the feelings felt could include beneficence, bulk, power, sentience and immanence. Category 4, the subjective form of intensity, could include the sense of spirit revealed through the material, positive values associated with the Earth Mother and the expressive power of great art.

Responding to category 2, in figure 38 I see the black shadow that separates the head from the coif in conjunction with other prehensions, such as the bright, warm light, the gesture of pouring-offering, and the downcast eyes. The black shadow outlining the face separates it into a mask-like icon. This concrescence is guided by sympathy (positive feelings, both bodily and mental, of concern for, and conformation to, the objects and actual entities of my concrescence), with associations of pouring-offering, domesticity, earthiness and beneficence. The feelings derived from these associations contribute to my individual satisfaction in the concrescence of the face as an actual entity. For instance, my realization of deification in the face informs the way I take up other objects, such as the breads and the milk, and make them into symbols of goodness and beneficence under the aegis of deification. All these feelings pass to a wider generality, a sense of the benign, of sustenance and of care that pervades Vermeer's woman, combined with conceptual feelings of the power and value of art to express a socio-emotional repository of meaning and experience in which we wish to continue to participate.

> The concrescence, absorbing the derived data into immediate privacy, consists in mating the data with ways of feeling provocative of the private synthesis. These subjective ways of feeling are not merely receptive of the data as alien facts; they clothe the dry bones with the flesh of a real being, emotional, purposive, appreciative. The miracle of creation is described in the vision of the prophet Ezekiel: "So I prophesied as he commanded me, and the breath came into them, and they lived and stood up upon their feet, an exceeding great army."[8]

The self-creation of the actual entity is thus guided by its ideal of itself. The realization of the milkmaid as an image symbolizing sustenance, wholesomeness, and an agent or repository of deity transforms cultural stereotypes into a synthesis with the impact made possible by Vermeer's artistry, much like the impact of Ezekiel's image. Our embodied experience is called to action by the patterns of art, whether felt as good, bad or indifferent. The vitalized milkmaid with her qualities of bulk and earthiness can be synthesized into an actual entity of a substantive, beneficent Earth Mother that forms the purposive, appreciative ideal.

> The breadth of feeling which creates a new individual fact has an origination not wholly traceable to the mere data. It conforms to the data, in that it feels the data. But the how of feeling, though it is germane to the data, is not fully determined by the data.[9]

Whitehead goes on to say that it is by the inclusion and exclusion of subjective forms that the character of the feeling of individual fact is determined as it is derived from the data. My subjective forms in realizing the notion "beneficent and powerful Earth Mother" exclude notions of fatness and coarseness that might otherwise attend the image. The notion of a beneficent, powerful Earth Mother is not fully determined by the data, but is a subjective way of feeling the data. The application of Whitehead's scheme can help us identify the feelings that meet us in viewing the milkmaid so that we can clarify our responses.

Actual Entity and Concrescence

> Thus an actual entity has a threefold character: (1) it has the character "given" for it by the past; (2) it has subjective character aimed at in its process of concrescence; (3) it has the superjective character, which is the pragmatic value of its specific satisfaction qualifying the transcendent creativity.[10]

In figure 38, the milkmaid as actual entity has (1) a character "given" for it by one's embodied knowledge of benign cause and effect, of European social and religious history, and of light and colors, and by the particular strain feelings induced by the bulk of the milkmaid, the geometry of shapes, and so forth; (2) a subjective character aimed at in its process of concrescence, a process in which one feels that the milkmaid symbolizes a sanctified Earth Mother; and (3) a superjective character — Vermeer's creation, "Earth Mother" — directed by feelings of deification, goodness and power, and notions of great art united in a realization of useful understanding which, for me, affirms a positive belief that socio-emotional optimism is as fundamental to the basis of human "being in the world" as the "daemons" of fear and anxiety emphasized by Heidegger and other Existentialist philosophers, if not more so.

Concrescence and Prehensions

Consider my previous example of making "famous" guacamole. According to Whitehead, the first analysis of the actual entity, guacamole, into its most concrete elements is to visualize it as a concrescence of prehensions, which have originated in its process of becoming. We remember that all analysis is an analysis of prehensions. Each prehension consists of a subject, in this case, for my actual entity, guacamole. There is a datum of good seasonings, with which I pull the taste of the ingredients all together, and a subjective form: how my subject prehends the datum, for example seeking the taste of my proven recipe.

In Vermeer's *Milkmaid*, I have prehensions of breads that look like peasant wooden shoes. The subject, breads-shoes, is conditioned by the datum, peasant Earth-Mother. Breads-shoes prehend the Earth Mother datum with the notion of sustenance linked to a benign agency.

Prehensions of actual entities involve "physical prehensions" and "conceptual prehensions." Neither type is necessarily conscious, and both types may initiate positive or negative feelings. Negative prehensions are eliminated from feeling as long as they can be relegated by positive prehensions.

But negative prehensions are not always so relegated. I closely examine my writing pad. It is a more unpleasant than pleasant shade of yellow-green. The yellow-green is a physical prehension, since by staring at it I respond with bodily changes, such as feelings of slight nausea and faint anxiousness. I would respond with different bodily changes to a soothing, muted white or to a black that seems restful or deadening. The yellow-green initiates a conceptual prehension in that the particular color, recognized as an eternal object with its connecting maps that form associations linking the past to the present, invokes a feeling of mild nausea. I hypothesize, using prehensions that become conceptual feelings, that living in a room painted in this color would be strange and unpleasant. In this context, my negative prehension of the color refuses to be inoperative.

Subjectivity and Subjective Forms

For Whitehead, the private (subjective) ideal qualifies the concrescence. He accounts for many species of subjective forms that effect the private ideal. There are emotions, purposes, valuations and impulses to continue feeling, which are called adversions, aversions (avoidances of feeling), and so on. These subjective forms coalesce through the lens of one's private ideal.

In the Athena collage (figure 11), I include the photograph of Athena in a ground designed to convey a sense of "adversion," so that parts of the ground continue selected feelings initiated by Athena. For instance, I design thrusting spears that pick up on the driven expression of the face and the forward projection of the helmet. I feel a subjective form of "being driven" mapped on to a conceptual feeling of "eventual destruction of the race" as a purpose. To recognize this conceptual feeling and the irony of being driven to self-destruction in spite of the intelligence and sensitivity of the race represents my private ideal.

The limitation whereby each of the actual entities felt are reduced to the perspective of one of their own feelings is imposed by subjective unity, which requires a harmonious compatibility in the feelings of each phase in the process. For example, in Athena, the actual entities of the eye slit as a black void, her fixed stare without volition, and the helmet's aggressive geometry and connotations of war are given subjective unity by my conceptual feeling that Athena is driven to self-destruction as a metaphor for the human impulse toward war. Physical feelings derived from the thrust of Athena's helmet and bottomless void are intrinsic to my creative conclusion. Whitehead conceives of a primary phase of simple physical feelings as a kind of machinery by which creativity transcends its past experience, and yet remains conditioned by past experience to become the actual world in its new impersonation.

Consider my initial feelings of thrust that I derive from Athena and her helmet. These feelings fill my concrescence with embodied experience. I process my initial physical feelings of thrust into conceptual feelings of aggression, movement and the passage of time. I also have feelings of aggression and piercing induced by the geometry of the helmet and death from the eye aperture of the helmet. I orchestrate all these feelings into a symbol of a drive toward death. Emotions are aroused by these physical feelings as well as by conceptual feelings. My present concrescent experience: The actual world in its "new impersonation" with its felt vitality is colored by the world already actual. The objectivist tradition would deny the importance of qualitative emotion or feeling of concepts that determine the creative movement of the past into the present.

Duration

Perception requires that we limit perceived data to form a concrescent unison. Whitehead gives the term "duration" to such a

Figure 39. Herb Greene, *Texas Man* (Detail)

unison. He speaks of it as a cross-referenced slice of the universe as focused through actually perceived data. A duration is a sensed simultaneity. In the Athena, a duration might include the angular outline of the helmet, the eye aperture, the "cosmic" texture of the bronze, and the eye and profile of Athena from which I have generated a datum of stellar space combined with self-destruction. A duration is a distinct natural entity of perception. It is not an abstract period of time, but is the actual time of connecting the actual entities via the datum and the qualifying subjective point of view.

In perceiving a duration we notice that the events that comprise it are not clearly demarcated. They shade into one another, so that for any event brought into focus, there always remains an awareness of a beyond whose qualities we do not discriminate. In doing collage, I use the ground to help identify and give expression to some of those qualities that are prehended during a duration. For example, I repeat and amplify the colored, textured patina of the helmet and face in other parts of the collage. As stated previously, this is to suggest the idea of Athena emerging from stellar space, and that prehensions of death in Athena's image may be causally linked to Athena's emergence from the cosmos represented in the painted ground.

> A duration is a complete set of actual occasions,
> such that all the members are mutually contempo-

rary one with the other. This property is expressed by the statement that the members enjoy "unison of immediacy." The completeness consists in the fact that no other actual occasion can be added to the set without loss of this unison of immediacy.[11]

Durations are unique to each act of perception. In the detail of *Texas Man* (figure 39), I have placed the man with birdlike aspects and the bird so that the pointed shapes of the man's hair, mouth, underarm and shirt pockets can mingle with the pointed beak and feathers in a unison of immediacy. The gobbler-goiter folds on the man's neck contribute to his birdlike aspect and act as a sign of negative contingency. In the unison of immediacy, one can feel the man to be bitter, dejected, vulnerable, physically weathered and yet defiant. The bird could be aggressive or defensive. We can experience these various feelings as if they stemmed from comparative durations.

Datum

During perception, the objectification of selected prehensions can relegate the full constitution of the perceived events into a subordinate relevance. Some objectified component in the perceived entity assumes the role of organizing how other aspects of the entity are channeled into compatibility.

Consider the perception of Rorschach blots. The datum is a

detail — a real component — among the vague shapes of a Rorschach blot that allow viewers to see objectified entities based on the viewer's previous experience and current intentionality. The ambiguous stimuli of the shapes in the blot are directed by the anticipatory feelings and conceptions of the viewer that are initiated and formed by the reference frames of the datum.

I remember reading about an experiment using identical Rorschach blots. Participants who were hungry found food objects in some of the actual details of the blot, while participants who had just viewed a horror movie saw monsters.

> Each entity arises from a primary phase which is in
> some respects settled: the basis of experience is
> given.[12]

Thus no experience can be entirely new. Some given component, which may be subject to genetically inherited, as well as learned dispositions, is acted upon to become a datum. For example, in the Athena, I transform my past knowledge of volition, intelligence and war into the idea of the race being driven to destruction by focusing on the eye-abyss, helmet and Athena's fixed stare to produce a datum. In further explanations of the datum, Whitehead notes that the character of an actual entity is governed by its datum, which both limits and supplies meaning to a concrescence. He relates this mental process to that of an organism being dependent on its environment. Applying this generalization to *Texas Man*, I coalesce thoughts and feelings stemming from the bird and man into a governing datum. The datum is dependent on my selection from the shapes, patterns, colors, objects and subjects that are presented for my selection in the two photographs. I process sharp, tension-producing shapes and body language as signs of hurt and defensiveness to supply the datum of my concrescence, where feelings of the vulnerability, hurt and frustration of the man become paramount.

Societies

Whitehead defines the concept of societies as a recognizable pattern of features by which we organize a concrescence. Societies refer to components of an event, such as the perceived fingers of a hand, which we utilize to maintain the identity of the hand. The reiteration of societies is necessary to provide an emphasis that is strong enough to dismiss contrary elements. Thus the organization of societies is implicit in the determination of actual entities and of a concrescence. For example, in *The Jewish Bride* (figure 23) the sum of the characters of various societies of actual entities — the hands and fingers with their messages of tenderness and trust, the sleeves and garments with their sense of warmth and spatial complexity, the peace and detachment of the faces, the protecting arms of the husband suggesting responsibility — provides a massive emphasis that is capable of dismissing the overt sexuality of the hand on breast into a negative prehension. Feelings of bonding, tenderness, responsibility and protection dominate feelings of assertion and sexuality, yet allow the latter feelings to remain as potent ingredients in contrast. I have not found Whitehead's clarity or depth of understanding of this concept in other philosophic schemes. For example, Merleau-Ponty is close to Whitehead when he says, "Perception is just that act which creates, at a stroke, along with a cluster of data, the meaning which unites them — indeed which not only discovers the meaning which they have, but moreover causes them to have a meaning." [13] But Merleau-Ponty lacks an analog to Whitehead's event theory, which allows us to break down an actual act of perception into its elements of concreteness.

Nexus

> A nexus is a set of actual entities in the unity of
> their prehensions of each other, or — what is the
> same thing conversely expressed — constituted by
> their objectification in each other. [14]

The feeling of calm in Vermeer's *Woman Reading a Letter* (figure 14) stems from the stability of the figure, the balance of proportions, the quiet, graded light felt palpably as it washes the wall, the calm color harmony, and the calm concentrated interiority of the woman reading. The objectification of calm in these members of the nexus is the result of a common element of form (recognized as the quality

of calm in the Vermeer) arising in the various members of the nexus by prehensions of calm in other members. These prehensions impose the realization and continuation of calm because they are maintained by positive feelings rather than thwarted by negative feelings. Both positive and negative feelings may be stimulated by conscious or unconscious guidance, and may be processed by individuals with various responses. For me, Vermeer's representation of calm in figure 14 represents one of the great achievements in art because of the expression of "time held," the sheer physical and mental harmony I feel, and the power and poignancy of the cosmological, religious and sympathetic human ethos that I feel and can read into it.

Objects and Abstraction

For Whitehead, the word "object" means any entity that can be felt and objectified. My *Collage with Vermeer's* Girl in a Red Hat (figure 40) and the *Mayan Maize God* (figure 41) show figures that project sentience. In both, sentience is expressed as a potential capacity for thought not yet called into action. Data such as open lips initiate the feeling of sentience. Such a feeling can be treated as an object. As such, it becomes a transcendent element characterizing that definiteness to which our experience has to conform.

Further, when we recognize sentience as an object, abstraction enters into perception. Thus to recognize an object is to abstract

162

Figure 40. Herb Greene, *Collage With Vermeer's Girl in a Red Hat* (Detail)

Figure 41. *Mayan Maize God*

from its prehensions. In the head of the Mayan Maize God, parted lips could just as well be associated with adenoids and a dull intellect. But in context with the downcast eyes that are without pupils, we are likely to feel submission and the impersonal, and with the strong feeling of awe that is projected by the face we can dismiss adenoids as a negative prehension and let our feelings be dominated by sentience, awe and submission. The strength of this particular

image resides in our ability to retain the focus of each of the several feelings — awe, sentience and submission — in the concrescence and continuing through the satisfaction.

The Mayan head with its long Mayan nose and upturned Asian-Mayan eyes is framed by a headdress, indicating aristocratic, royal or deified status. These cues contribute to notions that the face represents societal belief rather than a personage or portrait. Thus the objects "awe" and "submission" in the face of the Maize God become transcending elements, definite forms to which our experience (Mayan, late twentieth-century social American, adenoidal, and so forth) has to conform or be rejected.

In figure 40, the parted lips and the object sentience are involved in a more subtle event structure with more terms to consider. The young woman's eyes are directed toward the viewer. Their expectancy and possible aggressivity compel our attention. At the same time the young woman is not yet committed to action. Her parted lips are members of a pattern of highlights and shapes that evoke notions of limpidness, spaciousness, pearl-like translucence, and the necessity and luminousness of light. The lips, though beautiful, are expressively ambiguous. In context with the face and bodily gesture, they convey a hint of displeasure, which contributes to the "stand-back" expression of the face. Physical feelings of arrest, thrust and parry are evoked by the direction and shape of the woman's hat, by the three windows in the tapestry behind her hat with their arresting pattern and look of wide open eyes, and by the forms of the lion's-head chair terminals, which I see as resembling clenched fists. These feelings harmonize with the woman's expression of ambiguous reserve and surprise, and provide forms of definiteness even more complex, if less powerful, than in the Maize God example of awe and sentience. Vermeer involves us in complex ambiguities. Is the woman about to greet or to rebuff? Suffused with feelings of immanence, where is she going and from whence has she come?

We can consider sentience as an object in that we recognize its sameness throughout some duration. But objects like nouns (sentience) also change, since the object can have diverse relationships in diverse events, as demonstrated in figures 40 and 41. Whitehead's interpretation, whereby an objectified feeling, such as a particular sentience, can be recognized as an object, constitutes a necessary advance over European philosophy, which treats feelings as mere secondary qualifications of a primary reality that can be given only by external material.

In my *Collage with Vermeer's* Girl in a Red Hat (figure 42), I am struck with prehensions of assertiveness, movement, arrest and sentience in Vermeer's painting. I want to design forms in the painted ground that amplify my findings. In Whitehead's terms, I will be reflecting on my prehensions and attempting to design societies that are required to eliminate contrary elements. The strong feeling of arrest stems from the diagonal thrust of the boldly proportioned hat, which is heightened by the head turning to meet the viewer's gaze. The rather androgynous, perhaps startled face of

the girl appears off-putting. Only the top rail of the chair is visible, making it seem a barrier to the viewer. The lion's-head terminals on the chair can look like fists. Within a nexus these cues suggest feelings of both aggressive-defensiveness and standing-off, while interacting with the feeling of breathy sentience evoked by the face.

My hand-painted additions include a diagrammatic figure running and reaching toward the spatial enclave that frames the girl. The vague, bulbous forms of this figure respond to the modeling of the girl's earrings, lips and neckpiece. The figure's bulbous breeches remind me of male dress during Vermeer's time (Or was it during the Elizabethan period?). An image of a large chair shown in quasi-perspective reinforces the notion of spatial depth so pronounced in the Vermeer. Small images of human figures in seated or standing positions carry out my cubist intention of showing several aspects of, or references to, an object simultaneously. The large profile image of a face mingles with images of a hat and lips, in response to the prominence of these features in the portrait. Adjoining, and to the left of this profile is a small, vaguely female figure dominating a frame or box as if to reiterate the girl's dominance in the room implied by Vermeer. I attempt to unify these contrasting details by including societies of bulbous, highlighted forms and of bodily gestures such as running, sitting and reaching. All these details indicate my attempt to recognize the complexity of the actual data in Vermeer's image, and to attempt to respond in a unifying painted ground symbolizing a sampling of my "paintable" cognitive experience.

The "Universal" and The "Eternal Object"

Eternal objects are memories of colors, geometric forms, behaviors of organisms and everything we know from embodied experience and recover from the past. The mind turns the potentialities of definiteness from this recovered past into the novel actuality in the present. There are no novel eternal objects because they are the carriers of the past. Eternal objects are always felt components of a concrescence. We receive eternal objects in the process of perception and reconstitute them into a fresh realization.

The status of an eternal object is different from that of a universal. A universal is defined as a timeless, unchanging, final construct or qualification that is not subject to the vagaries of mind or evolution. Examples are Euclid's geometry as timeless and immutable law, and God as a changeless entity; a constant all-knowing and controlling force. As universals they are fixed features, subject neither to new knowledge, nor to change. An eternal object, however, is subject to the evolutionary process of a living mind and memory. For example, because of different cultural experiences and even possible developments in the evolution of color receptors in the eye, the meanings attached to certain colors for Americans living today would not be congruent with the experience and meanings of the same colors for artists who painted the Altamira caves thousands of years ago.

Whitehead has replaced the idea of mere sensation or thought needing nothing but itself to exist with the process of concrescences. According to Whitehead, the concrescent process coordinates experience garnered from different times and places. The human mind coordinates this history into closures of thought and feeling (including the thought potentials of past, present and future) concerning subjects. This process depends on the concept that for the mind, apart from the prehensive unifications involving subjects, including stones, roses, Euclid's geometry and God, "There is nothing, nothing, nothing, bare nothingness."[14]

What a contrast to Sartre in his book *Being and Nothingness*, claiming that consciousness is pure, undifferentiated being, without structure and existing in itself and for itself. For Whitehead, the universe would exist if humans were not present, but we cannot know it, nor can we know Euclid's geometry or God or shoelaces without the interventions and experiences of our living minds. Whitehead states how the notion of self-contained universals and entities in themselves in the Western tradition follows from two premises. The first premise takes objects, as primary substances qualified by secondary attributes, as the final expression of how objects are known to experience. The second premise is the acceptance of Aristotle's definition of a primary substance. A stone is always a subject and never a predicate, and always the passive receiver of attributes. This is equivalent to saying that the color gray cannot itself act as a subject in a response to the stone, or that the jerky motions of the Energizer bunny cannot be acted on as a

Figure 42. Herb Greene, *Collage with Vermeer's Girl in a Red Hat*

subject that is qualified by our experiences of pink, fur, sunglasses, embodied experience of body language, cartoons and miniatures, and comparisons of ourselves to animals. Whitehead holds that the subject-predicate distinction is one of human reason that does not express the structural situation of nature that he describes in his theory of events.

Whitehead rebukes the traditional distinction between universals as absolutes and particulars as attributes. He admits two classes of entities. One class consists of actual entities misdescribed by the philosophic tradition as "particulars." The other class consists of forms of definiteness which Whitehead terms "eternal objects," misdescribed as "universals" by seventeenth and eighteenth-century sensationalist and today's objectivist thinkers.

I have discussed Whitehead's treatment of how the misconception of the universal entered into modern thought through the "sensationalist" philosophy of the seventeenth century. I have attempted to show the influence of this doctrine on the attitudes of some twentieth-century artists, and believe that this misconception is the root of much "nonobjective art" — art that can quickly lose interest for so many viewers and that propagates an excessive subjectivity, which encourages viewers to find the "path of enlightenment" in a single, straight, black line running across a white canvas. Of course, we all attach emotional significance and narratives to symbolic forms that fashion, social consent, superstition and intellectual status supply with appropriate appetitions and justifications, such as the status conferred by some on upper class vocaliza-

tions of vowels and consonants in Massachusetts, Nike World's use of Nazi designs, the dolls in voodoo medicine, or the image of the Holy Mother in some perceptually-ambiguous object or reflection. Nonetheless, both loss of interest in some minimalist art and unchecked subjectivity cannot be attributed merely to Philistines in our midst. I close this essay with a few comments on Whitehead's explanation of causes rooted in the "sensationalist" tradition.

Strength of aesthetic experience is based on long-repeated and deeply established meanings of subjects and objects, such as light, darkness, budding plants, human and animal nature, motherhood, freedom from slavery, nuanced eroticism in lips by Vermeer, or the latest satellite photograph of incredible activity of the sun's surface, that are brought forth in concert with fresh feelings and concepts and reconstituted in an act of concrescence. Sense presentation requires vivid details triggering such already richly mapped entities to establish an individuality with its significant embodied background, which Whitehead calls an "it". Whitehead stresses that the sense of an individual "it"[15] can be distinguished from its qualitative aspects. Even a dog smells in order to find out if a person is that "it" to which its affections cling, and Roland Barthes, in his book *Camera Lucida,*[16] can claim that his favorite photograph of his mother barely brings him to touch the outlines of his fondness for her. The emotional significance of an object divorced from its qualitative aspects is at the base of family affection and the love of particular possessions. Such examples illustrate how the power of an already-harmonized background of experience can inform a sense object.

Perceptual situations, such as a square of color on a canvas as the presentation of an essence in itself, while allowing the viewer to meditate on the color, merge with it or be repelled by it, according to Whitehead, cannot conflate a real history. It can only present "sensation and a top dressing of conjecture . . . agreed upon by social consent if you are a high brow intellectual when you follow the current reactions of Greenwich Village and Harvard, if you are American, and of Bloomsbury and Oxford, if you are English."[17]

> Thus, the basis of a strong, penetrating experience of Harmony is an Appearance with a foreground of enduring individuals carrying with them a force of subjective tone, and with a background providing the requisite connection. Undoubtedly, the Harmony is finally a Harmony of qualitative feelings. But the introduction of the enduring individuals evokes from the Reality a force of already harmonized feelings which no surface show of sense can produce. It is not a question of intellectual interpretation. There is a real conflation of fundamental feeling.[18]

Personally, I would rather enjoy a Rothko square of soft and rich ultramarine blue on my wall than a dull-olive and brown toned, uninspired, eighteenth-century landscape painting from Europe. But what Whitehead is talking about here is not that "realism" is superior to "nonobjective" art, but how complexity and depth of experience is established through perception. It is a conflation of feeling that holds our interest in Vermeer's *Girl in a Red Hat*, a conflation that depends on our creating harmony from already-harmonized feelings about details that may indicate male-female relationships, body language, deep space with its intimations of immanence, limpidness and sentience, as well as color relationships. The mind's ability to create harmony is at the base of realizing an actual entity. This ability is the pragmatic outcome of perception.

The issue of harmony in the case of a blurry square of color on a canvas has been raised not to suggest that blurry square is without interest, or that concentrated or distilled aesthetic forms, such as Brancusi's *Bird in Space* or Japanese calligraphy, which do elicit body metaphors, rhythms, change and complexity, cannot evoke strength of feeling based on deeply-harmonized experience. The issue is to call attention to a misconception about universals that is uniquely a product of the Western tradition in interpreting the act of perception, and that continues as a questionable influence on aesthetics, as well as philosophy.

Having said this, I wonder if I have said anything because one could argue that Ingres' notable painting in the Louvre of Napoleon as Emperor, looking like a resolute baby dressed in royal robes, with Roman wreaths as props, should be a triumphant accretion of meaning when compared to a blurry square of color. And yet, for me, the painting of Napoleon, in spite of fine finish and splendor, is, in the end, ridiculous and probably was considered so when the picture was painted by at least those not in thrall to the aspirations of the state and high culture, the reason being that we cannot harmonize the felt categories as anything more than propaganda. Thus, for all his genius as a draftsman, Ingres' portrait is mostly a triumph of craft. My guess is that, like the dog sniffing for its master, harmony in higher human mental satisfactions, such as art, must be felt in terms of appetition and continuation (subjective aim) toward a desirable end. In the photo of Anne Frank, my concrescences of curiosity, expectations of the young, femininity and historic Nazi time, directed by my subjective aim to find value and significance in the events of the photo, represents such an end. My problem with modernism's blurry squares of color and Ingres' *Napoleon,* with its attempt to represent ideal types of the heroic and an Emperor's infallibility, is that I believe the desired end is framed by untenable assumptions inherited from both rationalist conceptions of absolutes and romantic conceptions of ideals.

CHAPTER TWENTY

Feelings

The difference between Whitehead and classical, rationalist philosophers is confirmed by Victor Lowe, Whitehead's biographer.[1] He tells us that Whitehead's scheme was not about abstract entities, such as mathematical equations or the logical propositions of philosophers intent on limiting meaningful experience to schemes of language, but about explaining the final concrete entities comprising the actual world. Whitehead held that while molecules and atoms exist quite apart from the individual psychology, nature exists to us by way of our response to the world through sense perception. For him, the question was how directed and precise thought applies to the fragmentary continua of experience, and how the correspondence is effected. Lowe believed that Whitehead wanted to satisfy common sense about perception, not contradict it, as he held classical rationalism to have done with its subjugation of feelings and suppression of the fact that, during perception, we "see things in terms of their relationships to other things."

For myself, one of the most original of Whitehead's concepts about perception and images is the role and importance of strain feelings. A strain is a feeling response to the geometric components in an event. In a strain, qualitative elements other than the geometric forms express themselves as qualities implicated in those forms; for example, the sharpness of a cube, the softness of a curve. Strains are among the initial felt responses to a visual form in a process where other things become ingredients in a concrescence of the form. A shape may seem weak or strong, active or static, swollen or deflated. Through synesthesia, even our reactions to the sounds of words such as "rose" and "toes" are tied to the experience of strain feelings. "Rose" sounds fuller, softer and more rounded than "toes."

In this section I take up Whitehead's analysis of feelings as the underlying components of human experience. As an alternative to Kant's critique of pure reason, Whitehead presents his theory of organism, in which he aspires to construct a critique of pure feeling.

The body provides the origin of experience that is necessary to all strain feelings and to all subsequent thinking. Since Whitehead,

Figure 43. Vermeer, *Head of a Young Girl* (Detail)

there have been an increasing number of studies on the role of the body in thought and feeling. Among the most seminal that I have read is Maurice Merleau-Ponty's *The Phenomenology of Perception*, published in 1946. In this book, the author gives a developed critique of omissions and misconceptions about bodily feelings as the foundation of thought in the philosophy of Descartes and other classical rationalists. Unlike Whitehead, Merleau-Ponty gives detailed accounts of experiments and clinical evidence, such as the experience of a "phantom limb," to bolster his presentation. Further evidence in the ensuing decades, including the more recent work of cognitive scientists Mark Johnson and George Lakoff, has expanded and verified the role of the body in perception and language. Neurologist Antonio Damasio explains how lesions to specific areas of the brain's emotional centers are found to reduce or disable rational thought connected to the disabled areas.[2] He also cites experiments showing that when monkeys see certain shapes, such as a cross or square, the activity of neurons in early visual cortices will be topographically organized in a pattern that conforms to the shape the monkey is viewing. This may indicate how strain feelings enter into cognition. A shape is transmitted to the visual cortices, imprinted or "mimicked," and then "mapped," or connected to appropriate networks of stored and embodied experience.

Strain feelings are strictly inherited from previous body functioning. Briefly, this means that our awareness is dependent on a reconstitution of the body's experience of similar forms, such as curves or pointed shapes, which is then coordinated during the concrescence and later stages of cognition. Strain feelings have a great influence on our emotions and are preponderant as we engage sensory data before the conscious realizations of the thought process can occur. Whitehead describes the "withness of the body" as the carrier of strain feelings. This bodily transmission is an ever present, though elusive, element in our perception of presentational immediacy. "It is by reason of the body, with its miracle of order, that the treasures of the past environment are poured into the living occasion."[3]

Thus, in perceiving the lips of *Head of a Young Girl* (figure 43), we initiate feelings of the geometric forms and texture of the lips with moistness, color and other contextual prehensions of the surrounding face. We feel the lips' rounded fullness as smooth and swelling. The curve of the upper lip feels somewhat languorous to me. The left end of the upper lip, extended "unrealistically" beyond the lower lip, is designed by Vermeer into an exaggerated downturning point in order to feel piercing, tightened and withdrawn in contrast to swelling roundness. We may not be consciously aware of these feelings, which Whitehead calls "simple physical feelings," but recognition of their contrasts in our felt response to the lips culminates in our more complex feelings of poignancy, sentience and sensuality. The recall of strain feelings as embodied experience is necessary to components of Whitehead's eternal objects (entities transmitting the contents of the past that appear in the process of forming fresh, actual entities), such as particular realizations of fullness, piercing and poignancy that we conceive of as entity-like feelings and ideas. The process involves mapping these particular strain feelings onto domains of pre-harmonized experience that characterize our conceptual feeling of poignancy.

Damasio[4] indicates how we activate a cerebral representation incompletely, or activate it without attending to it. This situation helps to explain why we have difficulty in reaching precisely the same satisfaction upon repeated exposures to the same data, as in the lips example. It also suggests how others with different experiences of lips, the Western tradition and gender issues may process strain feelings into different conceptual feelings about lips.

Like Republicans and Democrats differing over uses for the treasury surplus, most of our perceptual responses are conditioned by entrenched subjective aims or ideologies, which screen for preconceived meanings that may have little connection to the actual data being considered. I once left copies of my collage, which contained Barocci's study for the *Head of the Virgin* (figure 12), on the counter in a copy shop while I attended a parking meter. As I returned about a half-minute later, a woman in her forties had placed her purse to entirely cover my prints. As it became obvious that I was looking for the prints she removed her purse with a "harumph" and a look of disdain. My guess is that, in a glance, she had prehensions of inappropriate sexual references in context with Barocci's corporeal yet "sacred" virgin. Yet, other women, admittedly

dinner guests, have said the painting encouraged "inspirational" and "pro-feminist" feelings.

Back to strain feelings. In figure 44, Larry Burroughs' photograph of American troops in Vietnam, I experience almost visceral, physical (strain) feelings of being pulled into the pictured events because of the exaggerated and elongated perspective. The "pull" of the perspective, the prehensions of urgency, confusion, bandages, pain and more, can cause me, via subjective aim, to feel that I am almost physically "pulled into" the tiny lips and nose protruding from the bandaged head, which, for me, have become a distilled focus of pain and hurt.

Whitehead comments on how feelings, such as strains, merge into concrescences and consciousness.

> Consciousness originates in the later stages [of a concrescence] and illuminates these stages with greater clarity and distinctness. A simple physical feeling is the most primitive type of an act of perception. . . . Owing to the vagueness of our conscious analysis of complex feelings, perhaps we never consciously discriminate one simple feeling in isolation. But all our physical relationships are made of such simple physical feelings (including strains) as their atomic bricks.[5]

In figure 44, the angular, wounded arm, caught in an elongated perspective that only the camera could capture, ends in a hand

Figure 44. Herb Greene, *Vietnam*

twisted in deformity and anguish. I process both these features as "atomic bricks" — arresting and appropriate contrasts informing my feelings of the badly wounded marine, the bandaged heads and cradling marines. It may not be possible to discriminate any one physical feeling or mental concept of these details in isolation, yet my complex concrescence of pain, concern, confusion and even more complex feelings of poignancy, evoked by the marines who carefully, tenderly lift the wounded man, are based on primitive strain feelings of these details as they are processed into conceptual feelings.

> Important feelings of strain involve complex processes of concrescence. They are accordingly only to be found in comparatively high-grade actual entities. They do not in any respect necessarily involve consciousness. . . . But we shall find that the behavior of enduring physical objects is only explicable by reference to the peculiarities of their strains. . . . [T]he growth of ordered physical complexity is dependent on the growth of ordered relationships among strains.[6]

That feelings (including strains) form the foundation of human rationality is not a widely accepted proposition. Yet, when we misconstrue the operations of feeling, we misinterpret the nature of human experience as it contacts perceptual data. In using visual images to initiate a description of feelings, I hope to illustrate

categories of feelings that Whitehead designates and show how these types of feelings are inseparable from thought and are subject to analysis. First, we must understand Whitehead's concept of the "superject" and how it expands conventional understanding of an object, such as a stone, and our notions of one's point of view of the stone.

Superject

> In the philosophy of organism, the subject emerges from the world — a "superject" rather than a "subject."[7]

In classical thought, a stone is perceived as a passive object defined by separate qualities, such as its smooth texture and gray color. In contrast, Whitehead's theory proposes that the data of the stone (that it is flint and not granite, its polished texture, outline, color and heaviness) are met with feelings that are governed by a selection of prehensions limited by a datum, which is a prominent guiding feature or features that begin to focus the selection of a subject. The recognition of an arrowhead by the geometry of its edges and facets is an example. The datum, in turn, is guided by an overview, which is called a superject. Only through the operations of these controls does the datum progressively attain the unity of a subject. For instance, as the stone's edges progressively attain the unity of an arrowhead, we are not yet finished with the process. A superject, however faint or strong to our consciousness, determines the final outcome of the concrescence. Is the stone thought of as a prehistoric arrowhead, and is the superject influenced by the intentionality of an archaeologist looking for clues to support a demographic theory, or of a contemporary historian contemplating the subjugation of native peoples by firearms?

During the process of concrescence, the color, shape and other signs of content become potentials to be felt. What is felt becomes either a subject with connections to the world from which it arises, or an object that can direct creative action in forming new concepts. Order in the concrescence is produced by harmony in the objective data (what Whitehead calls "the objective lure").

In *The Jewish Bride* (figure 23), the complexity and degree of order in the datum and the exceptional harmony in the objective lure are responsible for the depth of feeling that we can experience in this painting. The datum can be the iconic married couple. The objective lure can be the harmonization of the humanly expressive, yet icon-like figures that stand for preferred archetypes of male and female marriage partners, the tender hands, the ample robes, the warm color harmonies, the use of gold with its connotations of both light and richness, and of other reference frames like commitment, cosmic universe, and the image-schemata of the sleeves that symbolize "many into one." All these entities can enter into the objective lure as "objects" whose indeterminateness has been submerged by the subjective unity of the superject, which, for myself, may be roughly described as "the feeling of full and mature love and marriage as if arising out of an infinite and benign universe."

The superject is an obvious and powerful concept conditioning thought, but one that has not been adequately explored because it is usually subsumed by the conventional notion of "one's point of view." In Kazuo Ishuguro's novel, *The Remains of the Day*, the protagonist, a quintessential English butler who had been in service to Lord Darlington for several decades, is motoring to Salisbury on a holiday granted by the new American owner of Darlington's estate. He stops at an overlook to survey the landscape. Meditating on the scene, he finds that it possesses the qualities of equanimity, reserve and greatness that he strives to attain in pursuit of being a "great" butler. This observation-proposition is actually the result of a superject-overview, which projects his sense of self into a powerful feeling of "English quiet grandeur." With Whitehead's theory, analysis of the superject allows us to get at more of the actual feelings and motives that condition "one's point of view". Although we may be unconscious of all the operations of subjective aim, it is not reserved for complex aesthetic feelings that wrest us from the routine, as in the examples above, but is required in the formation of any concept or feeling.

Whitehead writes that "feeling" is a technical term used for the basic, "generic" operation of passing from the objectivity of the data in the perceived event to the subjectivity in the mind of the enduring personality to the actual entity in question. For an example of this transfer let us consider the globular terminal at the end of the map pole in Vermeer's *Woman Reading a Letter* (figure 45). The terminal is modeled with soft yet vivid gradations of dark blue. Its tonal contrast against the light-washed wall is the most heightened such contrast in the painting. The subjectivity of my concrescence of the globular terminal can be described as the transition between my feeling the configuration, shading and color of the terminal as objective data and my subjective feelings of verisimilitude, quiet and arrest arising out of the painting of the terminal. Its clear yet mysterious modeling speaks of light falling on a material object to reveal a depth of human feeling. In this description of the globular terminal I have not mentioned all the members in my nexus of verisimilitude, quiet, arrest and human feeling in the painting that have influenced my response. I would not come to these determinations without having both consciously and unconsciously formed supporting feelings from other data, such as the map, the woman's garment and face, and the wall, that are also light-washed and rendered with an exactness that contributes to a sense of "truth." But it is the more vivid tonal contrast of the globular terminal in context with the integration of these other harmonized prehensions that instigate and confirm my response, just as, in like manner, my prehensions of the fetus image (figure 45) are harmonized in my concrescence of the pregnant woman as a symbol of ongoing life.

Conformal and Conceptual Feelings

There are three successive stages of feeling in Whitehead's analysis: a phase of conformal feelings, one of conceptual feelings, and one of comparative feelings, which include propositional feelings. In response to the perceived object, the mind coordinates feelings derived from embodied experience to produce conformal feelings. Conformal feelings include responses to strains and other pre-organized, embodied experiences. For instance, the feelings of quiet and sanctity that we experience in response to Vermeer's *Woman Reading a Letter* can include audition. In the Rijksmuseum I watched a woman, who had been spiritedly talking to a companion, lower her voice to a hush as she approached this painting, contracting her posture and sublimating her gestures. It was as if she had appetition to conform to a sense of quiet, sanctity and rarity projected by, and associated with, the painting.

In addition to the stasis of the map pole, I can also feel its motion, as if the pole was a spear thrust across the canvas. Its abrupt stop has the impact of an exclamation point. Thus I realize a definite limitation of a conformal feeling, and I experience a subtle but important negative conceptual feeling that enriches the final phase of the concrescence. The motion and force implied by thrust is held in balance with feelings of quiet and stasis, and gives more efficacy to my propositional feeling of "time held at an instant."

Vermeer often produces powerful feelings of arrest and

Figure 45. Herb Greene, *Collage with Vermeer's Woman Reading a Letter* (Detail)

movement, as in *Girl in a Red Hat* included in my collage (figure 40). We can attribute this to the Baroque ethos to express movement, and to Vermeer's use of a light box to produce elongated perspectives and his uniquely flattened patterns. The contrasting strain feelings of elongation in perspective and of flattening in the same painting encourage us to transform our embodied experience of these feelings into conceptual feelings about arrest, movement, flatness and depth.

Propositional Feelings

For Whitehead, it is more important for a proposition to be interesting than for it to be true. Truth may add to the interest, but truth is relative and its mere statement may or may not lead to further productive action. For instance, in Hamlet's speech, "To be or not to be . . .", it is not the truth condition that informs our interest, rather it is the suggested contrasts among categories of life, death, action and destiny.

A propositional feeling is a feeling whose objective datum is a proposition. The origination of a conceptual feeling with a predicative pattern or intention produces a propositional feeling. Conceptual feelings require embodied experience called up by the components of the proposition with its potential image-schematas, as in Athena (figure 11) with her "volitionless eye", aggressive and scary helmet, streaming hair and strong directional thrust, which

can be interpreted as "Athena being driven". Propositional feelings can only arise in a late phase in the process of concrescence. In *Woman Reading a Letter*, the feeling that the dark blue map pole is a symbol of verisimilitude is a propositional feeling.

Comparative Feelings

Comparative feelings dominate higher phases of experience. In figure 45, the sense of arrested motion that I derive from the map pole's stasis, abruptness and horizontal movement becomes a conscious perception as I integrate intellectual feelings and intuitive judgments about arrest, time, calm and verisimilitude. These felt contrasts are integrated comparatively to contribute to my propositional feeling that serial time has been suspended and Vermeerian "time held" has been achieved.

My intuitive judgment is that the feelings of calm, verisimilitude and arrest also contribute to my propositional feeling of "time held at an instant." I have an anticipation of this feeling derived from this painting and other works by Vermeer. This appetition has become an element in the Vermeerian sense of "time held" that I seek. I am able to process already-harmonized meanings of "time held," and to feel this apperceptive element in the concrescence. Thus apperception becomes a major tributary feeding the developing subjective aim.

Another type of comparative feeling is derived from what

Whitehead calls "physical purposes." The subjective forms of physical purposes are, in Whitehead's terms, either adversions or aversions, that is, appetitions for or against the continuance of a conceptual feeling. These appetitions are not conscious unless they are integrated with conscious perceptions or intuitive judgments. For example, in *The Shadow Hand in the Vermeer* (figure 15), I process strain feelings of softness and power derived from the forms of the large, yellow-tinted fingertips at the left into conceptual feelings for continuation. I wish to continue these comparative feelings into other events in the collage, such as the soft curves of the sheep's head that, together with the head's soft textures, encourage the feeling of "gentle touch." Because of their large scale, the fingers can also suggest swelling and power. These feelings are derived from the physical and conceptual feelings of the overscaled fingers.

A Feeling is an Agency

Whitehead describes feeling as an agency by which other things are built into the feeling's subject as it forms during the process of concrescence. In figure 15, I attempt to represent feelings that arise in my response to the events — musing girl, austere sheep, bodily tissue, woolly textures and Vermeer's shadow-hand. The overscaled fingers, conceived principally as outlines, are thought of as a composite of other things — signs of physical touch, reaching out as if to present or understand, a beneficent anthropomorphic agent

that is larger than life, and the receptors or generators of warm and illuminating light. I attempt to symbolize these aspects as built into the constitution of the fingers as one subject. As Arnheim points out,[8] outline drawing can succeed because the completion allows us to fill the contoured shapes, such as my drawn fingers, in context with the rest of the collage, with ideas of substance — presenting and touching, and suggestions of sunlight, tissue and wool — through imagination.

Whitehead tells us that a feeling has five characteristics of determination. The first is a determinate subject. In the overscaled fingers (figure 15) the determinate subject concerns the fingers' large size and lack of corporeality, which, to me, suggests an association with the "godlike" as subject. The godlike shadow-hand in the headdress of Vermeer's woman has inspired my repetition of this theme. I try to present the fingers as a "subject" that includes other things — to touch, the act of presenting, the godlike, and the necessity of sunlight that I feel as I take up the perceptual cues of hands and fingers.

The second characteristic is the determinate initial data of the fingers, which, for me includes their soft curving outlines, soft yellow color which suggests sunlight, soft shading, and suggestions of denotative pointing, direction, presenting and touching. The third characteristic is my negative prehensions of the overscaled fingers. These include the feeling that they lack literal realism and that they are not as expressive as I wish them to be. However, I feel this lack of realism, in context with the realism of the sheep, girl and the Vermeer, contributes to the notion that the fingers are first of all denotative before they symbolize other things. The determinate objective datum of the fingers, or fourth characteristic, is that they are of superhuman size, reaching, touching, and presenting. The determinate subjective form is a subject arising and synthesized from aspects of events in the collage that participate in the "finger" nexus. These aspects draw on embodied meanings of touching, and of the "spreading or passage of feeling" symbolized by graded washes of color and references to an umbilical cord, bodily tissue, to approach as sacred, to understand and to present. That concrescences of these meanings should be represented by my design is the final determinate subjective form.

Conceptual Feelings Into Propositional Feelings

I have discussed the feeling of Vermeer's projection of verisimilitude in figure 45 and the role played by the map pole with globular terminal in creating this feeling. The pole also reads as an immobile feature that steadies the woman's figure and creates distinguished proportions as it defines the wall space made by the chairs, the table and the woman's garments. As I perceive the woman's figure in another version of *Woman Reading a Letter*, (figure 45), her tapered shape rises to her head like a tall pyramid. Stability is a conceptual feeling that has been transmuted from a strain feeling of the

pyramid. As a conceptual feeling it is concerned with infusing feelings of stability gleaned from other terms of the concrescence, such as the feelings of calm and the continuity of life. My initial realization of stability has turned into a conclusion (propositional feeling) that the woman's beauty and the ongoing life that she symbolizes continue feelings of stability into feelings about nature and human existence.

While the use of descriptive language in the example above limits meaning against the width of other possibilities that I may feel, and that others certainly will feel, in viewing the Vermeer, prehensions, with their inclusions of both thoughts and feelings that are amenable to description, allow us to penetrate meaning more than we habitually suppose. Digesting the outlines of Whitehead's scheme allows viewers with their own embodied experience and subjective aims to analyze their own feeling responses to Vermeer's image.

Physical and Mental Poles

Our feelings for a perceived object are invariably complex, although we necessarily and habitually simplify them in order to maintain familiar thoughts about them. In the detail of *Decoy Fish* (figure 46), after the circular black eye of the decoy fish, the most recognizable detail is probably the silhouette of its top fin. This fin is a piece of evolution to make us marvel at the mechanism and plasticity of cell

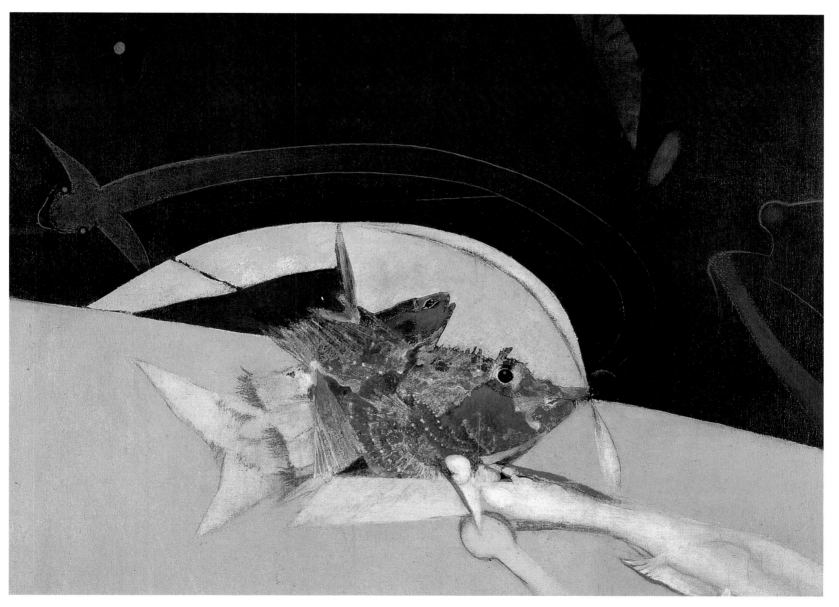

Figure 46. Herb Greene, *Decoy Fish* (Detail)

tissue. It has evolved to appear to a predator as a wounded fish and a ready meal. We feel strain feelings stimulated by the circular black eye. Because of context afforded by fish details, we process the black shape into an eye rather than a hole. The mental pole of the actual entity "eye" becomes relatively more important to the meaning of my particular concrescence of fish than notions of a circle. Yet both the strain feeling of the circular eye and the continuation of feelings of "eyehole" and "eye-fish" into creative closure remain to be felt in the satisfaction. Such creative closure requires valuation.

Valuation

Valuation in a concrescence is like examining my feelings about eating leftover potatoes for the third time. My mental pole introduces comparisons and valuation. My propositional feeling that the potato appears seriously unappetizing and knowledge that good bread is at hand condition my response. The mental pole in my decision has not merely reproduced the potato and bread data, but has acted to choose or avoid the potato. This valuation is the becoming occasion's determination of its own subjective form in response to the given data, and is facilitated by "appetition" with its incipient subjective aim.

> Appetition is at once the conceptual valuation of an immediate physical feeling combined with the urge towards realization of the datum. . . . For example,

"thirst" is an immediate physical feeling integrated with the conceptual prehension of its quenching. . . . All physical experience is accompanied by an appetite for, or against, its continuance.[9]

Whitehead goes on to say that, while conceptual feelings do not necessarily involve consciousness, consciousness must always involve conceptual feelings. Thus the urge for a glass of water involves a conceptual feeling, although we may not be completely aware of it any more than we may be conscious of the "stability" of Vermeer's woman reading a letter, even though we may feel her "stability" in our concrescence and as a presence in our satisfaction.

Intellectual Feelings Act to Heighten Emotional Intensity

The main function of intellectual feelings is neither belief, nor disbelief. The main function of these feelings is to heighten the emotional intensity in the conceptual feelings with which they are involved. They perform this function by narrowing possibilities to those that are most applicable to the directives of subjective aim. The proposition then becomes a lure for creative action. My prehension of the proposition, "The potato is stale," becomes a lure to get a piece of bread.[10]

Consider *Texas Man* (figures 47 and 39). Compatible prehensions of the man and the bird give closure to subjects such as defensiveness, the man's birdlike quality and the man's frustration.

Figure 47. Herb Greene, *Texas Man*

Compared to the bird's freedom of action, the "armless" man seems constricted and vulnerable. Processing these possibilities has modified my subjective aim. Prehensions of the bird's aggressiveness, freedom and defensiveness have become purposes or contrasts to be realized in the concrescence of the man.

Feelings and Their Subjects

In figure 39, my concrescence of *Texas Man*, "the bitter, dejected frustration of the man," is termed the "subject" of the feeling. If I abstract the subject "dejected and frustrated man" from my feeling of this concrescence, I am left with other possibilities for interpretation. Thus my feeling of "frustrated man" has to be a particular, inseparable aspect of my concrescence. This abstraction of a particular is an ingredient in the cognitive process as it responds to any event.

Non-Conformal Propositions

A non-conformal proposition can be admitted into the feeling of a concrescence. The result is that an alternative potentiality is synthesized with the primary meaning of the concrescence. This synthesis produces a novel creation. The novelty may add to or destroy order. It may be good or bad. But it is a new individual, or at least an old form that expresses a new function.[11] Collage dramatizes this action by forcing non-conformal propositions into a new

synthesis. The animated, herky-jerky movements of the toy bunny are contrasted metaphorically to the stereotyped, languorous gestures of the sophisticated, female coffee drinkers, as are the gestures and feelings of man and bird.

Propositions are not merely material for "logical" and "objective" judgments. If this were the case, then non-conformal propositions would merely be wrong and, according to Whitehead, they would be worse than useless. In their primary role, they enable the advance of thought by creating novel conceptions. Progress in art and science would not happen without nonconforming propositions. That they are subject to error is the price of progress. How propositions carry feelings into further concrescences is discussed by Whitehead as a process of transmutation.

Transmutation

Transmutation is the process by which our recognition of a pattern or other cue of organization of an actual occasion is transferred among two or more actual entities in a nexus. Transmutation ignores diversity of detail and overwhelms the nexus by means of some congenial and pervading uniformity. Thus we abstract (objectify) a recognized pattern while blocking out unwelcome detail. Recognition of the feeling of calm in Vermeer's *Woman Reading a Letter* is actually a transmuted feeling derived from recognizing compatible calm in diverse actual entities, such as the proportions of the wall, the stable figure of the woman, her face and the map, so that calm pervades the nexus. Transmutation allows nonconforming aspects of these actual entities to be dismissed.

> It is the mark of a high-grade organism to elimi-
> nate, by negative prehension, the irrelevant acci-
> dents in its environment, and to elicit massive
> attention to every variety of systemic order. For this
> purpose, the category of transmutation is the
> master-principle. By its operation each nexus can
> be prehended in terms of the analogies among its
> own members or in terms of analogies among the
> members of other nexus but yet relevant to it. In
> this way the organism in question suppresses the
> mere multiplicities of things, and designs its own
> contrasts.[12]

The complex comparative feelings at the end of the process of concrescence are almost always transmuted feelings. Such feelings are based on the mapping or channeling of analogous prehensions felt among relevant members of a nexus. In the example of *Woman Reading a Letter,* I prehend a feeling of calm in the nexus of the wall, the woman's stable figure, my reading of her interior life and the light as I screen out other potentialities of these actual entities in favor of calm.

Appetition

The role of appetition in the network of mental process is the root of intentionality and is repeatedly emphasized by Whitehead. Appetition becomes the flash of novelty in the living occasions of mental process that determines actual entities.

In *Texas Man* (figure 39), the downward-pointing shapes of the man's hair, eyes and mouth have similarities with the bird's beak. For me, the strains of these forms evoke physical and conceptual feelings of piercing and tension. Feelings stemming from these prehensions of the man and bird have produced a datum of defen-siveness. This is what Whitehead calls an "impure prehension." The datum "defensiveness" has become a proposition involving a physi-cal feeling derived from the "aggressive" pointed shapes and an intellectual feeling of defensiveness that have been presumed to indicate felt states of being in both man and bird. The photos of man and bird illustrate an indefinite number of eternal objects, such as shades of gray and black, clefts, feathers, beaks and noses, as well as different states of being and creaturehood. The abrupt integration of the strains of piercing shapes with reference frames of defensiveness and anger illustrates how a physical purpose has focused my appeti-tion upon abruptly selected forms of definiteness, such as defensive-ness, piercing, and feathery birdlike form, to initiate the flash of novelty: how the man and bird may be alike although they are different.

To orchestrate the ideas of sharpness, piercing and cutting, I allude to the sharpness of a thin, metal edge derived from the photograph of the car fender. A schematic, upraised hand grasps a white, fender-like pointed form. A bright red outline, with connotations of blood and a piercing cut, repeats the chevron of birds' wings. The grasping hand is the sign of my conceptual prehension, involving physical and mental aspects of cutting flesh, the man's missing arms and the sharpness of the fender.

Supplementary Stage

During the supplementary stage, contrasts are unified. Consciousness is a prolongation of the supplementary stage, in which we decide, choose and eliminate from the breadth of possibilities in the universe. Conceptual feelings, as described above in the grasping hand-car fender-cutting example, are required for conscious determination. Whitehead describes a further determining feature of this process.

Primitive Physical Experience Is Emotional

> The primitive form of physical experience is emotional — blind emotion — received as felt elsewhere in another occasion and conformally appropriated as a subjective passion. In the language appropriate to the higher stages of experience, the primitive element is *sympathy*, that is, feeling the feeling *in* another and feeling conformally *with* another.[13]

This subjective passion is exemplified by my transfer of feelings between man and bird in *Texas Man* (figure 39), my response to a grainy photograph of Lincoln (figure 55), in which I feel attributes, such as latent humor in his mouth line and gravity in his expression, and in the touching hands in *The Jewish Bride* (figure 23), into which I read tenderness, trust and responsible human love.

Vectors

Whitehead's concept of vectors, which underlies sympathy, is described by David Ray Griffin in *Mind in Nature*.

> Prehensions have a "vector" character. Using "feeling" in place of "prehension," Whitehead says: "Feelings are vectors; for they feel what is *there* and transform it into what is *here*." The notion of the vector character of prehensions is fundamental to Whitehead's attempt to describe the world as a multiplicity of actual things which are genuinely related. The notion that prehensions are vectors is a rejection of the doctrine of "simple location." Whitehead's doctrine that all actual entities have prehensions that are vectors constitutes his rejection of a materialistic view of nature.[14]

To viewers, a perceived object, such as a stone or the Nilsson fetus, represents a confluence of vector feelings transferred from events in other times and places into a concrescence. I attempted to describe this process in the chapters "Process" and "Metaphor." It is the transferal of conformal feelings of the past to the present, by vectors, that allows synthesis into fresh concrescences. For example, I perceive the map pole in figure 48 with prehensions of straightness, dark blue tones, highlights, shadows and globe. The first phase of processing conformal feelings of the map pole involves the feeling of strains, as my body conforms to the shapes of the pole, bringing what is there in the map pole image to my body-mind. I also feel a sobriety initiated by the dark blue color and feel the substantiality of the map pole. These are among the initial responses that are conformal feelings — one influencing another — as I proceed to newly synthesized feelings of verisimilitude.

I also experience conformal feelings as I take in the calm yet arresting proportions, the light, and the painted accuracy of the objects in the painting with which I initiate my feeling of verisimilitude. All of these transactions indicate the vector transfer of feelings from phase to phase of the emotional and intellectual buildup of my satisfaction. The strength and depth of feeling in Vermeer is, I believe, attributable to the intersection between two factors. One is Vermeer's ability to call up complex, positive propositional feelings, such as "life everlasting in a benign and ordered universe," "the spiritual present in the material," or "guilt-free sexuality." The other

is the strong individuality of both the conformal feelings and the physical purposes that are born of the "atomic bricks" in the details of his painting. For example, in *Head of a Young Girl* there are dramatically harmonized contrasts of the strain feelings produced by the spherical eyeballs and the sharp points of the eyelid shadows, as well as the assertive white brightness of the eyes and the black recesses of the pupils. There is a prehension of the girl's body turning away from or toward the viewer. We feel conformal feelings of both retreat and extension of the girl's body, and her intentionality. We process these contrasts into complex propositional feelings affecting the meaning of the girl's eroticism, poignancy, youth, assertion and withdrawal.

I feel a yet-to-be-described superject conditioning all the above-mentioned subsets of subject and feeling. Daniel Arasse[15] makes a substantive case that Vermeer's outlook on painting was heavily influenced by his Catholic experience. Vermeer's peculiar, blurred outlines in the subtle merging of the head of the young girl with its dark background are seen as showing a preference for light over outline — the essence of imitating the Creator. This mystical and religious "light" is explained by Arasse as the light of revelation. Bach's music expresses a depth of reason and spiritual assurance as feelings in unison. There is a similar unison of feelings in *Woman Holding a Balance*, *Woman in Blue Reading a Letter* and the *View of Delft*. But I need not believe in Vermeer's Catholicism to feel that in these paintings, his light, which touches my inmost nerve, and his ordering of thought, which touches my inmost mind, provide unwavering contextual qualifications for feeling my other realizations of the painting. The convincing fusion of faith and reason projected by Vermeer remains one of humankind's fascinating achievements.

In *Texas Man* (figure 47), the bird's wings are positioned so that the strain feelings of the wings can be contrasted with the feelings engendered by the man's missing arms. The bird's wings splay and curl to sympathetically contrast with the shocks of hair over the man's forehead. The beak-like shadow of his mouth, the winglike splay of his shirt collar, and the leathery folds of his neck remind me of goiters and buzzards — a certain negative correspondence with birds as opposed to positive correspondences of thrilling rhythms, as in spreading peacock feathers. Similarities in my subjective aims thus direct vectors of feeling toward one another within the nexus.

In *Texas Man*, I develop hook or talon-like shapes at far left and upper center that appear to be caught on a piece of the background forms. In context with the man, I see these forms as implying that he is immobilized or caught. His missing arms contribute to this inference. Without them he seems vulnerable. This propositional feeling also derives from the look of frustration on his face. The man appears powerless to change his situation. The talon-like shapes correspond with the beak, the implicit talons of the bird, and the pointed shapes in the face and figure of the man. Such are my

ruminations as I analyze prehensions, actual entities and feelings initiated by the man and the bird.

Whitehead characterized art as the imposition of a pattern on experience. We come to art alerted to seek a pattern to which our emotional and intellectual feelings can attach significance. Most of us can feel the excellence of the Parthenon's proportions. We may appreciate the entrance facade as an illustration of the golden mean and the Greek value of a preferred mathematical harmony. In *Texas Man*, I attempt to create a pattern that calls attention to how the mind might work to harmonize diverse actual entities such as "frustrated bird-man" and "defensive-offensive bird." Symbols of being caught and reiteration of the man's buzzard-like goiter attempt to present samples of the associations and mapped linkages by which perception and thought proceed. Whitehead employs the term "extensive continuum," discussed in the next chapter, to further describe how the mind negotiates among the diverse entities that comprise our perceptions and thoughts.

Feelings and Immediacy in Created Public Fact

> It is by reference to feelings that the notion of "immediacy" obtains its meaning. The mere objectification of actual entities by eternal objects (references to the past) lacks "immediacy." It is "repetition"; and this is contrary to "immediacy."[16]

Figure 48. Herb Greene, *Texas Man and Lenin*

But "process" is the rush of feelings whereby second-handedness attains subjective immediacy; in this way, subjective form overwhelms repetition, and transforms it into immediately felt satisfaction; objectivity is absorbed into subjectivity.[17]

While searching through the Farm Security Administration archives, I was drawn to a photograph of a farmer included in my collage *Texas Man with Lenin* (figure 48). The caption locates the place and time as Market Square in Waco, Texas, 1939. During the First World War, Gertrude Stein said that one could tell a soldier was American by the way he stood around doing nothing. The off-center posture of the man doing nothing but whittling struck me as particularly American. My latent expectations of a type of American posture found in the photograph — slouching, asymmetrical, and yet engaged — had been fulfilled with a quiet rush of subjective immediacy.

I placed a small picture of Lenin exhorting workers near the Depression-era farmer. The shape of Lenin's suit jacket and his trousers, cut off by the crude boards of the speaker's stand, seem to work with the shape of the farmer and his trousers that have been cropped by the photographer. Potential exists for cross-referencing thoughts and feelings about political conditions and time frames.

Whatever content the viewer imputes to the photos is necessarily carried along by strain, conformal and conceptual feelings derived from prehensions of the cropped shapes, rumpled suits, caps, banners, body language, awareness of political conditions, historic time-frames, and the "cutoff pants-banner" outlined by red and black at upper right. The "pants-banner" serves as a signal to be aware of mingling thoughts and feelings, and the process of choosing and rejecting from them. The cropped garments and "pants-banner" contribute to a datum of abruptness in processing feelings of immediacy.

Conclusion

By recognizing strains we can lift out our feelings and thoughts about shapes and other spatial relationships while excluding unwanted information. Strains, together with the other fundamental feelings (conformal, conceptual, propositional, comparative) and their subsets, give us tools to break down complex experience for analysis and communication. Whitehead suggests there are tools yet to be developed. In 1906, he presented a mathematics of cross-classification, which he called "projective geometry." In this system all objects can be analyzed for relationships in addition to those of topology, number and space. Remember, for Whitehead, any entity conceived by the mind, including any notion of number or space, is contingent on relationships to other entities. He prophesied that mathematics would assist us to understand and control our observations about the entities of aesthetics just as mathematics assists us to control our observations and conjectures about the physical world.

One can begin to imagine a terminology for calling attention to features, relationships and feelings that are apparent in the photos of the bird and the man (figure 47) that would increase communication beyond what ordinary language allows. For example, I can imagine large-scale photographs with sets attempting to individuate features that cause similar strain feelings and other sets of perceptual and associational identities. The inter-subjective paths of one's feelings between the bird and man may also be subject to some kind of calculus or schema from cognitive psychology. This doesn't mean that analysis will ever be adequate to account for the overview of Abbot Suger and the theological, cultural and technological realities that caused the shift from Romanesque to Gothic architecture, or to explain the complete chemistry of feelings induced by an Energizer bunny advertisement. It does mean that analysis can give us a higher degree of precision in identifying features of images and our reactions to them, and bring to bear relevant terms and discourses which, at the least, can assist us in knowing what we are talking about.

CHAPTER TWENTY-ONE

The Extensive Continuum

Whitehead holds that anything appearing to us as a physical reality, such as a stone held in one's hand or a mental reality, such as the thoughts initiated by Huck Finn's question "Why cant Miss Watson fat up?" involves the relatedness of prehensions.

For example, in responding to Huck's question, a non-English speaking foreigner who understands nothing of the question may barely recognize a plaintive, "question asking" tone in the speaker's voice and facial expression. A professor of American Literature might see Twain's compression, "fat up," as a progenitor of the shortened and abrupt syntax of Hemingway's early journalistic style; a revolt against the wordy, descriptive style of preceding nineteenth-century writers.

Prehensions, as we have described, are our initial sensory and ideational responses to any stimuli within our conscious-unconscious spectrum of reception. There are an indefinite number of potential selections of prehensions and actual entities in a concrescence of a stone or Miss Watson fatting up. The choice of which entities are to be actualized is directed by subjective aim, for no matter how much is determined for the concrescence by the conditions from which it arises, immediate decisions contingent upon the limits set by the datum and the overview of subjective aim are required to select and process our prehensions. During concrescence our decisions may be clear, vague or unconscious. They depend on our biases and beliefs peculiar to our individual experience that have been derived from the whole of our extensive world to which Whitehead gives the name, "the extensive continuum." In this way we breathe life and order into our prehensions of Huck Finn's question, a Euclidean theorem or a recurring dream of a strange city in which we attempt to find our way.

Definition of the Extensive Continuum

Whitehead's definition of the extensive continuum is that it is merely the potentiality for division. The realization of an actual entity —

the intelligent "Greek" profile of Athena or the fatting up of Miss Watson — effects this division. The objectification of the contemporary world via actual entities merely expresses the world in terms of its potentiality for subdivision in terms of the perspectives that any such subdivision brings into real effectiveness.[1]

In the phrase, "Why cant Miss Watson fat up?" the reader organizes suggested actual entities arising from the sequence of the words "cant," "fat," "up" and "Miss Watson" into real effectiveness. With the becoming of an actual entity, what was a potential in the continuum of space-time becomes actual. Whitehead allows that, for each concrescence, a limited or "regional" standpoint obtains. One's sense of a locus or period in space-time, such as an American culture that can respond to and understand Huck Finn and his language, would be an example.

The Extensive Continuum as a Symbolic Form

The extensive continuum is necessary to our understanding of the associations, linkages and overlappings among actual entities by means of which we describe the world. The continuum itself does not utilize shapes, dimensions or measurability. Whitehead shows that these properties are contingent on the structuring of events. For instance, the cognizance of spatiality is available only to high-grade organisms. Human concepts of space depend on an underpinning of already harmonized notions developed from the human experience of events, as when a baby learns not to reach for the moon — an experience that subsumes what the body-mind has learned so that it can later be reconstituted in the mode of non-sensuous perception and become referent to a variety of occasions.

Whitehead describes the extensive continuum as the one relational complex in which all potential objectifications can find their niche. Because it is extensive, it can weld many objects into the real unity of one experience, and it can connect the actual entities of the past with the actual entities of the present, as has been demonstrated in previous sections on process and metaphor. For purposes of graphic representation, the formal properties of the extensive continuum can be symbolized primarily by overlapping parts, continuations and contact, and by appropriate symbolic references.

For example in figure 49, *Collage with Cartier-Bresson's* Woman on a Bench, the woman seems to be suspended on slats streaming into the distance. We have a collision of unexpected experiential domains. Prehensions of tautness, hovering, the woman clutching her collar with references to chill and self-possession, her legs outstretched and floating on her cane, and other details, are to be harmonized with the perspectival movement of straight slats, which are also suspended (we do not see bench legs). We form actual entities, such as vanishing in the distance, suspension in space-time, reverie, and fading feminine elegance out of our prehensions. Notice how details such as the pearl ear drop, the flimsy gown seen below her coat and her aquiline features (on close inspection her nose

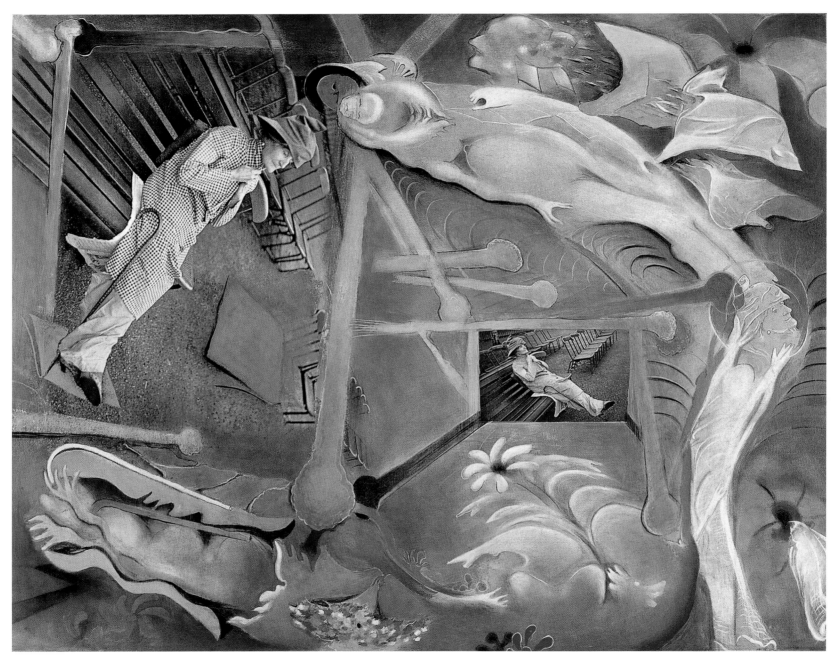

Figure 49. Herb Greene, *Collage with Cartier-Bresson's* Woman on a Bench

bridge has a bulge which can diminish the reading of her sharp features) can contribute to feelings of refined femininity, as does the fine scale of checks on her coat. The thin line of her mouth and sharp lines of her hat brim contribute to the formal harmony, which enables us to meld the many objects touched upon in the extensive continuum into the actual unity of one experience.

Regarding the woman, I also have prehensions of an apparition and of approaching death. I respond by painting a near connection of the woman's head with an elongated, semi-abstract, rather ghostly figure with a lifeless upside-down face just to the right of the photographed woman. I believe the monochromatic grayness of the photographs has contributed to my secondary feeling of ghostly apparition, as well as the age, "motion" and "suspension" of the woman. Above and to the right is a hand-drawn profiled head of the woman indicating reverie and ecstasy with flowers streaming from her hair. Next right is a reiteration of the newspaper upon which she sits, her hat, and a bit of gown and shoe. These details are potent to me in my initial process of concrescence. That the woman has a cushion suggests that she has frequented this bench more than once.

At lower left is a crude symmetrical figure indicating a coated or wrapped animal or plantlike creature sprouting "plant-hands." This figure is supposed to act as a metaphor of information processing suggesting more primitive typologies and storage categories upon which my concrescences are referenced. I am not satisfied with the design of this passage and hope to improve it.

In the detail of *Demonstrating the Extensive Continuum* (figure 50), I try to make an image that suggests both indefinite divisibility and unbounded extension, the defining properties of Whitehead's extensive continuum. This collage includes a photo of a Turner Venetian vista with airy, intricate, long perspectives, together with an especially dramatic perspective of camels and riders in a photograph by Carol Beckwith. Forms in the photos and the painted ground are shown in deep perspective with suggested overlappings and changed positions to suggest a space-time continuum.

The two photographs are placed to form a common horizon and are tinted with color to strengthen the harmonies between them. Each photo has a partial painted frame to highlight where the photo and painted background meet. This indicates the original spatial limits of each photo, suggesting that each represents a limited standpoint. Yet both frames open to the ground with its various details — spitting camels, human figures, fragments of architecture, a satellite view of the earth — suggesting an overlap of events in space-time and a widening multiplicity of standpoints. Each photo reads as if continuous with, or as having parts in common with, the other by reason of common prehensions and suggested overlaps — sand colored earth and water surfaces, long distance perspectives, bundled figures, and the associations of camels as ships of the desert. Deep perspective, with its implication of infinite space, among other possibilities, suggests infinite extension, supplied to a perceptual object by embodied experience. My painted boat images,

Figure 50. Herb Greene, *Demonstrating the Extensive Continuum* (Detail)

with their implication of apperception, suggest the mind pouring selected stored experience into a perceived object. Thus a symbol of apperception becomes another indication of extensiveness.

Prehending Events in a Four-Dimensional World

The world process involving extension consists of an enormous number of potential events whose prehensions only occasionally interact. The determination of compatibilities among interacting prehensions is shaped by subjective aim, and is qualified by an urge for creativity and novelty. For example, my subjective aim directs me to see the sand and water as related planes that support boats, camels and people. The physical world is a really a seamless web. We limit our attention to visual and mental fragments because our sensory mechanisms and our thoughts must necessarily be selective in order to manage and interpret pieces of the web. According to Whitehead, extensive relationships with their associational components are more fundamental to this interpretation than the more specialized spatial and temporal components. To think of the moon as an object embodied with meaning from knowledge of gravity, sunlight, rock texture, atomic scale, knowledge of solar system evolution and heat is more fundamental to embodied meaning than our formulas for understanding the distance from the earth to the moon, or how much human-lived time it currently takes to get there.

Extension is the most general scheme of real potentiality, providing the background for all other organic relations.[2]

I take Whitehead's organic relations to mean those that are inherent and that arise out of a teleological necessity attributed to natural processes. The ground in my collage, by intent, becomes an expression of extension, a symbol for the process by which we grasp and harmonize organic relations drawn from causal efficacy, including our scientifically-changing conceptions of space-time and geometry.

Thus the extensive continuum is the primary factor in objectifying experience. It allows comparison among actual entities with other events throughout the continuum of space-time. It explains how we are able to unify diverse references in the concept "Dentistry at Dawn," an intended humorous reading of a sprightly, sculptured assemblage of pipes, spheres and crescents, in comparison to a baby gate, dentist's tools and the moon or sun. The extensive continuum also allows us the freedom to reformulate our interpretations of data. At the turn of the century, hostile critics at the unveiling of Rodin's sculpture of Balzac described it as a dolmen, a snowman, an owl and a heathen god. Kenneth Clark[3] pointed out that these characterizations were all applicable, but that we no longer consider them as terms of abuse. Thus the mind is able to change the context and character of objects, subjects and actual entities by altering subjective aim and context within the possibilities offered by the extensive continuum.

The Concept of Becoming

Whitehead clarifies the idea of becoming. He limits it to the synthetic process of our mind as it forms feelings and concepts. Whitehead refers to the ensuing concepts and images as "creatures." They derive from the extensive world of which the body-mind harbors a certain concentration of potentialities. It is our awareness of prehensions of actual occasions coming together in the mind that unify these potentialities to become concrescences or creatures.

Whitehead's interpretation of extensiveness depends on reformulations of the atom made by physics through the 1920s. These formulations — principally quantum mechanics and the theory of relativity — have provided guiding images for Whitehead. Quantum mechanics introduced indeterminacy into interpretations of the atom. The more experiment pinned down the location of an atom, the less its speed could be determined. The atom could be described by its previous location or speed, but its future state had to be predicted in terms of probabilities. Relativity changed the concept of an atom from being simply located in a world of three dimensions to that of a four-dimensional world of space-time. Thus actual occasions and actual entities are conceived as creatures with an atomic character that derive from extension, relativity and quantum leaps. The mind is itself founded on this extensiveness.

Therefore actual occasions and events are seen to be subject to fluctuations of indeterminacy (A concrescence is never exactly repeated.) and the reformulation of space-time by relativity theory, in that concrescences draw on content from other places in space-time in nonlinear self-assembly.

Guiding images are cultural necessities. In *The Self-Organizing Universe*, Erich Jantsch[4] talks about guiding images in culture. He contrasts archaic cultures, with their myths of eternal return, to modern culture, where the experienced processes of the past and visions of an anticipated open evolution are directly grasped in a four-dimensional present. According to Jantsch, the time and space binding of consciousness of a sequential order of information — an order that corresponds to a specific sequence of events that had been presupposed by science from Newton until Einstein — is suspended. This results in a modern mental framework with similarities to the mental framework of archaic cultures, where cyclical time is a guiding image. In modern culture we have scientific evidence that events processed in the mind are connected not in a sequential, but in an associative mode, just as current neurobiology hypothesizes.

In figure 50, comparisons of the events of Turner's painting and Beckwith's photograph are not reducible to scientific explanations, yet interesting relationships occur among certain aspects of their events by association. For example, prehensions leading to the realization of perspective, space, infinity, water and sand seen as planes, and camels seen as ships, become ingredient in metaphoric associations, such as camels as ships of the desert. Associations assume primary importance to establish common forms of definiteness. All such forms are stabilized by eternal objects, as, for instance, the recognition of both the sand and the water as planes that can support weight, or the association of camels (ships) with gondolas. Such analogies result from embodied, structural necessities where eternal objects connect the events of the past with actual entities in the present process of concrescence.

With cubism and literary and surrealist stream-of-consciousness, the arts began to present experience as nonlinear. This attempt to image non-linearity corresponds to the four-dimensional present that has gradually become an important guiding image in science, as well as in art.

It should be emphasized once more that the extensive continuum is not a literal model of spatial relations among events. It is an abstraction derived from events. It is actual, however, because it enables us to characterize experience through prehensions and actual entities. For instance, in my design of figure 50, the rectangular, boxlike form (lower left) symbolizes my prehension of the actual entity "volume" initiated by gondolas seen as three-dimensional figures. I also have prehensions of boxlike perspectival volumes implied by the spatial limits and perspectives of the photos. I have processed these prehensions into an actual entity, "spatial volumes," directed by my subjective aim, which intends to dramatize volumes, perspective and extension.

Dividing an Actual Entity Into Component Feelings

According to Whitehead, the satisfaction in the realization of an actual entity can be divided into component feelings. There are two distinct divisions of feelings: the coordinate and the genetic. Coordinate division applies to the concrete data. For example, in figure 54 we can distinguish the feelings produced by the atmosphere of light, transparency and spaciousness from the feelings produced by the relative solidity and density of Turner's boats.

Genetic division applies to the concrescence. During the concrescence, prehensions are processed in their relationships to one another. The resulting actual entity represents a process where there is growth from phase to phase. This growth involves reintegrating data involving contrasts of actual entities, eternal objects and propositions in order to produce a complex unity with its own purpose. For example, one may realize actual entities of light, diffusion, emerging gondolas and architecture, together with the diffuse and impressionist handling of paint, as an idea that Turner is giving expression to the homogeneity of all matter.

Such genetic growth of a concept is not in physical time. While actual entities are creatures arising from the entire world of space-time, our mental realization of them as something actual takes place as if within a limited duration, or what Whitehead, borrowing from physics, will call a "quantum." This means that an actual entity is a realization of its own value, an expression of consistency held together by subjective aim — the sensed simultaneity or duration within events.

Physical time makes its appearance in the coordinate analysis of the satisfaction. The actual entity requires a certain duration of physical time for its realization. But the genetic process does not involve temporal succession. Whitehead explains how, during a concrescence, actual entities extend over one another. In this process the content of actual entities seems to implode from the continuum of space-time, as if all at once. The genetic process may have phases; for example, the phases of my concrescence of actual entities — warmth, light, amplitude and infinity — stemming from the husband's sleeve in *The Jewish Bride* . These phases also require the entire duration because the subjective unity that dominates the formation of the sleeve entities restricts the division of that particular duration. Whitehead's thinking on this subject is presented with excellent organization and clarity by Professor F. Bradford Wallach in *The Epochal Nature of Process in Whitehead's Metaphysics*.[5]

In figure 50, the photographs are overpainted with partial frames that open one to the other. The partial frames suggest different standpoints in the extensive continuum, and call attention to cross-referencing prehensions between each photo. The comparative feelings of Turner's "mid-nineteenth-century Venetian time" and Beckwith's "desert-nomadic twentieth-century time" illustrate a coordinate division of the concrete within the subjective unity as we include both photos within a duration.

To experience such temporal modes assures us that we experience a "real world" that stretches beyond our actual perceptions and yet is maintained within our grasp. Whitehead uses the term "epochal time" to describe how objectifications of time in each photo can be present and seem to extend over other potential objectifications, as if within the compression of a quantum. The bundled figures, plane of sand, camels-gondolas, and nineteenth and twentieth-century time frames exemplify such potential objectifications consonant with the subjective aim that produced it. In my collage (figure 50), this aim is to express something of the Whiteheadian "extensive continuum" as an idea.

CHAPTER TWENTY-TWO

Perception and the Body

As I look at my computer mouse, it takes me some seconds to think of how its shape and position are conditioned by my body. However, should I find myself on a tightrope ten stories above a city street without appropriate skills and equipment, I would instantly feel panic from compressing experience about weight, bones, distance, hardness, and fear of ending up smashed on the pavement below. Every perception is based on our accumulated experience of the body, although we are often unaware of this database unless we are shocked to it, as above. This chapter begins with brief comments on the body and the receptive phases of perception and ends with discussion of the final phases in which we generate the inexhaustible variety of bodily references that we apply to images.

> For animals on this earth, sense perception is the culmination of appearance. The sensa [the registrations of stimuli on the senses] derived from bodily activities in the past are precipitated upon the regions [perceived forms] in the contemporary world. [1]

According to Whitehead, Western philosophy has missed the main characteristic of perception: its enormous emotional significance. Instead of the passive reception of perceived forms that acquire meaning only by reflective thought, Whitehead finds that experiences inherent in bodily and mental functionings are actively transmuted as "affective tones" into perceived forms. My feelings for the black eye-abyss and angular shapes in Athena's helmet, or the pavement below my tightrope, represent such affective tones. We develop the ability to generate Whitehead's affective tones through growth of the body-mind.

Science shows how sense receptors in animals develop concurrently with their brains. In rats, each whisker develops with a specific cluster of brain cells. If a whisker is kept cut these brain cells fail to develop. In like manner, many of our brain cells develop as the body learns to coordinate experience gained through usage of its sensory organs and other stimuli-receptive structures — skin, musculoskeletal structures, eyes, ears, viscera — to establish the complexities of our emotions and thoughts as we respond to sense presentation through affective tones. Damasio[2] describes how feelings offer us the cognition of our visceral and musculoskeletal state affected by pre-organized mechanisms and by the cognitive structures that we have developed under their influence. Most important for the analysis of images, Damasio shows how, by juxtaposition, body images give to other images a quality of goodness, badness, pain or pleasure. Damasio has developed the concept of "somatic markers." These are body references that assist our deliberations by highlighting some options (either dangerous or favorable, balanced or unbalanced) and quickly eliminating them from subsequent consideration. These bodily markers also act as a booster for continued memory and attention. The neural landscape of this process is rarely stereotyped because the normal mind requires a steady flow of updated information from the changing states of the body. Damasio's authoritative and clearly-expressed accounts show how our biological drives, chemical changes, bodily states and emotions underlie thought and rationality, and, in my mind, give potent support for Whitehead's characterization of "affective tones."

Distinguishing the Phases of Perception

Common to all modes of perception in Whitehead's theory is the forming of prehensions into actual entities. Prehensions are the only means of determining any aspect of the shapes, sounds, smells, tastes and textures that inhabit our perceptual life. In all phases of perception, every prehension has both physical and mental aspects that Whitehead terms "physical and mental poles." For instance, my reactions to *The Origins of War* (figure 51) span both physical and conceptual poles of anxiety, fear, brain tissue, knowledge of helmets and Athena's "intelligent Greek profile."

A prehension initiates primitive physical feelings via strains, color sensations (including my negative prehension of the blue-green dye that was used to enhance the contrasts in the photograph of brain tissue) and various appetitions, including non-sensuous knowledge of fear and aggression, which causes physical and emotional feelings, however faint or vivid. Conceptual feelings issue from the mental pole and derive from the datum and superject — a synthesis of data selected from the perceived event and my subjective aim that has instigated feelings, such as the thrusting aggressive helmet as a sign of war and Athena being driven to destruction.

Ultimately the mental pole is also derived from bodily experience. A conceptual feeling of Athena's helmet in figure 51 is always informed by past bodily experience, such as the physical sense of a helmet's hardness and sharpness, as well as a conceptual sense of its protective and aggressive connotations. These body-mind prehensive phases remain as active components during both beginning and advanced phases of the original direction and amplification given by the datum and superject.

In figure 51, very disjunctive objects are shown at different scales. At the upper right is an electron photograph of brain tissue by

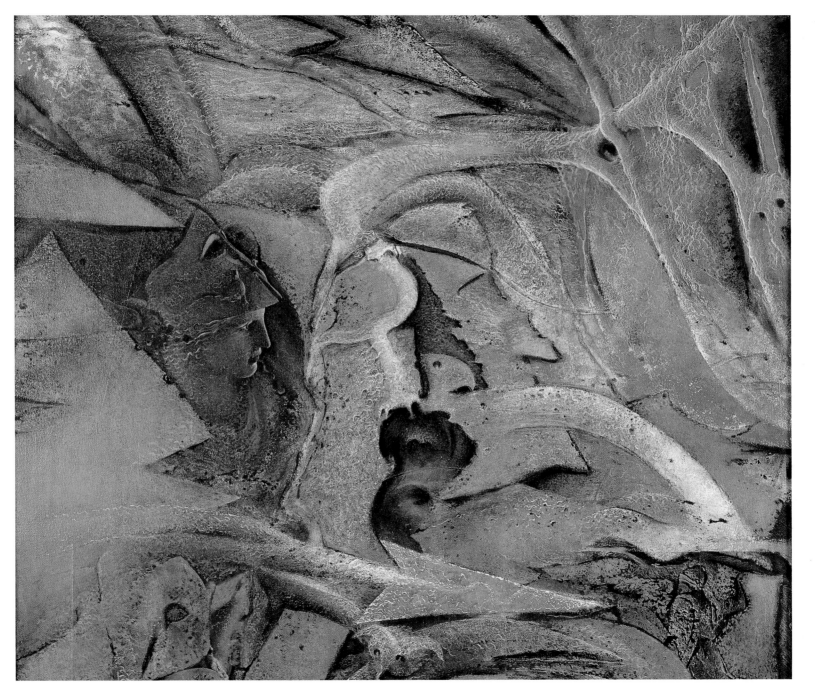

Figure 51. Herb Greene, *The Origins of War*

Lennart Nilsson. At the center is a hand-drawn helmet image formed by plates fracturing, revealing a fearful and possibly mindless creature underneath. In this image I am attempting to suggest that the creature inhabits the inner recesses of the brain, the limbic system where the most primitive feelings of fear are initiated. A spear, upper center, that could be read as thrown by Athena, is poised to strike the most visually significant area of brain tissue, keying into the idea of self-destruction. Initial primitive feelings include strain responses to the thrust and piercing angles of Athena's helmet, as well as surprise and a strange unfamiliarity upon viewing the fibrous forms of the neuron arms and the helmeted creature. The fibrous, dendrite-like tissue enveloping the neuron arms adds an intricacy without familiar scale. The notion of scale arises as a conceptual feeling that may be processed a number of ways, in context with the head of Athena. For example, I see it as a symbol of the vast, scaleless universe eliciting a component of awe. It may also signify that in the labyrinthian intricacy of the brain of Athena are instructions for the destruction of the race.

The nerve-like texture, the red touches and the recognition of brain tissue serve as reminders of the physiological aspects of the body, and the body itself as a reference frame. The fearful face under the fractured helmet personifies war. It represents a projection of fear, and the animal-human ambiguity indicated by the spear-carrying Greek warrior at lower left. To simplify the image, I reluctantly painted out an even larger spear-throwing warrior with a literal ram's head, which would have made the animal-human duality even stronger. These feelings of fear and animality — suggesting deep-seated mechanisms from which we are unable to escape — conform to my original grasp of the datum that is governed by a superject in which fear, aggression and self-destruction are retained to be contrasted with the sensitivity and intelligence of Athena.

Understanding the World as a Medium

Whitehead defines a perceptual experience by its systematic relationships to the body. Although these relationships may not be traceable, since the scale of our observation is limited, they involve certain geometrical strains in the body and a certain excitement in the body cells that produce qualitative feelings. This is not to say that the world exists only to stimulate our responses, but that, for perception, the function of perceived events outside the body is to excite these strains and physiological excitements within the body. Whitehead goes on to show how other means, such as mirrors and hallucinations, can produce similar results. He attempts to convince us of how perceptions are functions of bodily states transmuted to conceptual feelings of the object itself.

Whitehead's distinctions may seem mostly syllogistic, but if perceived events are contemporary happenings, then perception demonstrates to us an extensive continuum in which these happenings are qualified by the bodily states. This statement is an application of his premise that all things are extensions of, and within, the same physical field. Thus there is always some relevance during the interaction between the body and any perceived event. Whitehead writes: "The correct interpretation of this relevance is the art of utilizing the perceptive mode of presentational immediacy as a means for understanding the world as a medium."[3]

This proposition encourages me to link very disparate objects in doing collage. For example, *The Origins of War* (figure 51) includes photos of brain tissue and the bronze head of Athena. The texture of the plates surrounding Athena's face is painted to harmonize with the fibrous complexity of the brain tissue. Athena and monster are also overpainted with similar texture. By unifying these textures I implement a metaphoric idea in which all these disparate objects can have significant formal likeness to encourage intersubjective feelings that may be felt as relevant to each other. It is an attempt to express "understanding the world as a medium." If recognized, this idea would represent a high-grade propositional feeling. While I cannot be sure that I have accomplished a plausible representation to others, or that they would consider it important, I am continually drawn to the idea as a challenge to further effort.

Where does "understanding the world as a medium" get us? Whitehead writes:

The human body is to be conceived as a complex "amplifier" — to use the language of the technology of electromagnetism. The various actual entities, which compose the body, are so coordinated that the experiences of any part of the body are transmitted to one or more central occasions to be inherited with enhancements accruing along the way or finally added by reason of the final integration. The enduring personality is the historic route of living occasions which are severally dominant in the body at successive instants. The human body is thus achieving on a scale of concentrated efficiency a type of social organization, which with every gradation of efficiency constitutes the orderliness whereby a cosmic epoch shelters in itself intensity of satisfaction.[4] *PR 182-3 (1929)*

This is a lofty and, at first glance, wordy characterization that actually is amenable to common sense. I believe it will maintain its interest long after objectivists and deconstructionists would tell us that it doesn't mean much of anything. As I reread the passage, I am reminded that Whitehead was born in 1861 and considered himself to be an English Victorian typical of his age. His writing is sometimes characterized by dramatic rhetoric employed by late nineteenth-century masters of English, combined with efforts at scientific precision. I pause to let reader's come to grips with Whitehead's statement with an aside that bears on the body and the extensive continuum.

Gertrude Stein considered how people often become like their names. I have never admitted that anyone named Herbert can be an imposing physical specimen. What bothers me most is that my mother named me after then-President Herbert Hoover, even though she was to become, as I was, a Roosevelt Democrat. That I associate the name Herbert with obsequious butlers, or that my eighth-grade teacher called me Hebert, didn't help. In fact, I have always felt that my name kept me from becoming a great architect. If Frank Lloyd Wright had been named Herbert or Hebert, I believe it would have at least dampened his public self-certainty and his career. I would have had difficulties with Oswald or Abraham as names, and there are obviously other factors involved in diminishing or strengthening one's self-image, but we can see how Gertrude Stein became content with her name as an expression of her solid, compact physique and her assertive mind and personality.

In addition to the implicit references to the extensive continuum from which we derive such thoughts and feelings, I would point out the importance of one's physique and personality conditioned by expression through the body. Frank Lloyd Wright's short stature influenced his often-diminutive ceiling heights, as Mies Van der Rohe's large physique influenced his sense of large proportions, as in his Barcelona chair. Thus can the ideation of space, form and even cosmic epochs reflected by an ego, be conditioned by the body.

Figure 52 shows a detail of my collage painting *Fire Hose in Birmingham,* in which police "control" civil rights demonstrators in Birmingham, Alabama. The photograph at left, by *Life* Magazine photographer Charles Moore, has become world famous. At right, another outstanding photograph by Danny Lyon shows young women protesters in a Southern jail. There are suggestions in the photograph of rebelliousness in the girls who face us while clutching jail bars. To the rear, girls with faces turning away suggest the demure. One feels the arresting composition of the Moore photograph with its orchestration of physical force, determined resistance, pain and moral power. The rhythm and content of the figures — the woman with stiffened resistance and determined look, the man in the middle with hand silhouetted against his head, and the tall man bent by the water blast — provide a gamut of harmonized contrasts. This orchestration of resistance and bending is among the metaphors of the body collaged with my notions of justice, morality and suspicions of a prejudiced majority. According to Lakoff and Johnson,[5] much of our moral sense comes, via conceptual metaphor, from a broad range of experiential domains — religious, aesthetic, social, political and bodily. It is no surprise that we experience vivid moral feelings and judgments from the photographs above, whose details and aesthetic potency encourage our participation.

In the above example, my physical feelings are involved in conceptual feelings of physical force, bodily and mental resistance and wetness. Among my conceptual feelings, I notice associations of the tall African-American with stately, noble Watusi that I have seen in films. The jewelry, watches and woman's slip assist me to gain

Figure 52. Herb Greene, *Fire Hose in Birmingham* (Detail)

stable symbols, enabling me to return to my evanescent concres-cences of moral right and that these demonstrators are effective American citizens. Moral ideas are developed over a lifetime to become deeply involved with our sense of self-worth, religious and ethical values, and communal life. They are often weakened by rote use and self-serving manipulation. In this photograph, the shock, power, efficacy of the harmonized subjects, visual patterns and rhythms can initiate an abrupt and intense realization of one's moral feelings.

At the top left of figure 52 appear images of lips or a cut, colored pink and rose with gray and black. These images represent bodily tissue found on the insides of lips or of a wound, and some-thing of the fullness of certain African-American lips. Below the lip references, a large, stretched white form — a response to the tallest man — is shaped rather like the letter Y. The Y is a visual pun implying a rhetorical question, as if to ask, "Why is this event happening?" As I have alluded above, the concentrated orchestral efficiency of the details in the photograph contributes to an accumu-lating sense of visual and moral veracity. There is a fusion of mathematic pattern in the rhythms and gradations of black and white color with the concrescences of subjects, such as bigotry, force, resistance, bodily and mental pain, civil disobedience, wetness, hoses and police. The pattern focuses the viewer's attention and encourages the viewer to impose a synthesized order on the variety, content and feeling of the subjects.

Sensa Are Enhanced by Passage Into the Body

Whitehead speaks of a passage from lower to higher grades of satisfaction. This passage indicates the transition from the passive data outside the body to the more intense processing of meaning within the body. The reception, transmission and mapping of data gives way to the Whiteheadian "impulse of life" where energy is released in fresh forms. The selected datum thus acquires enhanced relevance and changes of character in its passage from the external world into the intimacy of the human body.[6] Such process enables the dusty texture of Athena's helmeted head (figure 11) to take on astral and cosmic associations, and the sunlight in the patterned harmonies of Vermeer's *View of Delft* (figure 53) to become, for Kenneth Clark, the novel form, "the light of the mind."

The Body and Possessing the World

Whitehead tells us that the most primitive perception is awareness of the body as functioning. Such feeling begins with a sense of the world inherited from the genetic, and experiential past. The body as inheritor of this past is a peculiarly intimate bit of the world. But it is only one of two aspects of being one's self. The other is to understand the actual world, known by the body-mind's possession of the actualities of that world through its embodied experience.

Apperception and Possessing the World

In the detail of *Demonstrating the Extensive Continuum* (figure 50), the painted ground surrounding the photograph gives details of diminishing perspective, gondolas, buildings, camels, riders, water and varying scale. Picking up on Turner's projections of distance, spaciousness, atmosphere, elongated perspectives and the ambiguously defined, wrapped and bundled gondolas, I draw a large-scale gondola at the lower right. This large gondola appears distanced from Turner's gondolas, yet at the same time has a commanding presence. At the lower left corner, a sweeping diagonal directs attention to Turner's gondolas, and confirms his exaggerated perspective and his unique touch in rendering atmospheric space and distance.

At the lower right, the prominence of the large, hand-painted boat and its fusion with the all-enveloping ground call attention to the notion of apperception — the filling in of the shapes and colors of Turner's gondolas given in presentational immediacy with the content of causal efficacy. Apperception is the transmutation of bodily experience, and linguistic and other forms of memory into the data of presentational immediacy that originates from "my possession of the world." To further suggest the play between presentational immediacy, causal efficacy and the mediating body as an idea, I attempt to make the painted ground compatible with the translucency of Turner's atmosphere and the indefinite boundaries of his gondolas, buildings and clouds. By color, exaggerated spatial perspectives, and a textural, "touchable," multidimensional atmosphere, an attempt is made to literally draw the viewer into the painting, as if to emphasize a physical, as well as mental sense of participation with the events in the painting.

Vermeer's View of Delft *and the Bodily Enhancement of Sensa*

In Vermeer's *View of Delft* (figure 53), bodily enhancements result in subtle yet powerful feelings to produce intense satisfaction. Considered by some to be the finest landscape painting in all of Western art, the painting's power makes it worthwhile to call attention to some of its effects that stem from bodily feelings.

In the painting, areas of reflected light register a series of contrasts. Note the bright, almost flesh-like surfaces of walls and roofs (1) at far right. The brightness is so vivid as to initiate a sense of bodily nerves and flesh, an effect similar to the bright, fleshy arm of the milkmaid (figure 38). Even though this sense is not produced by the sight of an actual piece of the body as in the milkmaid, it still engages a significant bodily reference by its heightening of sensation. Next, the yellow square of wall and the warm orange intervals (2) register as a distinct set of warmly colored rectangles; then, (3) the less bright but definitely warm set of red tile roofs that are receding at left; then, (4) the pale light on the Gothic church tower that mediates the sky with the warmer, darker tones of the surrounding

Figure 53. Vermeer, *View of Delft*

architecture. Finally, (5) the cool, blue roofs at right and the bright, white chimneys that accent the cool roofs and mediate the "fleshy" bright patch mentioned in (1). In these discrete tonalities, light assimilates in a structured society, like a chord capable of harmonizing and modulating a gamut of bodily experiences such as warmth, coolness, recessive and calming darkness, brightness and "fleshy" brightness. The result is a transmuted feeling of a complex and unified range of light, and of bodily states made more compelling by Vermeer's uncanny sense of realism and verisimilitude.

A similarly rich range of contrasts is present in the shading of the sky, the water and the dark foreground walls. The clouds, like my memory of the face of *Head of a Young Girl,* scintillate with the most subtle pointillist gradations, engaging both mind and eye to create a strong sense of reality, and of an "abstract" ideality both powerful and delicate. The same can be said of the reflective water. Where have we ever seen such limpid water or such vaporous clouds? As we gaze at them, our visceral-tactile experience is matched with the remembered experience of seeing actual sky, cloud, vapor and water. These atmospheric and fluid textures form an extremely strong contrast to the feeling of the masonry and the solidity of most of the buildings.

All of these tactile contrasts occur within a highly structured pattern of pointillist dots, proportions, sets and groupings that directs our interest to an abstract unifying order. Notice the pair of barges, arches, roof towers and women. These pairs are interspersed with important single entities — specific windows, dormers, arches and chimneys. These patterns and harmonies contribute to the sense of a potent yet mysterious order that we attribute to the picture. Mathematical generality is showing relationships without specific reference to concrete instance. The human mind has developed to respond to this order as an overlay integrating with good or bad bodily and conceptual feelings, as exemplified by the arresting and satisfying proportions of the Parthenon, harmonies of sound in music, or to whatever concrete instances are overlaid. No wonder Proust was moved to eloquent self-deprecation over the *View of Delft,* and van Gogh considered it to be the greatest work of art that he had ever seen.

At first glance one may not notice the dramatically free and ambiguous handling of space and the boundaries of objects in the *View of Delft* that is found in the Turner (figure 50). The geometric boundaries of building against building and building against sky are fairly definite. But there is much ambiguity within the textures and patterns of the masonry buildings, as well as in their intersection with the water. Upon closer inspection one sees the painting as a masterful artistic example of presenting both clear and vague sensa. As Whitehead states, clear and vague sensa are required for depth of satisfaction. In his terms, clear and definite objects can take their place in the foreground and become referent to the breadth and order of possibilities suggested in the vague background. Within the vagueness, a sense of connection and structured relationships to the clear objects is required. This condition is necessary for the immanence of relevant possibilities. Thus the body, with its ability to give to other images qualities of goodness, badness, balance, extension, and so forth, and that provides the ground underlying all symbolic reference, has developed with a mind that depends on the recognition of pattern to further its understanding of how contrasting entities can be connected and felt in togetherness. Using Whitehead's terms, I suggest that the *View of Delft* can be considered as one of the world's finest demonstrations of the mind's development toward the production of good within a finite unit of feeling.

In his essay, *Mathematics and the Good,* Whitehead tells us how pattern plays its part in that up rush of feeling that is the awakening of infinitude to the finite activity of coming to closures of meaning, such as Clark's reference to the *View of Delft* and its projection of "the light of the mind."

> Such is the nature of existence: It is the acquisition of pattern by feeling, in its emphasis on a finite group of selected particulars which are the entities patterned — for example, the spatial arrangements of colours and sounds. . . . The notion of pattern emphasizes the relativity of existence, namely how things are connected. But the things thus connected are entities in themselves. Each entity in a pattern enters into other patterns, and retains its own individuality in this variety of existence. . . . The point I am emphasizing is the function of pattern in the production of Good or Evil in the finite unit of feeling which embraces the enjoyment of that pattern.[7]

CHAPTER TWENTY-THREE

Public and Private

Around 1945 my high school friends amused themselves by thinking up humorous titles to abstract paintings. *Elephant Being Struck by Lightning*, I suppose, would not appear humorous to today's conservationists, but at the time they were responding to public uneasiness expressed in contemporary magazine and newspaper cartoons about what abstract art was supposed to mean. Currently a few critics say that art can mean anything one chooses, which would suggest that public meanings of art have lost their efficacy and that only private meanings obtain. In this essay I hope to avoid the extreme subjectivity of this position to present Whitehead's distinctions between the public and private aspects of the meaning of perceived events, which would include works of art, and to link his thought to the conditions that can shape both the disparities and the similarities among different viewer's responses to images. I finish the essay with examples of work by Picasso, van Gogh, Redon and Bacon to illustrate how projections of the private side of an artist's experience contribute to culture.

We are likely to believe that our thoughts about the shape, material and location of a spindle-backed rocking-chair that we see in the middle of a room derive from facts that are objective and, therefore, public. Other facts, such as the description of one's sentiment about the chair because it belonged to Abraham Lincoln or to one's grandmother, are usually considered to be subjective and, therefore, private. Whitehead's theory does away with the separation of causal facts, such as the history of the spindle-backed rocking-chair in Europe and America, emotional facts, such as my admiration for Lincoln and my sentiment for grandmother, and purposive facts, such as connecting the chair to a similar chair that appears in the photograph of the room in which Lincoln died. All facts — the shape, material and location of the chair, or the fact that it initiates emotional feelings — are based on prehensions of the events that initiated our response. Prehensions draw from the private side of experience and from possible interrelations among all events within the extended physical field that precipitate the public side of experience. This allows prehensions of a perceived event to commingle in the mind of the observer with prehensions of any other event.

The subjective aim of an individual imposes a private or subjective quality on prehensions and their ordering, but Whitehead has shown that both the private meaning and its expression via prehensions can be realized only because of the inherent publicity of the extensive continuum that was discussed in a previous chapter.

Take the example of the chair. Prehensions of its shape, material and the fact that it belonged to Lincoln or to grandmother have aspects that can be compared with prehensions of Lincoln, or of grandmother, or of both together. The shape of Lincoln's chair may remind me of the shape of grandmother's chair, and the compassion that I associate with Lincoln may remind me of grandmother's better nature. In this instance, I am able to dismiss my anticipated feelings of discomfort at sitting in the chair, or my suspicion that Lincoln was probably more sagacious than grandmother, as unwanted or negative prehensions.

These illustrations are struggling to be simple and slightly amusing. A more forceful example of prehensive publicity is the time my two-and-a-half-year-old son picked up a hammer, held it directly in front of his happy face and triumphantly and loudly blurted out "goddamn." My execution of home construction and repairs revealed a troubled side of my enduring personality. That there is an audience that can understand something of the humor and embarrassment of the suggested embodied meanings of such an

event — ineptitude, pain of hammer on thumb, temper, impatience, the innocence of a child, and the vast unspoken background that attends any event — indicates how much that is hypothetical to my private consciousness can be recognized as actual by an English-speaking public over the age of ten. Such meanings, drawing on imagination and the cross-mapping of experiential domains, (which are obscured or ignored by objectivist definitions of facts), have been shown to be shared, public and objective by cognitive scientist Mark Johnson in his *The Body in the Mind*.[1]

E. O. Wilson talks about genetic dispositions toward meaning as influences on the development of color vocabularies by different cultures. In both my architectural and artistic color preferences, I have a tendency to prefer muted colors, such as blues, greens, mauves, oranges and reds, contrasted to white. Bruce Goff noticed this while I was a student and showed me the work of English and Scandinavian book illustrators for comparison. My parents are from Northern Europe and I was raised in upstate New York, thus my genetic and environmental experience has a northern and temperate exposure. My Filipino computer consultant, reflecting a different culture and environment, successfully uses shades of bright yellow and green that I would never think possible. I have consciously worked to expand my color vocabulary in order to successfully use colors preferred by architectural clients and to harmonize colors with the photographs that I use in doing collage. Yet I am unable to completely escape my habitual color preferences. Thus I am concentrating on the interweave of public and private pressures on making color choices.

The Perceptual Process is Rhythmic

According to Whitehead, the perceptual process is rhythmic. It swings from the recognition of things that are public to individual private synthesis, and then swings from the private synthesis to the expressions and representations of public expression. The distinction between publicity and privacy in this cycle is a distinction of reason rather than a distinction between the data of concrete facts. Thus public and private sides of prehensions are not mutually exclusive.

We are often aware of a dialogue between public and private spheres as it occurs in our head. In Rembrandt's *The Jewish Bride,* I can cherish the expression of the public meaning, "mature love in a benign universe." It gives powerful closure to an expression of values — responsibility, connection to a universe in which sensitivity and morality have evolved, and an increasing sense of equality between men and women. My private satisfaction enables me to believe that the painting is a magnificent symbolic statement of these values and ideals down to their roots in Western civilization. I also doubt that I will ever see a finer, more concentrated statement, because the time and place has passed when that particular belief in a benign universe could be linked so convincingly with just those expressive represen-

tations — of light, richness, infinity, amplitude, warmth and immanence. Exuding from Rembrandt's early seventeenth-century representations of imagined Biblical and European clothing, these representations could not be reproduced by any artist living today, no matter the strength of his or her powers. Further, because of reading other sympathetic commentaries on the painting, I also believe that I am not the only one to have experienced such thoughts.

The Transcendence of Actual Entities

Whitehead tells us that there is no piece of data that is totally private. This is because we construct meaning in concrescences that are derived from public entities not present in the data of the perceived event.

> There is no element in the universe capable of pure privacy. If we could obtain a complete analysis of meaning, the notion of pure privacy would be seen to be self-contradictory. . . . [T]o be "something" is "to have the potentiality for acquiring real unity with other entities." Hence, "to be a real component of an actual entity" is in some way "to realize this potentiality."[2]

Whitehead's "potentiality for acquiring real unity" is effected by the interventions of actual entities such as "straightness" in other concrescent processes. If the entity "straightness" intervenes in a concrescent process transcending itself, it functions as an "object" (a sign that has been derived from the world and that can instigate further cognitive action). For example, I look at the edge of a picture frame and see that it is straight. I screen out potential objects that could be elicited by the color, material and ornamental details of the picture frame to fasten on straightness as an "object." By appropriating the eternal object "straightness" from the public world of straightness beyond my present perception, my notion of the picture frame has included my private conceptual feeling of public straightness as a transcending element.

Seeing and feeling one thing in another is the means by which we abstract the notion of straightness. It is also the means by which we create the metaphors that link all the various domains of experience. Language and all other classes of symbolic form depend on the process of transcendence to form actual entities. However, according to Whitehead, most scientists and logicians, up to and during the present century, have assumed that a simple, unambiguous subject followed by a simple unambiguous predicate represents the actual ordering of our observations and of understanding, in spite of every evidence to the contrary. Remember Whitehead's caution that Humpty-Dumpty does not precede the wall on which he sits.

For example, when Huck Finn asks, "Why cant Miss Watson fat up?" there is no way for the conventional subject-predicate structure to account for the links among the domains of feeling and thought that arise from cross-classifying the words "fat" and "up." The collage-like compression "fat up" combines the action and implications of verb, adjective and adverb, and becomes an experiential gestalt acting as a noun for an all-directional state mapped onto embodied experience about the scale and shape of our bodies, not merely the notion of a vertical "up." Gertrude Stein might have said that the compression "fat up" engages a flexible American mind that is prepared for the movement of content among the entities Huck, Miss Watson, fat and up. Stein created many multilayered examples of verbal collage in American literature, such as "Tender Buttons" and "Pigeons on the Grass, Alas." According to Stein, in a lecture contrasting American literature with English literature, the boundaries of American states are often straight lines across which Americans freely wander. That wandering, compared to the more insular English life, contributed to a mental flexibility to create new meanings out of inherited English words. Whether Mark Twain invented the phrase "fat up" or overheard it, the expression demonstrates how a phrase born in the privacy of an individual required an English-speaking public and, most probably, an American temperament, for recognition and appreciation.

To most Americans in 1950, usage of the word "hair" was probably confined to those meanings sanctioned by the dictionary. By the late 'sixties, the word "hair" could be used as the title of a Broadway musical, and refer to a clutch of cross-classifications of counterculture dress, images and attitudes. About 1950 several college classmates and I used the word "hairy" (a thicket-like mass of hair from which unseen, dangerous, wild and subversive potentialities might emerge) to describe some of the "far out" student designs in the architectural school at the University of Oklahoma. I thought this use of the word came from the student culture at Oklahoma, and that I, looking for public success as most of us are, had originated it. I read later, in a dictionary of American slang, that similar meanings of "hair" and "hairy" began in the teen culture of 1950 California. The slang meanings quickly swept the country, demonstrating a public readiness to utilize some of "hairy's" associations (transcendent entities). Slang terms dramatize, and then often devalue by unfeeling repetition and inaccurate usage, the process of transcendence and metaphor that form the generative base of thought.

The Antithesis between Public and Private

The antithesis between the public and the private is found at every stage in the analysis of an actuality. For example, as I perceive my hand every prehension — skin, color, underlying bone, the long length and grace of my fingers, their seeming lack of power — has public origins beyond the fingers in question. At the same time I know I have used my hand as a model for drawing hands as symbols of touching, or of trying to understand by reaching out. This is an obviously private aspect of my experience, and yet one that I cannot understand without recourse to public meanings. Whitehead subjects this situation to his theory of the prehensive unification of events.

According to Whitehead, the actual entities attending my hand represent overviews, or superjects. They represent a passage from known public facts to novel public facts; for example, the known public facts of hands and of understanding the world, to the novel, yet directed by subjective aim, public fact of my hand used as a symbol of my intentions of touching, connecting, understanding and longing. Public facts are coordinations within events. Obviously the actual coordinations from causal efficacy and the extensive continuum amid the complexities of individual minds can never be traced. Yet that many of us can agree that *The Jewish Bride* symbolizes a superject of "grownup love," or recognize that my outreaching hand can perform as a symbol of the attempt to understand, attests to the public's flexibility and power to cross-classify prehensions of the actual or imagined world and to agree on public meanings.

Examples From Collage Paintings

During the Civil War some Americans held Abraham Lincoln in contempt. They took up facts with public origins — that Lincoln had long arms, disheveled hair, homely and rustic appearance — and selected aspects of these facts to make into him into a gorilla in cartoons and verbal descriptions. This illustrates passage into a novel public fact. In Whitehead's terms, the making of a novel public fact — the "gorilla-Lincoln" — requires the formation of a superject that is derived from the public data of gorillas, Lincoln's hairiness and homeliness, and the subjective aim of those who wished to ridicule him. However, others act upon Lincoln's hairiness and homeliness with appropriate supplemental feelings and the subjective aims to produce another novel public fact — that Lincoln's supposed homeliness, in context with his deep-set, searching eyes, immanent humor in the structure of his mouth and tousled hair, is linked positively to his kind persona, originality and genius. An actual entity such as the "gorilla-Lincoln" or the "wise, kindly Lincoln" becomes a subject. Thus an actual entity is a genesis of self-creation and self-enjoyment of data that are at hand because they are public.

The detail of my collage *Lincoln* (figure 54) includes photographs of battle-ruined buildings in Richmond and a hallway in the house where Lincoln died. The painted, horizontal shapes under the ruined buildings and extending toward Lincoln convey an image of a tattered flag. The cropped photo of a Civil War battlefield, lower center, and the photo of war-ruined Richmond, considered as subjects, can stimulate feelings of the Civil War, nationhood, the heroic Lincoln, or other entities by which we map further associations and emotional feelings to the flag.

All my prehensions of these subjects have public careers even though they are first processed by my private, subjective forms. For example, in Lincoln's face I recognize the actual entities of assurance, gravity, stability, immanent humor in his lip line and awe in his overall aspect. His head, at larger scale than the other events, suggests importance. The large head, together with his expression of gravity and depth of character, and the pyramidal painted base that supports the head, suggest an overriding force (derived from strain feelings and metaphors of force, rising up and my knowledge of Lincoln's efficacy). I have a conceptual feeling that might be roughly expressed as follows: Rising up and out of the era indicated by the events of these photos is a certain coordination of facts and myths of American history. Lincoln's presence looms large. It dominates the scale of the collage and my conception of the era indicated by the photos in the collage. This private realization of Lincoln's dominance illustrates a passage into a novel stage of publicity.

Whitehead speaks of the subjective passion initiated by public facts, such as the photograph of Lincoln. In figure 54, such passion is appropriated from other knowledge of Lincoln and of the world. For example, Lincoln may have suffered from Marfan syndrome, causing the muscles in the right side of his face to sag. This condition is usually considered to be a disfigurement. But taken with his other features — the tall, sculptured head, the high forehead, the tousled hair, the chiseled, expressive, potentially bemused mouth and the exceptionally deep-set eyes — the sagging muscles provide contrasts that add notes of profundity, sadness and life to Lincoln's face. This photograph, with its head-on directness, austere aspect and fascinat-

Figure 54. Herb Greene, *Lincoln*

ing contrasts, more than any other public data about Lincoln, grounds my particular subjective passion for his character, his genius and his stature as an historic figure.

At Disneyland, I viewed a life-size representation of Lincoln. Management and designers seemed to be concerned that Lincoln's facial sag, warts, "twisted" mouth and "sadness" might cause negative prehensions among the audience. These would be inconsistent with their image superject of commercialized American nirvana. Disneyland's Lincoln, supposedly wax museum accurate, was and probably still is nacreous and innocuous, with all ambiguities and contrasts removed.

In the detail of *Lincoln #2* (figure 55), a fragment of Rembrandt's etching *Christ Healing the Sick* is placed in proximity to Lincoln's face. Lincoln was known as "Old Abe" and "Father Abraham." The latter sobriquet reminds us of the romance that many nineteenth-century Americans had with the Israelites and their prophets, a romance that influenced the names, dress and speech of the time. Although Lincoln was not an orthodox Christian, his comments and speeches often alluded to the language and poetry of the Bible. He spoke for human rights and individual worth with a voice that was pragmatic, moral, democratic and poetic. He is known for his acts of compassion and even extreme tenderness. Joshua Speed, Lincoln's first friend in Springfield, who married my wife's relative, Fanny Henning, and whose brother became Lincoln's campaign manager, gives an eye witness account.

Six gentlemen, I being one, Lincoln, Baker, Hardin, and others were riding along a country road. We were strung along the road two and two together. We were passing through a thicket of wild plum and crab-apple trees. A violent windstorm had just occurred. Lincoln and Hardin were behind. There were two young birds by the roadside too young to fly. . . . The old bird was fluttering about and wailing as a mother ever does for her babes. Lincoln stopped, hitched his horse, caught the birds, hunted the nest and placed them in it. The rest of us rode on to a creek, and while our horses were drinking Hardin rode up. "Where is Lincoln?" said one. "Oh, when I saw him last he had two little birds in his hand hunting for their nest." In perhaps an hour he came. They laughed at him. He said with much emphasis, "Gentlemen, you may laugh, but I could not have slept well to night if I had not saved those birds. Their cries would have rung in my ears." [3]

The Speed story reminds us of Lincoln's much noted compassion. Conceptual feelings concerning compassion and individual worth arising from facts and myths about Lincoln and Jesus can be considered as complex actual entities. Lincoln, like the purported Jesus, spoke with wisdom and compassion for the value of the individual. Jesus is often portrayed as being tall, bearded, long-haired, with a face both gentle and firm — characteristics that can be associated with Lincoln. Because of my knowledge of the Speed

Figure 55. Herb Greene, *Lincoln #2* (Detail)

anecdote, I form a peripheral association to St. Francis. In none of these categories do we say that the prehensions of Lincoln, Jesus, and St. Francis are congruent. We only say that processing certain prehensions of the three individuals can produce feelings of sympathy and historic sweep toward "a kinder, gentler nation" (to borrow from a recent political campaign) and a more compassionate world. By recognizing interrelations among selected domains of experience, such as compassion, haircuts, rhetoric and role models, we verify the extensive continuum which, allowing for grades of value, links all actual entities and creates the solidarity of the world.

For example, consider the linkage of Jesus to Lincoln as if it were a scenario unfurling in space-time. I think of public attributions of Jesus concerning compassion and individual worth as an influence spreading through Western history, finding expression in a frontier society that produced an Abraham Lincoln. I think of Jesus and Lincoln as exemplars in my private, mythic version of the transmission of certain values in Western culture. These thoughts produce a complex propositional feeling capable of self-identity with its particular role in determining satisfaction.

Heedless of philosophic analysis, the creators of American television commercials build on public associations among very diverse subjects and objects that are linked by the extensive continuum. They also employ technologies, budgets and creativity that I often envy. One of my favorite television commercials for 1992 was an ad for Nike athletic shoes. In this commercial, an actor wearing a gorilla suit poses as Godzilla. The monster, tall as a twenty-story building, is shown halfheartedly wreaking nighttime havoc on a well-made cardboard model of a metropolis. A glowering Charles Barkley, perhaps the most formidable of American professional basketball stars at the time, appears wearing his uniform and prominent Nike shoes. He bounces a basketball as he stalks up to Godzilla, who is confused to see someone his own size. Barkley stares down Godzilla and slam-dunks a conveniently placed hoop as Godzilla recoils, falling backward into a fifteen-story building thus demolishing it. The final scene shows a back view of the bulky Barkley, with shaved head, bare arms and legs, his arm around a hairy and chastened Godzilla, walking slowly away from the ruins. In a quiet voice, Barkley asks Godzilla if he ever thought about wearing shoes (to improve his game), leaving viewers with an implied image of the monster — who over the years has acquired a bad guy-good guy reputation not altogether dissimilar to Barkley's — clad only in basketball shoes by Nike.

For viewers who share in the appropriate implicit backgrounds, this commercial, like the Energizer Bunny, provides vivid and humorous cross-classifications made possible by the publicity of associations. In this case, gorillas, monsters, notions of destruction in cities and on the basketball court, fright, relief, conciliation and the hyperbole about the powers of basketball shoes, all help to enrich the satisfaction. A documentary film on making this particular commercial showed that the design interventions — sets, camera angles, positions of the actors and their facial and body expressions — were carefully revised and edited to produce a masterful outcome.

Partly in reaction to overwrought or sentimental literary associations born of the Romantic movement, to abstruse allegories, to the vagaries of theories and fashions in art, and by an objectivist determination to eliminate ambiguity and metaphor from rational thought, most advocates of modern rationalism have come to denigrate the process of making associations as the feeblest order of mentality. This is often a misconception, because while a particular association may be imprecise or even wildly inappropriate when applied to a particular situation, the publicity of associations is the lifeblood of the mind in its interactions with the extensive continuum via Whitehead's eternal objects. Further, as Whitehead says about logical inconsistencies,[4] if we wait long enough within the continuum of space-time, what is inconsistent can become consistent. Obviously, that inconsistencies can become consistent does not mean that within the vastness of the universe they necessarily will, but the principle remains. In Whitehead's universe, conceived as interacting events where some aspects of any event may be linked some aspects of other events, perusing the shapes of the earth's continents to find consistencies as the causal evidence for continental drift is one example. The reversal of inconsistencies in humor, for which we hardly have to wait at all, is another.

The important points about the formation of associations

during the perceptual process are their contribution to satisfaction when recognized as contrasts within identities rather than as incompatibles, and their effectiveness as prehensions with connections to the world, without which the results of even simple abstract concepts would lose their connection to reality. In closing, I want to take up causality in the subjectivity of painters, which has been of widespread cultural interest.

The Subjective as a Public Fact

John Berger, in his book *The Success and Failure of Picasso,*[5] criticizes Picasso's portrait of Mrs. H. P., painted in 1952 (figure 56). Berger contends that there is no rendering of shock, lyricism, emotion or sensation, at which Picasso usually excelled. Nor is there the stimulus of a structural invention, as in so many of his cubist paintings and sculptures. Berger is not trying to draw attention to an incidental failure by Picasso, but to his tendency to indulge in mannered expressions of his own art when he lacked a sufficient interest in his subject. Picasso, a rare child prodigy in drawing and painting who had the skills to paint anything, at times lacked conviction about what to paint. Picasso himself spoke of the many "fake Picassos" that he executed.

To quote Berger in his analysis of *Portrait of Mrs. H. P.*:

So much is happening in terms of the painting — the hair is like a maelstrom, the legs and hand

Figure 56. Picasso. *Portrait of Mrs. H. P.*

Figure 57. van Gogh, *Portrait of Trabuc, Attendant at St.-Paul Hospital*

painted fast and furiously, the face with its strange, abrupt hieroglyphs of expression — but what does it tell us about the sitter except that she has long hair? Unhappily, it is about *being painted by Picasso.* And that is the extremity of mannerism, the extremity of a genius who has nothing to which to apply himself.

To show how much a portrait that can be likened to Picasso's portrait can say, Berger includes a van Gogh portrait of 1889 (figure 57). In this painting we see the animated, almost frenetic brush strokes and outlines that we have come to associate in van Gogh's work with energy and the expression of some intense psychic presence. The painting can suggest an incandescence of inner life and angst to the verge of madness.

Such is the complex datum of public meaning communicated by van Gogh's private subjectivity, our awareness of his mental infirmity and our knowledge of the world. His visualization of these states has become an established public fact. The most important role of the artist's projections of subjectivity in culture is that they can assist us to give shape to both the public and private sides of their meaning so that we can contemplate them. As Berger points out, Picasso's subjectivity gives us access to his Spanish roots. Picasso talked of his work in terms of a series of destructions. "I do a picture and then I destroy it." Picasso did not believe in progress and was ambivalent about bourgeois society. Berger bases his observa-

tions on the fact that Spain never evolved a middle class to parallel that of the rest of Europe. Spain remained an essentially feudal society in which social change could only be envisioned as an act of destruction against oppressive forces. Berger's insights show how Picasso, as evidenced by his work, was torn between accepting and rebelling against bourgeois and capitalist values. Berger provides a fresh lens with which to view an important formative influence on the subjectivity of possibly the most gifted painter of the twentieth century.

Curiously, in spite of Berger's extended treatment of Picasso's subjectivity and fascination with himself as being more important than his work, Picasso is more often thought of as a great innovator, draftsman and creator of enigmatic images, lacking the warmth and introspection of preceding masters such as Rembrandt or Titian. Picasso's works do not give evidence of a personal struggle with demons, as with van Gogh, or of a personal visionary or metaphysical outlook, as with William Blake or Morris Graves. Rather, many of his works express a sense of, "Look what I can do." This points to a subjectivity of an ego enamored with the power of its possessor.

Ego without fresh content in painting is of a more limited public interest than, say, Redon's projection of personal triumph — a sense of self moving from darkness into light. Redon's parents placed him, as a young child, to grow up in a loveless and lonely rural environment because they believed him to be epileptic at a time when epilepsy was considered to be a social stigma against the family. Redon, at least partly in response to childhood despair, worked entirely in black and white until the age of thirty-five. His surreal creatures of this period were an indication of a mysterious humanity emanating from his black charcoals of "human-faced" spiders and hooded figures. As Redon became noted for luminescent and wonderfully colored pastels of flowers, he continued to use black in his palette. He constructed a strong metaphor of moving from darkness to an ecstasy of light — an expression of Redon's journey in healing himself. Undoubtedly, this timeless metaphor, as well as the sensory pleasure of Redon's colors and projection of spiritual feeling, have maintained and increased public appreciation of his work.

In contrast to Redon's subjectivity, in which we recognize hope and transcendence to spirit, Francis Bacon projects a unique sense of existential aloneness, dilemma and Sartre-like nausea in images. Bacon responded to the scale of destruction in Europe's recent wars and to photographs of death camps, and was influenced by Picasso's work in the 'thirties. With its slashing strokes and distortions, Picasso's work seemed, to Berger, to possess an intensity not yet seen in art — that seemed to merge the viewer with painted sensations of the subject. Bacon's painted screams, slashed faces and tortured figures force us to deal with the flesh, nerve and psyche of the human animal as Rembrandt's carcass of an ox hanging in a butcher shop forces us to deal with realities of raw flesh and death. When viewing Bacon's study of Isabel Rawsthorne (figure 58), I can feel the authority of his genius. The enormous gash of the neck and cheek jars me with force, sensation and the ambiguous imagery of pig, tongue and orifice, which suggests a wrenching of contrasts between the interior and exterior of a human-animal body. The contrasts set up by this seemingly spontaneous invention with the assurance of the intense, tiny eye, deft profile, slashed yet dignified lips and nose, convey a sense of dignity and of urgency.

Bacon projects unease and ominous portents that cloud our needs for hope and aspiration. I sometimes wonder if his vision will maintain its current interest if his own homosexuality and the subject of homosexuality become more biologically and morally integrated as legitimate parts of nature's spectrum. I may be conventionally-minded, but I find that many of his paintings that show explicit sex, drug injecting, tormented bodies, and heavy European existential gloom, partake of contemporary fashion for "rub it in your face" self-absorption and post-holocaust negativity about the human condition. I have noticed that in advertising art in the late 'nineties, one sees a lot of surliness and "extermination camp" makeup on the faces of models for clothing and cosmetics. One wonders if this trend is an extension of Holocaust fascination, fear of environmental destruction, road rage, power burgers, or what? However, Bacon's projections of existential angst and aloneness, which must always be with us, are not likely to lose their grip like the Romantic sentimental poses and allusions to death that characterized the funerary sculpture by Canova, who, in the 1820s, was

Figure 58. Francis Bacon, *Portrait of Isabel Rawsthorne*

considered the most accomplished and fashionably chic sculptor in Europe.

A growing awareness of an individual's heritage, environment and psychology has led to a near clinical interest in the private qualities of the artist's enduring personality. In Whitehead's terms, the body-mind is a concentrator of efficient organization in which orderliness of the world can be revealed. It is the enduring personality, with its ability to project its feelings, that permits the subjectivity of artists to reveal some of the more interesting and hard-to-reach expressions of this orderliness.

The creative role of the enduring personality is presupposed in a recent collection of essays by cognitive, neuro, biochemical, and physical scientists, including Oliver Sachs, Gerald Edelman, Roger Penrose and Freeman Dyson, in *Nature's Imagination,* edited by John Cornwell.[6] Without referring to Whitehead by name, they provide confirmations and elaborations of the shift from a deterministic, immutable and non-anthropocentric universe to Whitehead's dynamic, emergent, relational and holistic view of nature. It is a view where the subjectivity of the individual is appreciated within the spectrum of structure and openness, order and chaos, determinism and probability, constituted in the particles, events and history of our world.

CHAPTER TWENTY-FOUR

Consciousness

In his powerful rumination on the state of science and genetics, *Consilience,*[1] Edward O. Wilson tells us that consciousness is a specialized part of the mind that creates and sifts scenarios, the means by which the future is guessed and courses of action are chosen. Not a remote command center, consciousness is part of the system that is intimately wired to all the neural and hormonal circuits regulating physiology. It perturbs the body in precise ways with each changing circumstance, as required for well-being and response to opportunity and challenge, and helps return it to homeostasis when challenge and opportunity have been met. In another recent characterization of consciousness, *Philosophy in the Flesh,*[2] Lakoff and Johnson tell us that conscious thought is just the tip of an iceberg where at least ninety-five per cent of all thought lies below the surface of conscious awareness. Without this hidden presence giving shape and structure, there could be no conscious thought. Conscious thought and reason are crucially shaped by the peculiarities of our human bodies, the details of neural structure of our brains and the specifics of our everyday functioning in the world.

These summaries square with Whitehead, who, about seventy years ago wrote that consciousness is a resolution of physical, conceptual and propositional feelings streaming into awareness. These feelings flow from the reservoirs of our body-mind via our embodied experience expressed in causal efficacy, such as my awareness of my body as a perceiving self, or my knowledge that informs the sight of our slender, curvaceous bottle for salad dressing in which the cork pops out by itself every meal or two. My wife and I invariably find this event amusing, as do guests. It is as if a hat or head has flown off the anthropomorphic figure of the bottle. The sound of the pop also adds its appropriate references. Thus perceptions are received not neutrally, but with emotional and purposive subjective forms of reception. Consequently, perceived data are prehended as emotional feelings that are initiated by the act of perception. My understanding of Whitehead is that consciousness can only illuminate those elements of experience that have been considerably simplified and integrated, and that these elements have been processed by prior emotional and subjective forms. Applying the above tenets to the feelings and thoughts that are generated by the unexpected appearance of a large, hairy fly in your soup can suggest something of the situation.

The elements of our experience that stand out clearly and distinctly, such as mere sense awareness of the fly, are not its basic facts. Such facts are the derivative modifications (still connected to emotional and subjective forms, such as the thought of having eaten the fly) that arise in the process of concrescence. Subconscious thoughts and stimuli can be processed into neural representations that influence thought and feeling without our awareness. It follows that any actual entity can be known only in terms of a subconscious-conscious continuum, the elements of which remain connected to emotional and subjective content. In the case of the fly, the subconscious could include genetic dispositions to avoid nasty taste, pre-representational inputs, such as expected illness from disease, and representational inputs, such as the unappetizing, hairy and potentially germ-laden legs of the fly. Whitehead tells us about the synthesis of physical and conceptual feelings that are involved in the process.

All awareness, even awareness of concepts, requires
at least the synthesis of physical feelings with

conceptual feeling. In awareness, actuality, as a process in fact, is integrated with the potentialities which illustrate *either* what it is and might not be, *or* what it is not and might be. In other words there is no consciousness without reference to definiteness, affirmation, and negation. . . . Further, affirmation and negation are alike meaningless apart from reference to the definiteness of particular actualities. Consciousness is how we feel the affirmation-negation contrast (arising in the determination of particular actualities).[3]

This idea can be utilized to at least tidy the edges of the very untidy subject of consciousness and experience. Consciousness presupposes experience. It is a special element in the subjective forms of realized feelings stemming from experience. In the detail of my collage *The Immanence of Thought* (figure 59), one's consciousness can become absorbed with Vermeer's light. In my case, because of the reification of light in his painting, I seek to acknowledge something of my thought-response by making part of a circle at left, suggesting a muted sun, as well as a possible globe in response to the map. At lower left is a teardrop pearl-like form, suggesting prerequisites of light, shade, texture and outline that are necessary for visual perception. The immanence of pearls in my experience of Vermeer's work rises to my consciousness as I seek to acknowledge the lack of a pearl ear-drop worn by most of Vermeer's memorable women. Here I see a fashionable curl where I might expect a pearl. Thus in

Figure 59. Herb Greene, *The Immanence of Thought*

my collage I am expressing feelings of decision, and judging whether these feelings (of this and not that) are directed by the objective data in the image, or by my subjectivity, or by both conditions. Whitehead expands on the flickering consciousness as it might appropriate a pearl or curl in Vermeer's painting.

> Consciousness flickers; and even at its brightest, there is a small focal region of clear illumination, and a large penumbral region of experience which tells of intense experience in dim apprehension. The simplicity of clear consciousness is no measure of the complexity of complete experience. Also this character of our experience suggests that consciousness is the crown of experience, only occasionally attained, not its necessary base.[4]

The foveal image that allows us sharp visual focus is just one three-thousandth of the visual field. But within or outside the foveal image, the eye recognizes and responds to information of which we are not consciously aware, as in the case of subliminal inputs. The painstaking manner in which we have to focus on details in the visual field in order to move our conscious mind to think about them provides another illustration of the narrowness of consciousness. Our reliance on already harmonized experience to fill out the meaning of these perceived details also indicates the limits of consciousness.

Let us return to Vermeer's painting (figure 59) to illustrate how imagination may range within the limits of consciousness. We can be aware of subtleties in Vermeer's painting. We recognize the profile line of the head to possess uncommon grace and beauty. However, following this line closely over the facial features, one finds the nose perhaps too long for anatomical expectations. The lips are open and splayed and contribute to a feeling of breathy sentience, but the lips are shaped beyond the natural, as if curled back by pressing against an invisible, concave surface. The small reproduction does not permit a clear indication, but these exaggerations, including the extra length of the shadow from the eyebrow to the bottom of the eyelid, would cause a frontal view of the head to appear as abnormally distended and the lips as excessively puckered, as if seen in a distorting mirror. The high forehead with its continuing, upward-swelling outline is also slightly distorted. This body metaphor suggests that the direction and swelling-up is positive, fulfilling, powerful, yet eased. In this unforgettable profile, the splayed lips combined with the natal swelling of the woman are a sign of the potent yet subtle eroticism that I have previously mentioned. As a male I have attempted to allude to this eroticism by suggesting a rounded, nude female bottom at lower right.

At upper left is an image of a book slipping off a table, acknowledging the book that Vermeer has placed at the very edge of the table in his scene. This placement reminds of wine glasses that Vermeer has placed at the very edge of tables in other paintings. One

234

can only speculate on Vermeer's intentions here. My guess is that Vermeer liked to tighten feeling in this way, as in the *View of Delft*, in which he pointedly places a barge mast in the very center of a black window in the background architecture to contrast with the relaxed asymmetries of dormers, windows and chimneys. The assurance of Vermeer's composition allows such moves to attract our curiosity, and form contrasts to heighten the impeccable balance that he projects.

One of my motivations in doing collage is to give expression to the notion of mind rising to a state of consciousness, moving from the unconscious to the liminal to the conscious, and back again to the unconscious, as in figure 59, where a double profile attempts to acknowledge the sense of ongoing life conveyed by the pregnant woman. The smaller, slightly upturned head following the larger, down-turning head links a sense of the vaguely feminine youth with a liminal sense of dignity derived from the profile of Vermeer's woman. The recognition of a subject fading in and out of focus is a transcript of our actual perceptual thought process and represents a positive idea for interpreting the collage. The unconscious in art has been popularized as expressing the subversive, the repressed and the irrational, as in much Surrealism. What I am trying to express is the idea that an unconscious-conscious gradient is involved in any normal act of perception; for example, in figure 59, where I have used shades of pink and rose in reference to my associations of those colors with female children, interior organs and fluids, physiological

feeling, and feminine sexual parts.

Whitehead considers the individual, personal order that each of us brings to bear on a perceptual act in the immediate present. In such acts there is wide variation in the range and strength of realized order, knowledge and qualitative feelings. We may be aware of our perceptions but remain unaware of our thought process. We attend to some detail of abstract thought, or an immediate emotion, while ignoring the rest of the world. We are extremely discursive with our attention, which ranges from various states of sleep to varying degrees of alertness. In addition, we remember details from experiencing an act of perception that we did not appreciate during the original act. Whitehead makes other important points about the limits of conscious perception and its role in the thought process.

> When we survey the chequered history of our own capacity for knowledge, does common sense allow us to believe that the operations of judgment, operations which require definition in terms of conscious apprehension, are those operations which are foundational in existence either as an essential attribute for an actual entity, or as the final culmination whereby unity of experience is attained![5]

The general case of conscious perception is the negative perception, namely, "perceiving this stone as not grey". The "grey" then has ingression in its full character of a conceptual alternative.... Consciousness is the feeling of negation: in the perception of "the stone as grey," such feeling is in barest germ; in the perception of "the stone as not grey," such feeling is full development. Thus the negative perception is the triumph of consciousness. It finally rises to the peak of free imagination in which the conceptual novelties search through a universe in which they are not datively exemplified.[6]

The creative use of the negative perception that is described above by Whitehead can be illustrated by Malcolm Kirk's photograph of the painted face of a New Guinea tribesman, which I have used as the centerpiece of a not-yet-finished collage painting, figure 60. The stunningly painted face, surfaced with clay and color, is a vivid statement of cosmology at one with the human body, and elicited in me a nagging negative perception. The eyes of the man are not looking into the camera. They have a glazed, faraway look, as if indicating distancing and estrangement from the fierce, bright, beautiful face, as if the mind of the man is in existential limbo or expressing inner distress over posing for a camera and a culture that is largely incomprehensible to him. Anthropologist and neighbor Jim Meyers notes that the rules of war for these tribesmen call for a halt to battle at the onset of rain to protect their body paint from dissolution. I found the look of the tribesman's eyes so at odds with the presence of iconic paint that I felt compelled to darken them and smudge their spot of bright reflectivity in order to harmonize

conceptual novelties arising from their look with novelties arising from the painted face. If I had enough imagination I would have left the eyes untouched and designed mediating forms that could catch the existential dilemma that characterizes the actual event recorded by the photographer.

It is as if one caught a highlighted Whitehead, seated in his darkened study at his dark wood desk, surrounded by dark wood shelves lined with books from floor to ceiling with his eyes glazed, bored and with faint anticipation of yet another faculty meeting on protocol for graduate students.

The following analysis of Vermeer's *Woman Pouring Milk*, which is included in my collage, *The Becoming of Consciousness* (figure 38), takes up several of Vermeer's painted gestures in order to show something of their subtlety and power. Our response to them draws on the subconscious-conscious continuum. The milkmaid as Earth Mother, transcending that worn cliché, belongs with Vermeer's highest artistic achievements. The realism of the textures, colors and outlines of the forms in the painting is assured, and gives us open and accessible pleasure. Yet almost every shape and color seems to call for significance that lies beyond conscious apprehension. We feel an urge to search for this significance.

A milkmaid has become a prosaic subject, but Vermeer has endowed his milkmaid with a timeless mythos. She is a powerful Earth Mother whose strength and being convey a sense of nurture, sustenance and caring. These are archetypal images partly explained

Figure 60. Herb Greene, *A Man in the World*

by Wilson's concepts of epigenetic necessity — how genetic dispositions such as bodily security, warmth, sustenance and curiosity, or understanding the world, are developed through culture into symbols of a deified nurturing Earth Mother.

The milkmaid's body is carefully positioned. Her head turns into her shoulder/arm, which leans toward the pitcher's black orifice, the table and the breads. Her body curves with continuity and a feeling of concern, as if she is administering with her protective power. A thin stream of milk (a wide stream would disturb the feeling of tranquility) lies within the focus of this orchestration. The complexity of thought and feeling stemming from this thin stream of milk is characteristic of Vermeer's ability to charge every discrete gesture and piece of the *mise-en-scene* with a lure to consciousness in search of conceptual novelty, as in the contribution of the thin stream to a feeling of tranquility, and in the feeling of concern in the body language of the milkmaid.

The wall in back of the milkmaid's figure is unbroken, allowing her monumental presence to dominate the space, adding to her power as a symbol. Her downcast eyes and parted lips are signs of sentience and obeisance. Her face suggests a mask hiding its significance, and also an icon that represents earthy roots within its manifestations of deity. It is separated from its surroundings by a deeply incised shadow, a black gap that sets off the face from the white coif. This gap emphasizes the sense of the face as a hieratic mask by its separation from the maid's figure. It is among the first

and strongest prehensions that I return to over and over, seeking to uncover its significance. My sense of the entire picture is that it is a quiet yet powerful orchestration of archetypal aspects — "goodness," "sustenance" — and a receptacle for idealizations of a mythic, god-directed peasant anima.

The realistic white coif is painted as an epiphany of light. I feel deification in the super-intense light that the coif reflects. The thick, rolled-up sleeves speak of physical work. The color contrasts of her bare forearm arrest us with pronounced physical and conceptual feelings. They remind us of Rembrandt's *Slaughtered Ox*, with its representation of flesh and sinew, but in this Vermeerian context, no trace of death lingers. The arm is a detail that gives a visceral and conceptual surge to feelings of physical strength, the sensation of color, and to connotations of peasants that are suggested by the milkmaid.

The warm-colored breads and the resonating orange of the milkmaid's jacket combine to suggest wholesomeness and goodness. Wilson[7] cites research showing how the human response to color may be processed with other reference frames in the brain and is epigenetic in origin. I have read in a forgotten source of studies of human subjects that led to the use of muted shades of orange in restaurants for their decor and accessories to stimulate feelings of health and appetite. The prominent, black cleft that divides the jacket gives a sense of thickness and substance, and enforces the black of the pitcher's orifice. Directed by prehensions of wholesome-

Figure 61. Herb Greene, *The Becoming of Consciousness* (Detail)

ness and sustenance, this cleft also reminds me of a great furrow in a harvest field of golden grain in a painting by Breughel that also projects wholesomeness and mystery. The incisive thickness of the furrow is consonant with the depth of the black shadow that separates the coif from the face, the thick crusty breads, and the bulk of the woman herself. Evocative harmonies are fleshed out by processing feelings of substance, sturdiness, deified light, bodily warmth, social value, and so on. The basket and bright metal container on the wall seem to call out for some other conceptual novelty.

Although this is difficult to see in the reduced scale of a reproduction, the woman's face shows Vermeer's use of open bulging curves to shape and qualify eyes, chin, lips and nose. In context with the bulky body, the peasant costume, the rough-textured face and the breads, these shapes suggest a coarse, earthy, "peasant" character. At the same time, these circular shapes diminish to become spherical, pointillist beads of light, probably adapted from their appearance in Vermeer's pinhole light box, with which he highlights and unifies other features of the painting, such as the breads, basket and the pitcher. The resulting breads create a gamut or range of similar incidents to which one can attribute the unifying conceptual feeling of "many into one." The artful stage-setting of vessels, breads and the peasant garments interweaves other harmonies of color, shape and subject. For instance, the breads range from full rounds to small pointed loaves shaped like peasant wooden shoes.

Finally, I have omitted what is for me a major consideration in viewing this painting. The complexity of harmonies and inferences, and the sculptural power of the milkmaid's figure and face, seem a unique accomplishment in art. I can think of no other artist who has created an invention so powerful, so different from his other work and so fully mysterious. After all that I can say by way of explanation, I am held by the work's inexhaustible presence. Speaking for myself, Millet's peasants and Rodin's tragic burghers seem almost simplistic by comparison. My appreciation for the Vermeer is heightened by this propositional feeling. And yet mystery is the recurring feeling as I analyze this milkmaid. I do not believe that the painting projects a single originary message or overview. Rather, there is a dialectic of feelings moving through Vermeer's intense expressions of the sanctified, wholesomeness, beatific light, sustenance, power, bodily life, and so forth. For all the feelings of cohesion in the painting, to me, Vermeer's milkmaid intentionally projects the idea that there are limits in our ability to consciously apprehend the world. This proposition forms a poignant and profound contrast to Vermeer's ability to project "the light of the mind" as a rational yet mysterious presence, to borrow from Kenneth Clark's praise of the *View of Delft*. This light, reflected in the concentration of clarity, order and sanctity amidst the projection of pervading mystery that surrounds the origins of meaning of such objects as the incisive shadow that sets off the face from the luminous coif, the beaded shoe-breads, and the deified peasant face, expresses the contrasts that make this work so special.

Figure 62. Herb Greene, Untitled (Detail)

In this detail of a collage with Sayyed Nayyer Reza's photograph of a nine-year-old girl and an elderly friend in Lahore, Pakistan (figure 62), I am most interested in the older woman's face. How do we assemble such positive feelings of kindness and love from such vague yet subtle and precise cues: the dark, tiny shadows of her eye and apparently toothless mouth? On close inspection the eye of the young girl contributes equally. When one zooms in to eliminate hair, garments and all other details except the above mentioned, the strength of this realization of love and kindness does not lose any of its power. Perhaps it gains power. Of first importance to me is the wrinkling of the elder woman's face. It is as if this detail sets a substrate conditioning all other contrasts, such as the meaning of the gaze and the positive smile. The leathery texture of wrinkles can remind of elephants as well as of the aging body and warmth of spirit within. I keep having to push away negative prehensions: the picture is too sentimental, too obvious. Returning to the aged profile I continue to affirm my enjoyment. There is something about referencing the mental domain of age and its associations with oncoming death that forms necessary contrasts to the domain of the richness of human life indicated by the smile and look. It is as if our experience of the events in the photograph is strengthened when we can harmonize thoughts and feelings about what a thing is with what it is not.

According to recent findings in neurobiology, we would be shortsighted to think of our responses to experience, including art,

as final closures, and I would not interpret Whitehead's use of the terms "final satisfaction" and "many into one" as anything more than our desire and need for temporary closures as we process feelings in our higher experiences and move on to our next thought. During a lifetime we alter contexts and find new vantage points in our response to art. During my mid-twenties, enamored of Bartok, Stravinsky and Ravel, and resistant to norms of artistic excellence from the Renaissance to the Moderns, I found pomposity in passages of Beethoven's Fifth Symphony, as did Wallace Stegner's narrator in his novel, *Crossing to Safety*. By my mid-fifties I had acquired most all of Beethoven's music. I had gradually become enamored of his heroic spirit, intellectual range, lyricism, and the historical, socio-political contexts in which he wrote. These latter interpretations provided reference frames that allowed me to position "pomposity" as a negative prehension subservient to my "evolving" subjective aim.

Whitehead's concept of subjective aim does not lead to final, fixed closures. It, too, involves the process of continual regrouping of connections in the mind. Wilson[8] asks who, or what, within the brain monitors its vast networking apparatus.

> No one. Nothing. The scenarios are not seen by some other part of the brain. They just are. Consciousness is the virtual world composed by the scenarios. There is not even a Cartesian theatre . . . no single locus of the brain where the scenarios are

played out in coherent form. Instead, there are interlacing patterns of neural activity within and among particular sites throughout the forebrain, from cerebral cortex to other specialized centers of cognition such as the thalmus, amygdalla, and hippocampus. There is no single stream of information brought together by an executive ego. There are instead multiple streams of activity, some of which contribute momentarily to conscious thought and then phase out. Consciousness is the massive coupled aggregates of such participating circuits. The mind is a self-organizing republic of scenarios that individually germinate, grow, evolve, disappear, and occasionally linger to spawn additional thought and physical activity.

CHAPTER TWENTY-FIVE

Creativity / Novelty

Whitehead uses the term "novelty" to mean anything that is fresh, original and innovative. Novelty runs the gamut from good to bad, but it never refers to the cheap or merely clever. In Whitehead, novelty is critical to the valuation of a concrescence.

A concrescence is always becoming and never completely in the past. It is at once a creature (Whitehead's word for a mental creation produced by the body-mind of an enduring personality) and a condition for creating novelty. It is unfettered, and includes the enduring personality's experience of the entire world. Whitehead holds the aims and selections of a concrescence to be inexplicable without a creative force within us derived from the universe from which we have evolved. This force, expressed in mental operations, directs choice in a reaction to the world of possibilities. It governs aesthetic and moral consistency and the origination of novelty during a concrescence. Whitehead refers to this agency as "the consequent nature of God" in deference to the historical concept of God as the giver and organizer of life, and as the agency that is necessary to evoke the intensities of harmony leading to realizations of beauty, moral feeling, peace, truth and other higher mental satisfactions. Whitehead links creative novelty to the transfer of past knowledge and feeling to the comparison of choice realized in the concrescent processes in the present.

"Apart from God, eternal objects [knowledge of the past yet to be realized in the present] . . . in the actual world would be relatively nonexistent for the concrescence in question. For effective relevance requires agency of comparison, and agency belongs exclusively to actual occasions," which are the prerequisites for creating the actual entities necessary to make concrescences and comparisons. Whitehead's metaphor of God as an agent of comparison and aesthetic and moral decision differs from the Judeo-Christian maker and ruler of everything in the universe. Whitehead's God is indifferent to the demise of the dinosaurs by a meteor strike or the death, pain and destruction caused by a Hitler. Rather, God is "the subjective form of refreshment and companionship; the notion arising from the timeless source of all order."[1]

Whitehead describes God as an immanent potential requiring human imagination to divine the requisite cause for aesthetic and moral consistency, which continues to develop in an evolving world. Unlike our very remote ancestors, we look out to a myriad of colored shapes of autumn leaves or the play of surf and process these as experiences of aesthetic value. We are more than practical beings when we spend tens of thousands of hours meticulously cleaning oil spill-soaked sea birds. We are affirmed when we see moral good prevail over evil, and when we choose to nurture and cherish feelings of love. We can suffuse the shapes of the human body with complex objectifications and mathematical harmonies to create art. We have feelings of attraction for another combined with conceptual feelings of falling in love. Even the recognition of a gorgeous sunset involves such conceptualization and realization. We feel the color, space and light based on appetition in the present to continue our enjoyment. We entertain a datum or focus that is conceptually prehended. That datum may include the preservation of feelings (initiated by conceptual feelings) about the causes of the saturation of the sunset's color, or our knowledge of our need for the sun's energy. Thus God's immanence in the world is verified by an urge toward harmony in the future based on appetition in the present.

The self-determination of feelings and concepts into concrescence and satisfaction is always imaginative in its origin. The causation of the process is the inflow of the actual world, characterized by our choices among particular components with their own feelings and intensities. The effective unities of the subject are felt and reenacted by this fresh and novel concrescent subject. The reenactment phase, however, merely conforms to the patterns of the past. The new subjective valuation requires the work of novel conceptual feeling. Here, aesthetic, moral and other choices conditioned by the enduring personality come into play.

In the twentieth century, in reaction against historical representations of the religious and spiritual in Western culture and to swim in the "sensationalist-objectivist" mainstream, many modern artists have avoided all but the most abstract symbols of spirit. Yet most of us ascribe spiritual values to the beauty and wonder we find in a nature which includes ourselves. Nature is a process that, to most of us, seems miraculous and awesome, a process with which we want to express empathy and in which we want to participate. But some among the elites that champion modern art are like mid-century Marxists. They have been, at best, indifferent to fostering expressions of this ever-present human urge, favoring instead an agenda stuck with a God-is-dead materialist ideology. The events of the Anne Frank photo and the Redon print in my collage (figure 63) provide a sense of life's renewal, of spiritual values, and a venue for a Whiteheadian interpretation of God I think many viewers can appreciate.

Redon has turned his drawing on its side, as if he suddenly

sensed a feeling projecting out from Ophelia's upturned head through the cluster of flowers. This decision indicates novel conceptual feeling in Redon's invention. On its side, the vase of flowers becomes dissociated from the expected, and evokes a sense of drifting and passage. Redon's *Ophelia* expresses both inward feeling and feeling projected outward, while allowing us to overtly behold the process. Ophelia's eyes are closed, her face directed as if following or projecting both internal force and the flowers themselves. The body as a container, which this "force" can either emanate from or penetrate into, is a root metaphor of a conceptual feeling that Ophelia and the flowers are caught up in some ecstatic and spiritual flow of energy.

One can feel certain affinities between Redon's *Ophelia* and Anne Frank. Anne looks out, aspiring, expectant, with hints of the portentous. She appears young, sensitive and intelligent. Dark circles under her eyes contribute a certain gravity and morbidity to her expression, just as the dark spaces between Redon's flowers suggest a gravity and mystery that underlies their warm, glowing colors. Whiteheadian "vectors" of feeling within us move from the warm, mysterious, dreamy face of Ophelia to the flowers, and from the flowers to her face. One searches for correspondences among the events of flowers, Ophelia, the preening, "caring" birds and Anne Frank. There is something spiritual and poignant in Anne Frank's expression, with its prehensions of youth, expectation, longing, searching, and a gaze to a future world. I eliminate my prehension

that the right side of Anne's hair looks rather like the profile of a black spaniel in order to feel the possibility of redemption through the suffering that I identify with Anne. I also eliminate prehensions of the commercialization of Anne Frank by playwrights and others who have "modulated" her diary and story to soften and hide her witness to the darker realities of human barbarism and cruelty in a living present. I feel an element of sadness associated with Anne's death can be transformed into an element of triumph, because the loss of her life, which held so much promise, has so positively effected the lives of millions through her diary and her photograph. I also feel triumph in the Redon, a sense of imagination realizing a vision of the spirit. The photograph of preening gulls in figure 63 shows the interdependence of creatures — the necessity of caring that evolution has produced — and reminds us, in particular, that white sea birds, with their graceful, soaring wings, have become symbols of spirit and release in human culture.

How to explain the resulting harmonized feelings that refer to such a diversity of events? It is inexplicable without recourse to Whitehead's principle of novel concrescence, the elimination of unwanted detail to produce aesthetic consistency. Finding consistencies between the Redon, gulls and Anne Frank does not constitute an exercise in indulging my romantic imagination. Such consistencies are public, available to everyone, to be reconstituted by the creativity of individual viewers.

Through the harmonies of prehensions, the ideas of quest,

Figure 63. Herb Greene, *Homage to Anne Frank*

hope, triumph and redemption conveyed by the Anne Frank photo can commingle with the spiritual movement, ecstasy and triumph in Redon's *Ophelia*.

Most people feel that there is some kind of directing agency in the world of ecological dependency, and that a world of abundant and incredible natural beauty is not wholly explicable by mechanistic models. Whitehead's principle represents a rational explanation of this world without depending on supernatural causes. Neither capricious nor punishing, Whitehead's God is capable of preserving all that is valued by the human mind, transforming disjoined multiplicity with its oppositions and diversities into concrescent unity. Here, Whitehead reveals his ties to Coleridge and the English Romantics. By the very nature of the drama of life and death on Earth, most of us will always seek deeply harmonized symbols of this kind of unity in the contexts of death, rebirth, triumph and redemption.

In his emphasis on the role of novel appetition, Whitehead tells us that growth of intensity in this function is marked by prehensions of theories. In the Anne Frank photograph I prehend aspiration, intelligence and morbidity. I have an appetite to support or enlarge these themes to convey my prehension of theory (a propositional feeling). The components of Anne Frank's facial expression act as a structured society to which I attach a host of feelings — feelings about her being in the world and about her death at the hands of the Nazis. I am reminded that we carry these potentials, or ingredients

of feelings, within ourselves, to be reconstituted and released by some intense coordination of their symbols that are appropriate to our concrescence. This snapshot of Anne Frank, with her uplifted head, out-looking gaze and dark circles around her eyes, taken in an automatic photograph booth, has helped to immortalize Anne for millions. To me, the other photos taken in the same series made her look like a teenager, perhaps Jewish, perhaps impish, but without the distinctions that move me and, I presume, the editors of *Life* and many of their readers.

We can feel a sense of worth beyond the merely perceived events in Anne's photo. We can enjoy this sense as an overpowering element in the realization being experienced. In my processing of the image of Anne, it is "in this way that the immediacy of sorrow and pain is transformed into an element of triumph. This is the notion of redemption through suffering, which haunts the world. . . . Thus the universe is to be conceived as attaining the active self-expression of its own variety of opposites — of its own freedom and its own necessity, of its own multiplicity and its own unity, of its own imperfection and its own perfection. All the 'opposites' are elements in the nature of things, and are incorrigibly there. The concept of 'God' is the way in which we understand this incredible fact — that what cannot be, yet is."[2]

For Whitehead each category of existence requires other types of existence for its explanation. There is a sense that we cannot know or feel a thing without incorporating contrasts with its opposite and a gamut of things in between. The discordant multiplicity of actual things "requiring each other and neglecting each other, utilizing and discarding, perishing and yet claiming life as obstinate matter of fact, requires an enlargement of the understanding to the comprehension of another phase in the nature of things. In this later phase, the many actualities are one actuality, and the one actuality is many actualities. Each actuality has its present life and its immediate passage into novelty; but its passage is not its death. This final phase of passage in God's nature is ever enlarging itself."[3]

According to Whitehead's interpretation of process, each cognitive act has the potential to reassemble and unify our universe. In the Anne Frank photo, the unification can involve the expression of a particular immediacy of expectation, hope and suffering. This realization perishes, only to enlarge itself by becoming ingredient in the evolutionary stream of thought that produces our evaluative feelings of Anne, an evolution that has come a distance in sensitivity and understanding from our ancestors of even fifty centuries past. For Whitehead, the highest realization open to the human mind is the free creation of actualities involving contrasting actual entities, such as we find in the photograph of Anne Frank.

CHAPTER TWENTY-SIX

Symbolic Reference

We usually think of a symbol as an object that stands for a meaning not explicitly present in the object. A dove holding an olive branch, for example, is a symbol of peace. For Whitehead, symbol making starts not with "dove branch-peace" as a known entity in a lexicon, but earlier in the perceptual process, with the transfer of meaning from the vast embodied background of causal efficacy into the bare sensa of presentational immediacy. We tend to oversimplify perceptual objects by failing to distinguish the complicated transfer of meaning between these modes. In visual presentational immediacy, shapes and colors of the dove and branch give no information about the past or future. They merely illustrate discrete portions of the presented, perceived duration of events. The past influences the concrescence of actual unities of experience and our projections about their future. The interplay of the perceived data and the interpretations of my concrescence of "blue sky," where the prehensions of the color blue, atmosphere, space, light and underlying earth share common components among their sense data and their meanings, provides an example.

In Whitehead's scheme, the process of concrescence, directed by a datum and subjective aim, finishes as a creative act. My determination that the blue sky signifies a good day for a picnic, continuing drought, blue spectral scattering when the sun is high or sensual enjoyment, or can act as a symbol of "good life," demonstrates such creativity. Further, at its inception the act of concrescence utilizes the pure modes of presentational immediacy and causal efficacy, which are not subject to judgment and are incapable of error. However both possibilities exist in making symbolic reference. For instance, I have the same feelings of blue sky when looking at the sky reflected in a mirror; or depending on whether I am hungry or frightened, I see a food object or a monster in a Rorschach blot. In general, human perception is subject to error because it is interpretive.

The animal body of the viewer from which the perspectives are focused is the origin from which the scheme of extensive determinations of our past or "embodied" experience of sky, space, the color blue or scientific knowledge of blue is finally constituted. Hence the difficulty of recovering non-biased, "objective" meaning from this vast meandering scheme through the limitations of human mental equipment. Yet, as we must, we accept our present determinations of blue sky as if built upon an objective foundation of experience. While sense perception dominates our experience, Whitehead observes our main interest lies in hidden, embodied experience.

> It stands out that what we want to know about, from the point of view of either curiosity or of technology, chiefly resides in these aspects of the world [schemes of extensive determination] disclosed in causal efficacy; but what we can distinctly register is chiefly to be found among the percepta in the mode of presentational immediacy.[1]

Presentational immediacy is an outgrowth of causal efficacy. It requires high-grade symbolic reference, with variety and vivid distinctness of sense presentation. While low-grade organisms, such as amoebas, respond to their environment by advancing, withdrawing and incorporating rudimentary subjective aim, as far as we can tell they do not engage in a process of symbolic transfer that enables parrots and chimpanzees to arrange colored blocks and learn hundreds of human words to make a variety of meaningful sentences from them. The more primitive types of experience are concerned with sense reception and not sense perception. It is only in sense perception, enjoyed by high-grade organisms, that the sensa are perceived as qualifying some external region of space. The initial response of visual perception is the transfer of feeling tones from the organism to these external regions of space

> The crude aboriginal character of direct perception is inheritance. What is inherited is feeling-tone with evidence of its origin: in other words, vector feeling tone. Thus perception, in this primary sense, is perception of the settled world in the past as constituted by its feeling-tones, and is efficacious by reason of those feeling-tones.[2]

The settled world of the past is carried into the present by eternal objects, such as the blueness of the sky. Symbolic reference requires that the connection between the two modes, presentational immediacy and causal efficacy, be effected by the identity of eternal objects ingredient in both of them. Blueness, which permeates components of the color, atmosphere and space of the blue sky, is such an eternal object.

Whitehead Applied to Dali

How might Whitehead's scheme, based an prehensions, feelings, transfer of the past via eternal objects, and the generation of symbolic reference out of causal efficacy be applied to the

Figure 64. Dali, *Soft Construction with Boiled Beans / Premonition of Civil War*

Figure 65. Goya, *Saturn* (Detail)

determinedly "bizarre" narratives of European Surrealist painting? Let us consider a Dali masterpiece, *Soft Construction with Boiled Beans* (figure 64), sometimes referred to as *Premonition of Civil War*. This painting is a near-overwhelming demonstration of creating thoughts and feelings of ecstasy, pain, destiny, decay, self-destruction, frenzy, fluctuations and reversals of meaning, the surface of the earth, sky, and other characterizations, such as the tiny "bourgeois" man whose "bust" appears at the top of the bony, gnarly, arachnid-like hand at lower left, and whose complex symbolic possibilities, fueled by the contexts of the painting, I will shortly take up in detail.

When I saw the original picture I was jolted by the sheer power of Dali's imagination and technique. This work overcame any doubt I had about his genius as a painter due to his notoriety for falling out of department store windows and into the newspaper headlines, and due to my concern that too many of his works seemed like "trade-mark productions" of his style rather than genuine explorations into the irrational and the unconscious. Among the ideas that *Soft Construction* gives us is the indelible ground of the earth's surface and the adjoining atmosphere as the ultimate stage for human existence. How many times have we thought of ourselves traversing or gazing out at this setting for our lives? Consider Dali's sky. Eternal objects of "hard" and "soft," saturated blueness and whiteness, pale, luminous and delicate whiteness, and "perfect" cloud detail in commanding spatial perspective transfer my past experience of clouds and sky into "solid" feelings of clouds and sky. I have prehensions of historic time, destiny and beauty in the handling of sky, clouds, light, shadow and form, which provide poignant contrasts to prehensions of the grotesque, decay and frenzied self-destruction. As I reflect on the painting I believe that Dali must have studied Goya's *Saturn* (figure 65) with empathy. Both paintings exhibit a Spanish ability to image self-destruction that connects me to Berger's insight on Picasso's "Spanish destruction," which was discussed in Chapter 2. The elongated and fluid "knee-arm-desert dune" at upper right of the Dali much resembles the attenuated knees and elbow of Goya's *Saturn*, except the Dali knee-leg stands on the torso of its dismembered body in mocking triumph. There is a prehension of the ridiculous in the Dali that parodies the frenzy of self-destruction. Such is the complexity of the embodied experience of strain feelings, body metaphors, propositional feelings (recognition of triumph in the standing leg) and categorizations of history and the world that causal efficacy can bring to one's concrescences of Dali's knee.

Like other painted objects in Dali's works, his compelling rendering of texture, shapes, colors and light give us prehensions of permanence, even from the sky. All the better to contrast with prehensions of decay in the human body merged with a desert landscape in which details become exposed bones, entrails, rocks, gnarled tree, human figures and "anamorphic-like" distortions of human skulls and facial profiles. Notice the bony face of the featured, stretched-back woman. The left side of her face is formed into a self-satisfied profile face, as if found in a cloud, while the jaw is formed into a fragmented skull. At bottom center of the painting is a limb-torso. At the left end of the torso is a head facing up that is decaying, bony and mountain ridged. A tiny, face-up, human profile with vacuous smile appears at the right end. The animated beans could be maggots scurrying for sustenance. All these forms are held together with an undeniable symphonic mastery of form and color.

Underlying Dali's essay is his preoccupation with a long history of European art that has attempted to show the objects of both actual vision and imagination as durable, substantive and concrete. Dali's "realistic" modeling of light and shade, and his black shadows that take on a graphic-symbolic life of their own — becoming caves, figures and sensuous, curving lines — will, I think, become ever less puzzling in their break from realism as expression of the subjective-objective duality, and of metaphor as the necessity of seeing things in terms of other things, becomes ever more recognized in culture. See the vise-grip of the grotesque hand — stony and gnarled, with human figures as fingers — squeezing, pulling the hyper-extenuated breast with engorged but spent nipple. This detail is powerfully orchestrated with the bony rock formations of the woman's neck and face, which is pulled back in a smile and grimace of sexual pleasure, as if the creature is in ecstasy over its own pain as it pulls itself apart. Notice how the neck-head formation sits on the shoulder-breasts-arm-leg image, where the shoulder and breasts complete a human figure supine on the sand. One can enjoy the sensuous outline and recognize the supine figure extending magically into the projecting arm-leg.

Are the abundant and intricately worked "subliminal" faces and figures in the face of Dali's woman structurally similar to the shadow-hand in the Vermeer? For me the question raises the problem of merely applying logical categories to the actual world without sensitivity to the varying contexts in which the "hidden" images are found.

There are structural similarities, but there are differences in the ways in which one applies values to the individual events in each painting. Believing, as I do, that both paintings exemplify peaks of human creative power, I am finally more sympathetic to the Vermeer. It is focused through a reference frame not of mere sentiment, but of projecting the feeling that optimism and spirituality are even more important for culture and human development than is the recognition of human anxiety, fear and our tendencies for self-destruction. There is a projection of Telesian tactility, or sense of touchable texture, in *Woman Holding a Balance,* encouraging feelings of affect that is lacking in Dali's *Premonition.* I am also more surprised and interested by the hidden hand in the Vermeer. The large scale of the hand and its unexpected juxtaposition with the "beatific" face of the woman strengthen my mapping of harmonized meanings. With the Dali, I know to look for "hidden" images and transformations as "rules of the game" stemming back to Giuseppe Arcimboldo in the sixteenth century, who was famous in Europe for composite human figures built up of plant and food objects, and whom Dali admired for his double images and fastidious technique. Thus we are in pulsing or calm dialogue with our subjective aims as

we commit to our apprehensions and satisfactions. Unlike my response to the Goya (figure 65), I lose some energy in my closures of Dali's projection of self-destruction because I have intermittent negative prehensions of the comic and the ridiculous intruding into his caricatured grotesques.

These comparisons are not to diminish Dali, who in this painting takes my breath away. Consider how we fill the bust of the "bourgeois" man with meaning (located at the top and center of the bony creature-hand at lower left). This tiny detail provides an excellent starting point for the symbol-making mind directed by datum (his cowed indifference and neutrality), superject (the self-ravaging human creature), and subjective aim (the terrors, subconscious underpinnings and ironies of human self-destruction). The viewer concludes that the man is neither held by the apparition's hand, nor does he appear to be standing on the land. We are not sure if the man is walking toward, backing away from, or is oblivious to the apparition. His body and head bow, suggesting humility and powerlessness. He is lighted and scaled to appear as if connected to the conventional scene of houses, villas and towns in the far distance. His rumpled suit and trim goatee suggest he is an urban "everyman," in thrall to Dali's pessimistic allegory of the human condition. Thus my preference for Vermeer only indicates that, because of my values, instincts and Whiteheadian lenses that assist me in examining my feelings, if I were allowed only one painting on a desert island it would have to be the Vermeer.

Figure 66. Herb Greene, *Senator Barkley at Buchenwald*

Senator Barkley at Buchenwald

Getting back to particulars of building symbolic reference: Figure 66 shows details of a collage with photographs of Senator Barkley, mannequin fingers and a Texas town square on a Saturday afternoon in 1939. Barkley stands over a stack of corpses at Buchenwald. In this collage I want to call attention to the interplay of presentational immediacy and causal efficacy in the process of deriving meaning. I have painted much of the space surrounding the photographs as a surface suggesting blotched skin and dirty sheets. The skin refers to the desiccated bodies in the photograph, and the sheets refer to the dirty clothes and tarpaulins that appear between the gaunt and attenuated limbs. Outlines of limbs, mannequin fingers, tattooed numbers and gray, yellow, umber, black and red colors are given in presentational immediacy. My intuition is that these facts and categories will lend direction and harmony to the implosion from causal efficacy. The grayed yellow for urine, sickness and the stigmatized Star of David, the red for blood and angst, tattooed numbers for Nazi dehumanization, and so forth. Other feelings and thoughts derived from causal efficacy could be: knowing that the skin of victims was sometimes stretched into lamp shades; that mannequin fingers and corpses are without feeling; and that stained sheets cover unspeakable acts. A severed tongue is caught on a bony projection, enforcing the idea of unspeakable acts. Blood, bones and body parts act as cues of the original data of the corpses, and of the human body that necessarily qualifies perception.

More than just protection against the cold, Barkley's layers of civilian clothing suggest to me democratic authority and something of civitas, in contrast to the ultimate degradation of the camp. He seems numb. His face, even at a distance, shows sadness and incredulity. The photograph of mannequin fingers suggests numbness, an eternal object consonant with feelings of numbness produced by Barkley's expression and a presumed response to the stack of corpses. A creature-like painted arm holds a tarpaulin, as if shielding bones, bodies and the emerging photograph of a Texas town square. This photo is a device to include feelings of the contemporaneous and disengagement, in contrast to the immediate fact of the Nazi horror. To me, it also serves as a reminder of the tribalisms, ignorances and prejudices of a world that looked away. Again, via the extensive continuum, such associations arising out of my concrescence count as objective experience in my understanding of the death camp scene.

In the photographs of Barkley and the Texas town square, there are correspondences between the isolated figure of Barkley and the solitary statue in the square. Their clothing and spatial settings support liminal feelings of authority and civitas. There is the bronze military officer and Barkley's layered clothing, which, in black and white, appears homogenous. My positive feelings for Barkley are influenced by my knowledge of his authority as a public representative, and the humanity of his facial expression. I include the town square primarily for its American prewar setting, and the people sitting or standing as single figures and in small groups, which allow for interpretations of insularity and disengagement. These allusions allow my feelings about American isolationism to contrast with feelings about the Nazi camp experience.

Repetitions and Symbolic Reference

In figure 67, *A Great Profile* with Vermeer's *Woman in Blue Reading a Letter*, one can experience feelings of awe from the fetus image, which reveals the forming eye, brain case, and the profile of well-developed features of fingers and face of a potential human not yet ready for thought or conscious action. The dark form directly surrounding the fetus head could be a womb or another head with a shape corresponding to the woman's head. The curving, light blue band with dark blue outline is a repetition of the beautiful profile of the woman's forehead and of a pregnant belly. One intention is to link the iconic Vermeer with contemporary knowledge of what is actually going on inside a woman's womb, with the potentialities of symbolic reference moving from one photograph to the other. For me, in conjunction with recognition of the pregnant woman and fetus, there are prehensions of timeless awe in Vermeer's accomplishment that can commingle with prehensions of awe we can feel in the Nilsson image. Repetitions of the "beautiful" profile in different contexts of fetus, womb and head hold our attention and give our mapping mind directions during the clash and integration of information given by the different contexts. The repetitions assist us to make fluid yet meaningful etymologies of meaning.

The Process of Symbolic Reference

Figure 68 shows a collage that includes Turner's *Burial of Sir David Wilkie*. During the initial stages of perception, derivations from the painting's data lack clear definition into subjects and objects. For example, as I take up the ship, water and sky I feel the ship's blackness ambiguously as deadening, absorbing and repelling. I feel a milky light in the background. The past has been lifted into the present, but without precise differentiations. I then feel an enhanced precision where symbolic transference has occurred among distinct shapes. For example, I recognize the sharp black sails from their edges, shapes and context with the ship, and the fiery reflection in context with the surrounding dark sea and the "detached" aft portion of the hull. The subtle actions of self-preservation among the actual entities "sail shapes," "masts" and "blackness" are becoming possible. In this later phase, flashes of conceptual originality appear. For example, I feel the fiery reflection as a vertical stabilizer that anchors the ship, emphasizing its strong feeling of stasis. I also feel the beauty of the luminous, milky sky as a contrast to the inky blackness of the ship and sails. The decisive blackness of the sails with their cutting shapes feels ominous, directed toward the idea of death (a flash of conceptual originality). This direction, given by my subjective aim, preserves my various feelings of death from blackness, burial scene, stasis and "piercing" shapes of sails.

The initial experience of milky white, blackness, strain feelings of the sails and the burial scene has been analyzed by my imagina-

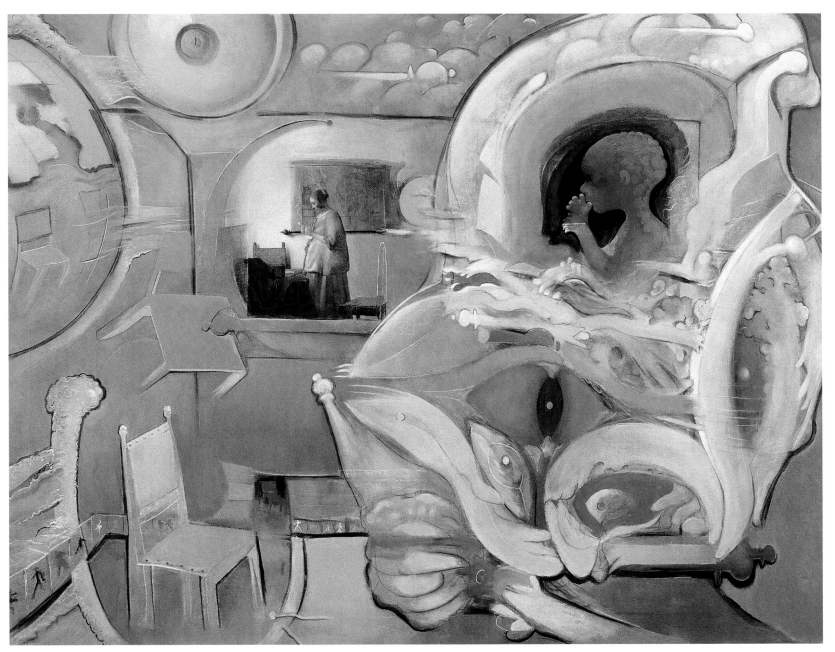

Figure 67. Herb Greene, *A Great Profile*

tive realizations of their potentialities. My experience has been reorganized by this imaginative enjoyment and by judgment. Whitehead holds that the growth of reason comes into play as critical judgment disciplines imaginative enjoyment.[3] This describes my feelings of motivation as I attempt to understand my interest in Turner's mastery.

Expressing the Idea of Symbolic Reference

Turner's rendition of ship's paraphernalia, both precise and vague, contains various incidents. I grasp these as an entity that stands for the "many." At the same time the unifying, fuzzy black color field contains a multiplicity of ship details that I can read as an entity of "one." The set "many into one" assists me to recognize a gamut of "vagueness to clarity" in Turner's painting. This gamut can apply to objects, such as the sharp black sails, the vague intimations of ship railings and deck equipment, and to further unseen "immanent" contents of causal efficacy. The gamut allows for strong details in the foreground — ship's hull, paddle wheel, sails that appear parallel to the picture to enforce the sense of stasis, drifting smoke and feeling of death, all recognized as actual entities — to refer to immanent possibilities. For example, the inky black circle of the paddle wheel can possibly be felt as a mysterious black sun that is setting on the horizon, a conceptual feeling that can strengthen the feelings of death and burial.

Outstanding among Turner's contributions to painting and aesthetics is his development of the painterly expression of the set "many into one" to the point of its isolation and appreciation as a concept. This is a contribution to the growth of reason in the discipline of imaginative enjoyment. Because of the degree of abstraction that Turner reached to convey this idea, he is among the important precursors of abstract modern art. Turner also stands directly in the line of artists leading to the design concept of a complex manifold uniting many things. In *The Burial of Sir David Wilkie*, the encompassing field of blackness, with its suggestive gradations and incidents, expresses the diversity in the world entering into higher conceptual feelings. Of course, many great art works — for example, medieval Hindu temples, "mountains" covered with sculptures of all of life's manifestations — powerfully express the concept of "many into one." But what we are concerned with here is the development of the idea into a principle of abstraction. Western culture is becoming aware that harmony starts from perception issuing from the body-mind. The recognition of sets, groupings, non-Euclidean geometry, indeterminacy, the concept of immanence and other ideas from the cosmology and mathematics of Western culture are entering into our criteria of critical judgment in the discipline of imaginative enjoyment.

Figure 68. Herb Greene, *Inscape*

CHAPTER TWENTY-SEVEN

Order

Wilson tells us that the dominating influence that spawned the arts was the need to impose order on the confusion caused by intelligence. As previously stated by Whitehead, order in our perceived world is different from the given world because we adapt the given world to attain an end. In his discussion of how the perceiving mind creates order during a concrescence, Whitehead proposes that during the processing of actual entities we experience gradations of intensity among them because we envision this end. We have hunches and beliefs that effect how we choose and discard prehensions among various possibilities affecting a concrescence.

In my collage *Athena* (figure 11), adaptation for an end is expressed by the "subject-superject," roughly phrased as "the species driven to self-destruction, in spite of human intelligence." Because of the "astral" texture of Athena's helmet, face and the surrounding background, the origins of this destruction can seem rooted in the very stuff of the universe. We have apperception, or non-sensuous perception, in the building of the superject. The actual entities —

abyss-eye slit, aggressive helmet, "astral" texture, lack of volition, intelligent profile and "doomed survivors" — can be felt with gradations of intensity within my superject, or dominant ideal, which is contemplating the human drive to self-destruction.

Whitehead's notes that, to obtain order, intensity in a concrescence must be heightened so that the various components in a nexus can enter into feeling as contrasts and are not dismissed as negative prehensions. This fact provides one reason why Whitehead's scheme works poorly when applied to minimalist art, such as Rothko's rectangles of color and Mies Van der Rohe's facades of flat rectangles at the Illinois Institute of Technology. Differences in the details of these examples are too minor to elicit strength of feeling through contrasts. There is very little stimulus from which order can be created. Within the nexus of Athena and her helmet, there is a lot of stimulus to create order. I feel that the falcons adorning the helmet seem a bit comic in their representation, but I dismiss this aspect into a negative prehension of low-grade importance while maintaining my positive prehension of raptors as human symbols of predatory and warlike attributes. I overwhelm my prehension of the comic by the strength and the gravity of my prehensions in the previously described details of Athena, such as the "black abyss" of the eye-slit. My dominant ideal, with its appetition, has been evident in each phase of my process for harmonizing my feelings while making symbolic reference.

Intensity in harmonization requires the massing of contrasts. For Whitehead, order is a generic term that cannot be applied to the vague. The components of order in a concrescence are not viable until they are identified in the conceptual feelings of consciousness. One of the more notable aspects of Whitehead's theory is that each definite phase — the demarcation of an actual occasion, of a duration or of a concrescence — refers to a specific ordering for that particular phase. Thus order in a felt actuality is always tied to an enduring personality that imputes its own ideal into the terms of the concrescence. The idea of an absolute order becomes untenable. The attainment of order is partial, because it includes specific elements of disorder in the components of a concrescence. Order always coexists with disorder. There is not just one ideal "order" which all actual entities should attain. Whitehead attributes the notion of one ideal order to pedantry and the over-moralization of thought, like the dogmatic acceptance of absolutes exemplified by a medievalist who believes in an image of God at the top of a Christmas tree with fixed hierarchies of ornaments below. Whitehead attributes the

notion of a dominant ideal order that is peculiar to each actual entity to Plato, whose ideas have influenced him.

Referring to Plato as a progenitor, Whitehead finds abstract ideas like order to be static, frozen and lifeless. Ideas come to life in a living intelligence, an intelligence that stems from the individual personality exercising subjective aim. Continuing to acknowledge his debt to Plato by reiteration, Whitehead states that concepts of harmony and mathematical relations are required to explain the connections among things, as they are transformed into unities. This proposition is fundamental to order. Plato uses the term "receptacle," the matrix for all becoming, to refer to the vehicle in which connections among things in the world are made. The receptacle imposes a common relationship on all that happens, *but it does not impose what that relationship will be.* Whitehead has built on these ideas with his theory of prehensions and feelings within the extensive continuum. These ideas are in my mind as I attempt to create an image associated with a superject of order as it develops within my particular "mental space-time."

In my collage, *Plato's Receptacle* (figure 14), curving rectangles of the off-white passage generate a manifold, a symbol of the receptacle. I have selected warped rectangles as units to build up the manifold because their planes and boundaries appear as pieces of a continuum harmonizing with the wall plane, the map and its divisions, the back of the chair, the planes of the letter and the book that appears at the end of the table. The curvatures in the collage are

Figure 69. Frank Lloyd Wright, *Freeman House*

influenced by scientific conjectures about the bending of light rays passing through magnetic fields and the effectiveness of non-Euclidean geometry. The curves also express the body, sensuality and the urge toward Eros — ideas that suggest to me how I should "shape" my "receptacle."

I attempt to create a unifying "plenum-receptacle" that responds to the events in the collage. The plenum has been cut away to reveal a fetus, as if in a womb. Signs of female anatomy worked into the plenum lie in close proximity to the fetus. The form of the white plenum is designed to appear as a possible continuation of the "shaped" space in the painting. The asymmetry of the plenum and its adaptation to various events — globe, map, fetus and pregnant woman — is supposed to suggest that order arises out of the particular geometries, ideas and associations that are initiated by the events in the collage, as well as from my imagined, preferred geometry represented by curving lines and warping planes.

The architecture of Frank Lloyd Wright constitutes one of the most successful aesthetic expressions of a "receptacle." In the Millard and Freeman houses (1920-24) located in Hollywood, California, Wright creates a manifold out of small, sculpted, concrete blocks that form the space of the house, giving a powerful sense of the many becoming unified in the one. The diverse features of piers, soffits, walls, borders to wood floors, and beams of these Wright houses are all defined by the intricate blocks, some solid and some perforated, in which Wright's many harmonized applications illustrate adapta-

tion for the attainment of ends. The expression of continuity that unifies all the differentiations of form is one such end. In the Millard exterior, the delicate, sparkling texture and the vertical lines of the patterned blocks are in harmony with the scale, light, shadow and verticality of the surrounding vegetation. The mass of the house, which could be obdurate and off-putting if plain surfaced, instead feels scintillating and life-enhancing.

Both here and in the Freeman interior (figure 69), the purpose and meaning of the "manifold-receptacle" seems evident. The device fosters a conceptual feeling of order capable of entering into the superject conditioning our response. For example, we can be reminded of the reference frames of immanence, continuity and change — primary tenets of organic theory that Wright so often expounded along with relationship to the site and the expression of materials. In the interior of the house we experience the ordering of contrasts of light that stimulate our innermost nerve, from the pinpricks of the free yet ordered small perforations to the expanse of the visually free, mitred-glass corners of the room. The feeling of mastery in Wright's expression of the manifold and of light is so mingled with the enjoyment of scale, texture, space and notions of dwelling as if in a protected cave opening out to free vistas, and of resonances with a past that includes pre-Columbian references, that when one experiences the house there is a richness, indeed, a magnificence of ordering which strengthens these enjoyments.

A ruin as metaphor is an example of the plenum concept

used as an ordering device for architecture that includes the works of thousands of citizens participating in the building and design process over generations and centuries. Figure 70 shows an elevation drawing of a hypothetical center for government services located in a large, Southwestern city. Private and public office buildings that serve the bureaucracy are designed by individual architects. These buildings surround and connect to an elliptical-shaped courtyard formed by massive, nonparallel walls that are designed as features of ongoing public art. The walls have resemblances to local land and sedimentary rock formations, and allude to the ancient architecture of pre-Columbian America, Native American cliff dwellings, ancient Rome, and ethnic references deemed appropriate by the citizens of the city. The interiors and exteriors of the walls are designed as a continuing exhibition of the city's and region's history and its cultural arts and crafts. The intention here is to provide an ongoing narrative and ornament, and to include a high degree of public participation with spontaneous and indeterminate outcomes.

This building program aims to establish an American counterpart to the expression of craftsmanship, communal participation and cosmology in great buildings and spaces that we admire from the history of civilization, places such as the Piazza San Marco and Salisbury Cathedral. In this case, our cosmology respects the modern Whiteheadian view that some aspects of any event can be coordinated with some aspects of any other, and stemming from Heisenberg and quantum theory, both determinacy and indetermi-

nacy are required to establish how any event comes into being and how its future can be known. Thus in conceiving the building program, physical theory informs social and aesthetic theory, in that expression of democratic participation with future unpredictability becomes a principal goal to be achieved in the symbolic form.

The aesthetic and psychological underpinnings of the project are best explained by Professor Arnold Weinstein in his lectures, *The Soul & the City: Art, Literature, and Urban Life*.[1] Weinstein describes how Freud, interested in tapping and understanding unconscious layers of experience, conceived the city of Rome as a palimpsest with layers of script (buildings and sites) underneath the surface. To reproduce all the layers at once is not possible in physical reality, but is achievable in memory, language and art. A plenary vision of ruins of the city becomes a stimulus to find the "ruins" of the mind. This allows a recuperation of the destruction caused by the passage of time, reversing entropy. The artful image of the city's ruins helps us to recover the origins and stories of one's life. Thus the forms of the government center need to encourage the individual mind to become archaeological in intention. To retrieve a history of time, birth, death and rebirth.

The political intent of the program is both populist and elitist. The ornamental surfaces and displays include a wide spectrum of artistic contributions, ranging from the works of school children and art therapy classes for the elderly, to the works of master artists and contributions by historical societies. All such works would be

Figure 70. Herb Greene, Government Center for Tucson

done with the supervision of arts and architectural facilitators. Periodic replacement of selected surface ornament ensures fresh commentary, while the sale of select replaced pieces in the private sector fosters interest in antiques and crafts.

The method of building proposes a synthesis of our present high technology, an intermediate technology suited to small groups and special objectives, and the return of individual expression as ornament on architecture. The accretion of popular arts and crafts, together with the modification of spaces and forms designed to welcome alterations, make the structure a vehicle for the expression of cultural memory and renewal — a metaphor for the passage of time.

The architecture described could also serve as a long-lasting core and a nucleus for private development to increase tax revenues and improve quality of life. It can be designed as a backdrop for arts fairs, a crafts center, music, dance, theater and political rallies, and become the focus of tourism. Planning, execution and installation of major projects for ornament can be televised, subscribed, and then installed with ceremony.

Because I see the over-thick walls expressing mass and substance in contrast to the thin and glassy forms of much contemporary urban architecture, the Roman allusion seems to fit my predilection for mass, texture and history. (I very much admire Roman aqueducts, Roman brickwork and H. H. Richardson's massive Romanesque libraries, for the qualities of their stone, artisanship

and historical allusion.) The actual walls of the project would be made of concrete cast in shaped styrofoam molds with integral color and ornamental inserts made of ceramics, or any material that will weather acceptably.

Important masses of planting with fountains and waterfalls would be integral as ecologically-designed features. Restaurants, bookshops and craft sales, as well as galleries, are among the more obvious functions with potential for incorporation into the structure.

Again, the important objective aims to provide an architectural metaphor of continuity over centuries, while incorporating indeterminate participation and aesthetic and narrative contributions, and by making existential connections to the city that signify both stability and change. The understanding of order must necessarily be complex to encourage and satisfy the participation of our diverse population while accommodating an aesthetic expression of our knowledge of geometry, architectural tectonics, social psychology, mental process and architectural form.

There are precedents for such a structure. Lucien Kroll's work in France and Belgium shows what a talented and charismatic architect, as facilitator for the design decisions of contributors, has accomplished. The subways of Stockholm under the direction of Per Reimers, which utilized artists in the total design process, are also impressive. The ecological, social and economic implications, such as the creation of meaningful jobs beyond current free-market

Figure 71. Herb Greene, *Study for a Collage with Sartre and Giacometti*

opportunities, and a change in the current politics of the arts, suggested by this brief are important considerations that require argument beyond the scope of this writing.

In closing this chapter I want to comment on making order, stimulated by my prehensions of humor in an unfinished study, figure 71, for a collage that includes Cartier-Bresson's photographs of Jean-Paul Sartre and the sculptor, Giacometti. The latter is shown setting up an exhibition of his monumental and emaciated human figures. Watching a documentary film on Cartier-Bresson, I was captivated by his tall, thin and lithe body. He moved across the streets of Paris with the spring of a water bug. One wonders where and how he was standing when he took the picture of Sartre, which shows him from an angle that exaggerates his short stature in contrast to the tall man facing him. With the Giacometti we have, again, the height of the camera position. There are potential prehensions of humor in scanning the "short" statures of each artist in their respective surroundings.

Sartre appears worried. "Reflective" would be inadequate as a descriptive term because of the deep furrows in his brow. His eyes are intense, directed, concerned and definitely cocked. Our embodied experience sees cocked eyes as not natural, odd, and with potentials for humorous readings when mapped on to domains of reference, such as interpretations of right conduct and philosophy, which we associate with Sartre. Sartre's mouth is downturning — a sign of negative emotion. Prehensions of worry can seem at odds

with prehensions of Sartre's leisurely grasp of his pipe, his comfortable jacket with luxurious sheepskin collar and his "natty" scarf. For me there is something of a mismatch with these prehensions of comfort and urbanity with certain of our expectations of Sartre: his voyage with communism, history as a soldier, international intellectual force, activist and famous philosopher with his theory of bad faith, constant choice and decisive action in human affairs.

Giacometti leans forward. We know he is taller even though he looks short because of the camera angle, his bent posture, and the optical contrast with his super-elongated, sculptured figures. His rumpled suit and outbursting hair with textured outlines harmonize with the ethereal, attenuated figures and their eroded bodies. What we have here is another example of Cartier-Bresson's genius in recognizing and harmonizing formal visual patterns, such as textures, positions and outlines, to help us set off our awareness of deeply embodied states of being and knowing. Sartre looks like he habitually takes on the world's problems with outwardly directed seriousness and angst, although he may be losing steam as signs of middle age mingle with signs of comfort in our consciousness. With his sculptures, Giacometti gives us a commanding and dignified presence emphasizing the aloneness and vulnerability of the individual psyche. A near definitive expression of European and Sartrean postwar existentialism is apparent. My view is that Cartier-Bresson has recognized something of intellectual exaggeration in a serious sense that determines the outcomes of works by both Sartre and Giacometti. This conclusion may be in error, but at least Cartier-Bresson has recognized exaggerations and inconsistencies across experiential domains that enable us to find components of humor.

There is always exaggeration and distortion to prove a point in art. Even the *View of Delft* (with "natural" buildings, roofs, water and sky) which Clark describes as unaffected by any *parti-pris,* custom, convention or stylistic artifice, or the *Head of a Young Girl* (vivid lips, mouth and eyes, but no eyebrows) are distorted. They contain Picasso's "lies," or distortions that tell the "truth." But this is not to disparage existentialism in the 'fifties, as I might the sentimental romanticism of much nineteenth-century art. Personally, I find great interest in the European, and particularly French, intellectual tradition, which treats subjective states with extreme objectivity. Barthes' fondness for his mother and Descartes' separation of body from mind blend with Sartre's insistence on continuous conscious decision making and action in spite of the overwhelmingly complex animal and intellectual motivations that affect most human doubts, loyalties and actions, and that produce our innumerable compromises, inactions and wanderings. Much as my own feelings of pragmatism are incompatible with the idealism of much of what I take to be tenets of Sartrean existentialism, *vive la difference* as I attempt to find order focused by the goal of attempting to understand what I am seeing in terms of contrasts and identities through prehensions of physiognomy, humor, art, philosophy and history.

My primary addition to figure 71 is a cartoon frontal view of a long-headed Giacometti with "wild" hair that attempts to resemble both sheepskin and neural tissue. Notice the sharp leather triangles that terminate Sartre's pocket. The up-down arrow made by these pocket patches induce me to make arrows every which way. This is a conceptual reach on my part, a response to making Sartrean decisions all day long. Whether I can redo this sketch into a form acceptable to me remains to be seen.

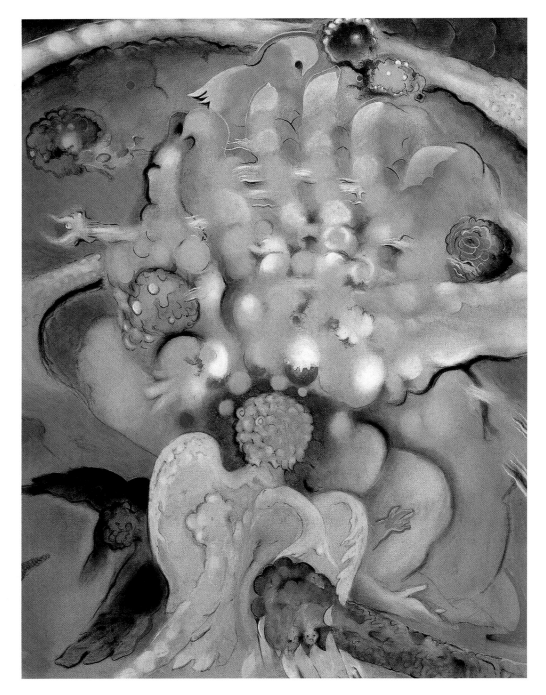

Figure 72. Herb Greene, *Icarus / Daedalus*

Epilogue

The noted arts theorist, Rudolph Arnheim,[1] sees the incompleteness of our mental imagery as a strength. It allows us to speculate about the image rather than replicating its exact form. As the mind has developed to search for significant form, it has a readiness to grasp such form from sketchy and incomplete cues. We can consider this characteristic of perception as it pertains to imagination. The power to imagine, with all its untold possibilities, is undoubtedly our greatest intellectual asset. And yet, when we consider actual attempts in the search for significant form in the works of individual artists, one can't help but notice the self-imposed limitations of the artist. Even a mold-breaking genius, such as Picasso, adept in sculpture, drawing, painting, other genres and multiple styles, faced discernible limits in his formal styles and what he expressed with them.

Will image manipulation by computers free our individual limitations? One of the mental and visceral thrills that I have experienced within the decade is seeing on television a computer image of familiar frontal view of Einstein's head. The accuracy of the details went beyond realism. The vast number and blending of pixels, and the bright light of the screen, produced an illuminated image that one could seemingly walk through and inhabit. But while I was excited by the image, I have yet to see computer art that has deeply moved me even in the special effects of movies. As I begin to work on a computer I can see possibilities in the blurs, stretches, clones, masks, blendings, changing perspectives and overlays of images that it allows. Computers and new imaging technology undoubtedly stimulate our imagination and offer many new opportunities for creating images.

But technology alone was not responsible for the stained glass at Chartres, and I doubt that computers, of themselves, will produce art that deeply moves us. We are moved by expressions of life and reality, colors and sensations, in context with already deeply-harmonized subjects and objects, those Whiteheadian "its" and our idealizations of them subsumed with appropriate mathematical pattern. I only wish I could return in a hundred years to see if such expressions have been accomplished with the aid of computers.

In the meantime, I find it exciting and gratifying to see recent scientific work, such as Edelman's and Damasio's interpretations of the neural mechanism. As Damasio writes,[2] when minded brains appeared, they developed to ensure the survival of the body as effectively as possible. Nature provided the solution of representing the outside world in terms of the modifications it causes in the body proper. Damasio and others anticipate the creation of representations of the structures of biochemical regulation in the brain stem and cortices, the viscera, the musculoskeletal frame, the muscular mass and the skin, the organ that constitutes the organism's body. Rather than diminishing the sense of self that some fear will result from advancing science, as with Nilsson's magnifications of the interior structures of the body, Vermeer's creative use of the *camera obscura*, and Degas' studies with the camera, such representations are likely to inspire new visions of life and humanity in art and enlarge our understanding of the self, as well as the world.

References

Chapter 1 Motives and Methods

1. Key, W. B. *Subliminal Seduction* (New York: Prentice-Hall 1973).
2. Levy, Andrew, "Play Will Make You Free: Reprising The Triumph of The Will in Chicago's Nike Town" in *The Americanization of The Holocaust*, ed. Hilene Flanzbaum (Baltimore: Johns Hopkins, 1999) pp. 211-224.
3. Edelman, Gerald M. in *Nature's Imagination* (New York: Oxford 1995) pp. 101-18.
4. Clark, Kenneth *The Nude* (Princeton: Princeton University Press 1956) p. 140.
5. Bateson, Gregory *Mind and Nature* (New York: Bantam Books 1979) p. 131.
6. Wilson, Edward O. *Consilience* (New York: Knopf 1998) pp. 127, 157, 246-7.
7. Price, Lucien *Dialogues of Alfred North Whitehead* (Boston: Little, Brown and Company 1954).
8. Noll, Richard *The Aryan Christ: The Secret Life of Carl Jung* (New York: Random House 1997).
9. Levi, Albert *Philosophy and the Modern World* (Bloomington: Indiana 1959) pp. 65-70. University Press 1959).
10. Gage, John, *J. M. W. Turner: "A Wonderful Range of Mind"* (New Haven and London: Yale University Press 1987) pp. 228-234.
11. Johnson, A. H. *The Wit and Wisdom of Alfred North Whitehead* (Boston: Beacon Press 1947).
12. Rifkin, Jeremy *Algeny* (New York: Viking 1983) p. 183-6, 188.

Chapter 2 Lenses for Seeing

1. Sontag, Susan *On Photography* (New York: Farrar, Straus, and Giroux 1977) p. 11.
2. Heidegger, Martin *The Metaphysical Foundations of Logic* Trans. by Michael Heim (Bloomington: Indiana University Press 1984) pp. 21, 28, 56, 125, 137.
3. Wolfe, Tom *The Painted Word* (New York: Farrar, Straus, and Giroux 1975).
4. Wolfe, Tom *From the Bauhaus to Our House* (New York: Farrar, Straus, and Giroux 1975).
5. Whitehead, A. N. *Science and the Modern World* (London: Cambridge University Press 1926).
6. Lakoff, George and Mark Johnson *Philosophy in the Flesh* (New York: Basic Books 1999) pp. 25-6, 265-6.
7. Price, Lucien (op.cit.) p. 367.

Chapter 3 Immanence and Figure-Ground

1. Cassirer, Ernst *The Individual and the Cosmos in Renaissance Philosophy* (Philadelphia: University of Pennsylvania Press 19) p. 26.
2. Koshkin-Youritzen, Victor *Pavel Tchelitchew.* (Fred Jones Jr. Museum of Art, The University of Oklahoma, 2002).
3. Lakoff and Johnson, (op. cit.*)* pp. 198-199.
4. Wilson, Edward O. (op. cit.) p. 60.
5. Lakoff and Johnson *Metaphors We Live By* (Chicago: The University of Chicago Press 1980) also *Philosophy in the Flesh* (op. cit.) p. 117.

Chapter 4 Athena

1. Eisler, Riane *The Chalice and the Blade* p. 113.
2. Lakoff and Johnson (op. cit., *PIP*) p. 198-9.
3. Stein, Gertrude, *Composition as Explanation* in *Selected Writings of Gertrude Stein* (New York: Random House 1946) p. 454-6.
4. Bateson, Gregory (op. cit.) p. 121.

Chapter 5 Barocci

1. Lecky, W. E. H. *History or the Rise and Influence of the Spirit of Rationalism in Europe* Vol. 1, p. 78.
2. Lakoff and Johnson (op. cit.) p. 56.

Chapter 6 Denotative Forms

1. Frankel, Carl *In Earth's Company* (Stony Creek, CT: New Society 1998) p. 32.

2. Langer, Suzanne *Mind: An Essay on Human Feeling* (Baltimore: Johns Hopkins Press 1967) pp. 165, 206.

Chapter 7 The Shadow Hand in the Vermeer

1. Snow, Edward *A Study of Vermeer* (Berkeley: University of California Press) p. 132.
2. Cassirer, Ernst (ibid.) pp. 146-7.

Chapter 8 Vermeer's Head of a Young Girl

1. Bohm, David , "The Implicate or Enfolded Order: A New Order for Physics," in *Mind in Nature*, ed. John B. Cobb and David R. Griffin (Lanham MD: University Press of America 1977) p. 37.
2. Talbot, Michael, *The Holographic Universe* (New York: Harper-Collins 19) p. 50.
3. Clark, Kenneth *Looking at Pictures* (Boston: Beacon 1960) p. 111.
4. Arasse, Daniel, *Vermeer: Faith in Painting* (Princeton, NJ: Princeton University Press 1993) p. 34.
5. Snow, Edward (ibid.) pp. 3,4.

Chapter 9 Hitler

1. Fromm, Eric *The Anatomy of Human Destructiveness* (New York: Holt, Rinehart & Winston) pp. 402, 414.
2. Whitehead, A. N. *Process and Reality* (New York: Macmillan 1929) p. 30.

Chapter 10 Texas Mother and Vermeer's The Love Letter

1. Clark, Kenneth *Civilisation* (New York: Harper & Row 1969) p. 206.

Chapter 11 Crying Frenchman

1. Damasio, Antonio *The Feeling of What Happens: Body and Emotion in the Making of Consciousness* (New York: Harcourt Brace 1999) pp. 48-9.
2. Clark, Kenneth *Moments of Vision* (New York: Harper and Row 1981) p. 10.

Chapter 12 Ships and the Feminine Gender

1. Wright, Sewall *Panpsychism and Science* in *Mind in Nature* (see Bohm, op. cit.) p. 79.

Chapter 13 Konorak/Giselbertius/Vermeer

1. Snow, Edward (op. cit.) p. 64.

Chapter 14 Terminology

1. Levi, Albert (op. cit.) p. 271.
2. Whitehead, A. N. (op. cit.) p. 226.
3. Damasio, Antonio (op. cit.) pp. 236-43.
4. Heidegger, Martin (op. cit.) p. 200.
5. Damasio, Antonio (op. cit.) pp. 230-244.
6. Murdoch, Iris *Existentialists and Mystics: Writings on Philosophy and Literature,* Edited by Peter Conrad (New York: Penguin).

Chapter 15 Process

1. Lakoff and Johnson (op. cit.) pp. 418-419.
2. Damasio, Antonio (op. cit.) p. 200.

3. Wallach, F. Bradford *The Epochal Nature of Process in Whitehead's Metaphysics* (Albany: State University of New York Press 1980).
4. Damasio, Antonio (op. cit.) pp. 160-7.
5. Lakoff and Johnson (op. cit.) pp. 24-5.

Chapter 16 Metaphor

1. Lakoff and Johnson (op. cit.) pp. 424-425, 536.
2. Whitehead, A. N. *Science and the Modern World* (New York: Free Press 1967) pp. 72, 113.
3. Farmer, John *Green Shift: Towards a Green Sensibility in Architecture* (London: Oxford, Butterworth-Heinemann 1996) pp. 159-65.

Chapter 17 Events

1. Gregory, R. L. *Concepts and Mechanics of Perception* (New York: Scribners 1974) pp. 86-129.
2. Whitehead, A. N. *Nature and Life* (New York: Greenwood Press 1968) pp. 20-22.
3. Waddington, C. H. *Whitehead and Modern Science* in *Mind in Nature* (ibid.) p. 145.
4. Arnheim, Rudolph *Visual Thinking* p. 91.
5. Langer, Suzanne (op. cit.) pp. 206, 208.
6. Bateson, Gregory (op. cit.) p. 126.

Chapter 18 Visual Patterns and Structured Societies

1. Wilson, Edward O. (op. cit.) p. 28.
2. Clark, Kenneth (op. cit.) pp. 125-140.

3. Johnson, Mark *The Body in the Mind* (Chicago, The University of Chicago Press 1987) p. 137.

Chapter 19 The Act of Perception

1. Whitehead, A. N. (*Process and Reality*) p. 321.
2. Oliver Sachs *A New Vision of the Mind* in *Nature's Imagination* (Oxford: Oxford University Press 1995) p. 107.
3. Wills, Christopher *The Runaway Brain* (New York: Harper-Collins 1993) p. 297.
4. Damasio, Antonio (op. cit. *DE*) p.146.
5. Whitehead. A. N. (op. cit. *PR*) p. 88.
6. Whitehead, A. N. (ibid.) p. 89.
7. Whitehead. A. N. (ibid.) p. 322.
8. Whitehead, A. N. (ibid.) p131.
9. Whitehead, A. N. (ibid.) p.131.
10. Whitehead, A. N. (ibid.) p. 134.
11. Whitehead, A. N. (ibid.) p. 491.
12. Whitehead, A. N. (ibid.) p. 127.
13. Merleau-Ponty, Maurice. *Phenomenology of Perception* (London: Routledge, Kegan, Paul) p. 36.
14. Whitehead, A. N. (op. cit. *PR*) p. 35.
15. Whitehead, A. N. (op. cit. *PR*) p.254.
16. Barthes, Roland *The Camera Lucida* translated by Richard Howard (New York: Hill and Wang, 1981).
17. Whitehead, A. N. *Modes of Thought* (New York: Macmillan 1938) pp. 148-9.
18. Whitehead, A. N. *Adventures of Ideas* (New York, MacMillan 1956) p. 363.

Chapter 20 Feelings

1. Lowe, Victor *Alfred North Whitehead: The Man and his Work* (Baltimore: Johns Hopkins University Press 1990) vol. 2, p. 268.
2. Damasio, Antonio (op. cit. *DE*) pp. 52-79, 171-5.
3. Whitehead, A. N. (op. cit. *PR*) p.516.
4. Damasio, Antonio (op. cit. *DE*) p. 106.
5. Whitehead, A. N. (op. cit. *PR*) p. 362.
6. Whitehead, A. N. (ibid.) p. 473.
7. Whitehead, A. N. (ibid.) p. 136.
8. Arnheim, Rudolph (op. cit.).
9. Whitehead, A. N. (op. cit. *PR*) p.47.
10. Whitehead, A. N. (ibid.) p. 416.
11. Whitehead, A. N. (ibid.) p. 284.
12. Whitehead,A. N. (ibid.) p. 483.
13. Whitehead, A. N. (ibid.) p. 246.
14. Griffin, David Ray (*Mind in Nature*, op. cit.) p. 127.
15. Arasse, Daniel (op. cit.) pp. 82-84.
16. Whitehead, A. N. (op. cit. *PR*) p. 234.
17. Whitehead, A. N. (ibid.) p.235.

Chapter 21 The Extensive Continuum

1. Whitehead, A. N. (op. cit. *PR*) p. 104.
2. Whitehead, A. N. (op. cit. *PR*) p. 105.
3. Clark, Kenneth (op. cit.) p. 320.
4. Jantsch, Erich *The Self Organizing Universe* (Oxford: Pergamon Press 1980) pp. 302-3.
5. Wallach, F. Bradford *The Epochal Nature of Process in Whitehead's Metaphysics* (Albany, NY: State University of New York Press).

Chapter 22 Perception and the Body

1. Whitehead, A. N. *Adventures of Ideas* (New York: Macmillan 1933) p. 314.
2. Damasio, Antonio (ibid.) p. 159.
3. Whitehead A. N. (op. cit. *PR*) p. 193.
4. Whitehead, A. N (ibid.) pp. 182-3.
5. Lakoff and Johnson (op. cit.) p. 333.
6. Whitehead, A. N. (op. cit. *PR*) pp. 125-6.
7. Whitehead, A. N. *Science and Philosophy* (New York: Philosophical Library 1948) p. 119.

Chapter 23 Public and Private

1. Johnson, Mark (op. cit.) pp. 173-93.
2. Whitehead, A. N. (op. cit. *PR*) p.324.
3. Speed, Joshua *Reminiscences of Abraham Lincoln* (Louisville, KY: The Filson Club) p. 25-6.
4. Whitehead, A. N. *Modes of Thought* (New York: MacMillan) p. 76.
5. Berger, John *The Success and Failure of Picasso* (New York: Pantheon) pp. 151-154.
6. Cornwell, John in his introduction to *Nature's Imagination: The Frontiers of Scientific Vision* (Oxford: Oxford University Press 1995.) p. 1.

Chapter 24 Consciousness

1. Wilson, Edward O. (op. cit.) p. 113.
2. Lakoff and Johnson (op. cit. *PIF)* pp. 4,13.

3. Whitehead, A. N. (op. cit. *PR*) p. 372.
4. Whitehead, A. N. (ibid.) p. 408.
5. Whitehead, A. N. (ibid.) p. 244.
6. Whitehead, A. N. (ibid.) p. 245.
7. Wilson, Edward O. (op. cit.) pp. 160-63.
8. Wilson, Edward O. (ibid.) p. 110.

Chapter 25 Creativity and Novelty

1. Whitehead, A. N. (op. cit. *PR*) p. 46.
2. Whitehead, A. N. (ibid.) p. 531.
3. Whitehead, A, N. (ibid.) p. 530.

Chapter 26 Symbolic Reference

1. Whitehead, A. N. (op. cit. *PR*) p. 257.
2. Whitehead, A. N. (ibid.) pp. 182-4.
3. Whitehead, A. N. (ibid.) p. 270.

Chapter 27 Order

1. Weinstein, Arnold *The Soul and the City: Art, Literature, and Urban Life.* The Teaching Company. Audio tape.

Epilogue

1. Arnheim, Rudolph (op. cit.) p. 140.
2. Damasio (op. cit.).

Index